Women of Strength

Also by Louis Baldwin

Hon. Politician: Mike Manfield of Montana
Jesus of Galilee
Oneselves: Multiple Personalities, 1811–1981
(McFarland, 1984)
Edmond Halley and His Comet
Portraits of God
(McFarland, 1986)
The Pope and the Mavericks
One Woman's Liberation
The Loves of Their Lives
Triumph Over the Odds
Intruders Within: Pueblo Resistance to Spanish
Rule and the Revolt of 1680

Women of Strength

*Biographies of 106
Who Have Excelled in
Traditionally Male Fields,
A.D. 61 to the Present*

by
Louis Baldwin

McFarland & Company, Inc., Publishers
Jefferson, North Carolina, and London

British Library Cataloguing-in-Publication data are available

Library of Congress Cataloguing-in-Publication Data

Baldwin, Louis.
    Women of strength : biographies of 106 who have excelled in
traditionally male fields, A.D. 61 to the present / by Louis
Baldwin.
        p.   cm.
    Includes index.
    ISBN 0-7864-0250-4 (sewn softcover : 50# alk. paper) ∞
    1. Women—Biography.   2. Women in the professions—
Biography.   3. Women civic leaders—Biography.   I. Title.
HQ1123.B35   1996
920.72—dc20   96-38693
                                                            CIP

Manufactured in the United States of America

*McFarland & Company, Inc., Publishers
    Box 611, Jefferson, North Carolina 28640*

To Ginnie,
with love

Table of Contents

Preface   xi

The Biographies

Boadicea
Leader of Men   1

Joan of Arc
Military Heroine   3

Elizabeth I
Able Ruler   5

Margaret Fuller
*First Woman Foreign
Correspondent*   7

Harriet Tubman
*"Conductor" of the Underground
Railroad*   9

Alice Eastwood
Accomplished Botanist   10

Nellie Bly
Crusading Reporter   12

Alice Hamilton
*Early Advocate for Safe Work
Environments*   15

Mary McLeod Bethune
*Founder of the National Council
of Negro Women*   17

Mary Roberts Rinehart
War Correspondent   18

Jeanette Rankin
First U.S. Congresswoman   20

Frances Perkins
*First Woman U.S. Cabinet
Member*   23

Anna O'Hare McCormick
Pulitzer Prize Winning Journalist   26

Eleanor Roosevelt
Nontraditional First Lady   28

Dorothy Thompson
Freedom Fighter   30

Amelia Earhart
Famous Pilot   32

Margaret Chase Smith
Maverick Congresswoman   35

Margaret Mead
Anthropologist   37

Barbara McClintock
*Winner of the Nobel Prize for
Medicine*   40

Clare Booth Luce
Powerful Politician   42

Margaret Bourke-White
Photojournalist   44

Maria Goeppert-Mayer
*Winner of the Nobel Prize for
Physics*   46

Rachel Carson
   Pioneer Environmental Advocate   48
Miriam Rothschild
   English Scientist   51
Rita Levi-Montalcini
   Italian Scientific Researcher   53
Jacqueline Cochran
   Outstanding Pilot   55
Millicent Fenwick
   Legislator   57
Dorothy Crowfoot Hodgkin
   Winner of the Nobel Prize for
   Chemistry   59
Mother Teresa
   Missionary to the Poor   61
Babe Didrikson Zaharias
   Athlete Phenomenon   62
Eva Crane
   Leading Apiculturist   65
Rosa Parks
   Civil Rights Leader   67
Katharine Graham
   Newspaper Publisher   70
Helen Thomas
   First Woman U.P.I. White House
   Bureau Chief   71
Marguerite Higgins
   War Correspondent   73
Rosalyn Yalow
   Developer of Radioimmunoassay   75
Flora Lewis
   New York Times Paris Bureau
   Chief   77
Elena Bonner
   Soviet Human Rights Activist   79
Patricia Roberts Harris
   Secretary of Housing and Urban
   Development   82
Shirley Chisholm
   First Black U.S. Congresswoman   83
Felice Schwartz
   C.E.O. of Catalyst   86

Margaret Thatcher
   First Woman Prime Minister
   of the United Kingdom   89
Jeane Kirkpatrick
   Ambassador to the United Nations   92
Lina Wertmuller
   Film Director   94
Althea Gibson
   Tennis Champion   96
Sarah Caldwell
   First Woman Conductor at the
   Metropolitan Opera   98
Violeta Chamorro
   President of Nicaragua   100
Barbara Harris
   First Woman Bishop   102
Sandra Day O'Connor
   First Woman Supreme Court
   Justice   104
Alice Rivlin
   Economist   106
Barbara Walters
   Television Interviewer of
   Celebrities   108
Ruth Bader Ginsburg
   Supreme Court Justice   111
Dianne Feinstein
   Liberal Senator   112
Jocelyn Elders
   Surgeon General   116
Ann Richards
   Texas Governor   118
Carla Hills
   U.S. Trade Representative   120
Edith Cresson
   First French Woman Prime
   Minister   123
Jane Goodall
   Primatologist   125
Geraldine Ferraro
   Vice Presidential Candidate   127
Sylvia Earle
   Marine Scientist   130

Barbara Jordan
Legislator and Orator   132

Barbara Mikulski
Politician   135

Elizabeth Dole
Cabinet Member   137

Hazel O'Leary
*Head of the Department of
Energy*   141

Eleanor Holmes Norton
Civil Rights Attorney   143

Lynn Margulis
Molecular Biologist   145

Janet Reno
*First Woman U.S. Attorney
General*   147

Maxine Waters
Congresswoman   149

Marian Wright Edelman
Senator   151

Wangari Maathai
Kenyan Political Activist   154

Cynthia Moss
Elephant Scientist   155

Pat Schroeder
Political Gadfly   158

Donna Shalala
*Secretary of Health and Human
Services*   160

Elizabeth Holtzman
Politician   162

Leslie Stahl
Television News Reporter   164

Molly Ivins
Political Commentator   166

Anita Roddick
Successful Businesswoman   168

Charlayne Hunter-Gault
Journalist   169

Marcelite Jordan Harris
Brigadier General   171

Faith Popcorn
Market Forecaster   173

Billie Jean King
Tennis Champion   175

Cokie Roberts
Political Commentator   177

Sharon Pratt Kelly
Mayor, District of Columbia   179

Nina Totenberg
*Outstanding Broadcast
Journalist*   181

Mary Robinson
Ireland's First Woman President   183

Antonia Novello
Surgeon General   185

Wilma Mankiller
Indian Chief   187

Diane Sawyer
Investigative Journalist   189

Connie Chung
*Television Network News
Anchor*   191

Judy Woodruff
Chief Washington Correspondent   193

Linda Bloodworth-Thomason
Television Writer and Producer   196

Hillary Rodham Clinton
First Lady   198

Joan Lunden
Television Morning News Anchor   201

Peggy Noonan
White House Speechwriter   203

Sally Ride
Astronaut   205

Jeana Yaeger
Record-setting Pilot   207

Benazir Bhutto
Pakistani Prime Minister   209

Anna Quindlen
New York Times *Columnist*   212

Sharon Matola
Zoologist   213

Susan Butcher
   Dogsledder   215
Maria Shriver
   Broadcast Journalist   218
Mae Jemison
   Astronaut   220
Katie Couric
   Television News Anchor   221

Rigoberta Menchú
   Nobel Peace Prize Winner   223
Susan Faludi
   Author and Gadfly   225
Maya Lin
   Artist   227

General References   231
Index   233

Preface

These brief profiles, presented chronologically by birth date, sketch the lives of some women who have made their mark in fields traditionally associated with men—not in literature or the arts, for instance, but in journalism, science, law, business, sports, politics. Achievers, in short, in this man's world.

The selection process suffered from an embarrassment of riches. For egregious oversights, a round of apologies herewith, with a reminder that, given a finite word count, choosing one means slighting another—for instance, Hypatia of Alexandria, who 1600 years ago lectured in mathematics, astronomy and mechanics, invented the plane astrolabe (predecessor of the sextant) and the hydrometer for measuring specific gravity, and who was brutally murdered by monks after being condemned by the local patriarch.

"Frailty, thy name is woman" is one of Hamlet's most famous lines. But evidently his experience was limited to those poor creatures at Elsinore, and surely the University of Wittenberg wasn't coeducational.

The Biographies

Boadicea
Leader of Men (died A.D. 61)

In A.D. 61, the Roman historian Tacitus tells us, the Roman occupiers in Britain suffered "a severe disaster." Indeed, tens of thousands—probably about 70,000—of the interlopers were slain, and several of their towns were burned to the ground, among them London. All this happened because a woman, a tribal queen of the fiercely resentful Britons, just couldn't take it any more. This was Boadicea, a.k.a. Boudicca.

Exactly when she was born is lost in the mists of nonhistory. She first appears in history as the widowed queen of the Iceni people of East Anglia, a huge redhead quite handy with a spear. The people of her island had been barbarously treated by the Roman military governor, Suetonius Paulinus, whose contempt for their bloody unattractive Druidic religion and his suppression of it infuriated the Britons generally and the Iceni particularly. "Suetonius imposed a garrison on the conquered people," according to Tacitus, "and destroyed the groves dedicated to their cruel superstitions, for it was part of their religion to spill captives' blood on their altars and to use the entrails in questioning their gods about the future." The Romans' fastidiousness is ironic, of course, given the gory tradition of their Colosseum.

Boadicea's husband had appointed the Roman emperor Nero as one of his heirs in the hope of avoiding Roman depredation. Nonetheless the Romans plundered his kingdom, confiscated his property, flogged his widow and ravished his two daughters, and reduced his extended family to slavery. The Iceni, although the most powerful of the tribes, had also been the most cooperative despite the Romans' religious wrack and ruin, and this final straw goaded them into a rebellion far bloodier than their religion. Boadicea, deeply and thoroughly incensed, rallied not only her tribe but also a great collection of tribes in the vicinity and beyond, gathering a horde of formidably armed and belligerently painted warriors that would number, according to a later Roman account, as many as 80,000. The Roman legions on the island numbered no more than 20,000—but they were 20,000 well armed, highly disciplined troops.

In the town today called Colchester the Romans, after driving out the Britons, had given possession of their homes and fields to various Roman officials, tradesmen, and money dealers, among them many veterans of the ceaseless Roman military expeditions. Without the occupying legions to guard it (they were otherwise employed in raids against the Welsh and on garrison duty elsewhere), the town's trespassing settlers were fair game for Boadicea & Co. They were massacred, every one, and their bodies left in the ashes that were all that remained of the town.

That massacre was followed by another when she led her Britons out to meet the Romans' Ninth Legion, fast approaching on a futile rescue mission. Her charged-up warriors overwhelmed the Roman infantry, killing every soldier—although most of the cavalry, doubtless thanking the gods for their greater mobility, escaped. Now she turned toward London, a busy, rich metropolis by the primitive standards of the time and place. Word of her unwelcome coming reached the town when Suetonius happened to be there with only a small armed-guard. Despite the terrified pleading of the townspeople for protection, he decided he'd have to leave them undefended while he joined a Roman force of some ten thousand now hastily en route to intercept the direful queen's huge war party. Although he offered to take along any of the townspeople who wished to join him, very few accepted this suicidal alternative to probable annihilation.

The others must soon have wished they had. They were indeed annihilated and the town was utterly destroyed. Leaving it to meet the Roman legions, the queen's men (and women too, incidentally) found the town now called St. Albans in their way. Another razing, another slaughter, and the town was no more. It was the third so visited, bringing the total dead, according to Tacitus, to 70,000.

But now facing them was not a town but Suetonius and his ten thousand, arranged in a very defensible position and lusting for battle. Outnumbered perhaps eight to one, they were counting on their tactical skill, their training and experience, their superior weaponry and celebrated discipline to win the day.

The Britons fell upon them in a fury, and that fury doubtless was their own undoing. It was, at any rate, no match for homicidal discipline. The battle was a bloody one, with no quarter given even to the women. Those Roman advantages had indeed won the day. Even discounting Tacitus' numbers, it's clear that Romans died by the hundreds, Britons by the tens of thousands. Thereafter, although Suetonius was in a mood for wholesale vengeance, he was replaced by a less militant governor who eventually arranged a truce with the Britons that introduced an era of durable, if uneasy, symbiosis.

After that great, decisive battle, however, Boadicea committed suicide by poison, ironically a Roman solution to disgrace. Winston Churchill, in his famous history, saw in Boadicea's rebellion "the crude and corrupt beginnings of a higher civilization blotted out by the ferocious uprising of the native tribes. Still, it is the primary right of men [and women] to die and kill for the land they live in… . Her monument on the Thames Embankment opposite Big Ben reminds us of the harsh cry of liberty or death which has echoed down the ages."

Joan of Arc
Military Heroine (1412–1431)

Who's the foremost military hero in French history? Probably not Charlemagne, Napoleon, Foch, or de Gaulle, but rather a simple peasant girl from the province of Lorraine, later to be known as The Maid of Orleans. No other commander, one historian has asserted, could "have led such a motley force against the English siege troops that surrounded Orleans and routed them in less than a week as the Maid had done."

Joan was born around 1412 in the village of Domremy to a plowman named Jacques d'Arc and a pious mother in a family of three boys and another girl (who died young). At the age of 13 she began to hear voices, later identified as those at first of God and then of France's patron saints, Michael, Catherine and Margaret, who appointed her to rescue France from the English invaders then occupying approximately the northeastern third of her country. Deep within that occupied territory was the town of Reims, northeast of Paris, where French kings were traditionally crowned. As a result Charles, the dauphin (crown prince)—whose father Charles VI had been so severely defeated at Agincourt by England's Henry V and who had died (like Henry) in 1422—had yet to be crowned. (On such foundations rests monarchy.) If the current English siege of strategically located Orleans, on the southern border of the English territory, could be lifted, a French army just might be able to force its way up to Reims for a proper coronation. But who in France could lift that formidable siege?

In May 1428 the voice-inspired teenager found her way south to the northernmost French fortified town and asked its commander to help her get to the dauphin and explain her mission, but he laughed her back home. She returned the next January, and this time, with some help from some sympathetic and patriotically hopeful townspeople, she persuaded him that she was not a witch and that she *must* see the dauphin. And so, in male clothing and with six soldiers, both for her protection, she made the eleven-day trip to the royal castle at Chinon, just west of Tours.

There the skeptical dauphin, no willing believer in disembodied voices, mingled at her approach with his courtiers in an effort at disguise, but she went up to him without hesitation and confidently informed him that, if empowered to wage war against the English interlopers, she would see to it that he'd be crowned at Reims. That tempting prospect, however unrealistic, overcame his skepticism, and he agreed. After several weeks of theological questioning during which she disgorged no satanic heresy, she was cleared for action, accoutered with the requisite arms and armor, and provided with a troop of several hundred men, including two of her brothers.

Arriving at Orleans in early May 1429 with some reinforcements but still heavily outnumbered, she seemed not in the least fazed by the odds against her. Within a week of several engagements she entered the city in triumph, with the English in full retreat (although she refused to pursue them because it was Sunday). A few days later she met the dauphin at Tours and urged him to let her escort him to Reims for the coronation. When he agreed, since it wasn't Sunday she took off after the English, defeated them decisively in a series of battles, and, liberating several fortified cities along the way, arrived in late June at Reims, where she was welcomed most appreciatively. The less adventurous Charles safely arrived some days later and was victoriously crowned in mid–July.

Thereafter things went generally downhill. Although she relieved many towns from enemy control in the ensuing months, she never did realize her goal of taking Paris—yet her efforts to do so at least resulted in a shaky truce with the Anglophile Duke of Burgundy that largely freed the land northeast of Paris from the English grip—except for roving bands of independent-minded Burgundians, whom she encountered in May 1430 during their siege of a town deep in the truce territory. Never shy about engaging personally in battles, this time she was captured. After being shunted about for several months between political pillar and ecclesiastical post, she was finally handed over in January 1431 to the gentle custody of the bishop of Beauvais, in whose diocese she had been taken, for the price of 10,000 francs, This was fine with the English, who were reluctant to get rid of anyone so popular without first discrediting her as a witch, or heretic, or whatever.

Over the next five months, in Rouen, her historic interrogations and trial took place. She stood up stubbornly to incessant harassment, badgering, and browbeating and maintained the inspired righteousness of her mission even during a bout of serious illness, but she finally succumbed and signed a document of abjuration. Accused of treason by her voices for doing so, she quickly recanted, submitting herself to the ecclesiastical court's judgment. The court, unable to find anything genuinely sorcerous or heretical in her stoutly forth-right testimony, at least had the decency not to charge her gravely on such grounds. They had to resort, however, to condemning her for wearing male attire, and it was for this heretical preference that, at the end of May 1431, she was burned at the stake.

Twenty-three years later, after the French had retaken Rouen and captured the records of her trial, she was retried, this time under papal auspices, and in July 1456 she was rehabilitated with much ecclesiastical pomp and circumstance. Many more years later she would be the subject of sympathetic biographies, in English yet, notably of those two apostles of religiosity, Bernard Shaw and Mark Twain.

And in 1920 she was canonized.

Elizabeth I
Able Ruler (1533–1603)

Poor Henry VIII of England. Not only was he hooked on Anne Boleyn, from whom he couldn't get what he wanted without marriage (with her father's support, she was one tough cookie), but he also desperately wanted a son to inherit his kingdom, not some weak, ineffectual female—and his queen, Catherine of Aragon, showed no promise of producing a son. And so, being a man of action, he divorced and imprisoned his wife, broke with the protesting pope of Rome, and married Anne—who, to his chagrin, gave him a mere daughter. Yet that mere daughter, Elizabeth—who inherited his red hair, vitality, resolve, competence, talent for oratory, and love of the arts—would rule as his eventual successor longer (45 years) and more ably and successfully than any likely son. More carefully calculating than he, more provident, closer with a shilling though not notably stingy, and politically more astute, she would essentially inaugurate the power and prestige of the British Empire with what came to be called her Golden Age.

Elizabeth Tudor was born in September 1533 in Greenwich Palace three years before her mother's execution left her with no family to speak of. In the eleven years after Henry's death in 1547 she received a thorough classical education at Cambridge, where she also learned to speak fluent French and Italian, passable Greek and better Latin, developing a linguistic ability that served her well later in dealing with foreign emissaries. During those years of waiting she also lived, in various palaces and for a while ominously in the Tower, as quietly and unobtrusively as possible through the intrigue-infested reigns of her sickly half-brother and militantly Catholic half-sister. After finally coming to the throne in 1558, she immediately restored Anglicanism to its primacy yet arranged a nonviolent if uneasy accommodation with the country's remaining Roman Catholics, although (or because?) her greatest fear in foreign affairs was that a combination of Catholic nations, particularly Spain, might forcibly try to replace her. In this connection, as a precaution, she managed to pressure the French into withdrawing from Scotland, where they had taken up unwelcome residence. Her efforts to take back Calais from the French, however, were decisively thwarted.

In this success in Scotland and failure on the Continent she was joined by Sir William Cecil, the prime minister who would work closely with her for forty of her forty-five years as queen. She appreciated his intelligence and ability and was able to keep him in office even though he was opposed by Robert Dudley, Earl of Leicester, perhaps the only man she ever really loved. Although a passionate woman, she was a very practical queen. She never married but used her presumed availability as bait in political situations. For many years, for instance, she stalled off Philip of Spain's Catholic aggressiveness by suggesting interest in marrying this or that Catholic prospect without ever letting things get really serious.

A domestic source of concern was Mary Stuart, Queen of Scots, who fled into England in 1568 after her subjects rebelled and whose claim to the English throne had just enough credibility and Catholic support to give rise to several conspiracies. Elizabeth put up with this for almost twenty years but finally signed the order for Mary's execution in 1587. Only a year later she learned that Philip of Spain had dispatched a formidable-looking fleet to English waters to invade, conquer and depose, and thus to restore Catholicism to the sceptered isle. When invasion seemed most imminent she visited the army awaiting it, riding on a white horse and sporting a white plume and stubbornly resolved, she told her anxious soldiers, "to live or die among you all, and to lay down for my God and for my kingdom and for my people, my honor and my blood, even in the dust." Luckily she didn't have to put this to the proof, for the Spanish armada turned out to consist of sluggish sitting ducks, easy prey for the smaller, faster, more maneuverable English warships, and there in the English Channel that was the end of that.

Thus largely relieved of that worry, she devoted even more attention to promoting the prosperity of her kingdom and to encouraging the arts, especially the literary arts in an age studded with names like Bacon, Marlowe, Spenser, Shakespeare. With her support, adventurers like Sir Walter Raleigh and Francis Drake roamed the world, sowing the seeds of empire. The Irish rebellion soured the general euphoria somewhat, and that of the Earl of Essex in 1601 embittered her final years with the need for her reluctant signature on another important execution order.

She died in March 1603. Since the Virgin Queen had produced no heir, she was succeeded by Mary Stuart's son, James VI of Scotland, who became James I of England. The incongruity was considerably softened by his imperious Anglicanism.

Margaret Fuller
First Woman Foreign Correspondent
(1810–1850)

In the mid–1800s there were no foreign correspondents, except in the sense of people living abroad who might incidentally write letters to American newspapers. Those American papers gathered their news of events in Europe almost exclusively from papers arriving by sea from England and the Continent. During the Italian revolution of 1848-49, however, Margaret Fuller, hired by Horace Greeley as history's first woman foreign correspondent and one of its first war correspondents, regularly reported from embattled Rome.

She was born in 1810 in Cambridgeport, Massachusetts, first of nine children of a lawyer who had served in Congress under President John Quincy Adams. He educated her quite severely, as he would have educated the son he'd wanted, giving her the ability to read Latin at six, in addition to nightmares and excruciating headaches. At fourteen she was sent to a boarding school, from which she emerged a sweet young thing, more or less.

Although her sex prevented her from going to college, her intellectual attainments were such that she became the first woman to be permitted to use the library at Harvard. After her father's death she moved to Boston, where she joined the freethinking Transcendentalists, and then moved to Providence, Rhode Island, for a teaching job that paid her well enough to help support her family. After a few years of this she returned to Boston and the Transcendentalists as the unsalaried editor of their paper, *The Dial*, and as a freelance writer.

Her first book, *Summer on the Lakes*, published in 1843, so impressed Greeley with its depiction of dispossessed Indians that he undertook publication of her second, 1845's *Woman in the Nineteenth Century*, which incited plenty of tumultuous controversy with its feminist demand for full equality: "We would have every path laid open to women as freely as to men. If you ask me what offices they may fill, I reply—any. I do not care what case you put; let them be sea captains if you will."

This book impressed Greeley's wife more than it did Greeley, and she persuaded him to employ its author for his *New York Tribune* as literary critic, and thereby as the first woman member of the editorial staff of a city newspaper. While stirring things up as literary critic, especially concerning women's rights, she also branched out into investigative reporting, for example in exposés of prison conditions at Sing Sing and the living conditions of prostitutes.

By 1846 Greeley had come to the unprecedented conclusion that his paper needed an American to serve as a full-fledged foreign correspondent in Europe.

Since she had been living with the Greeleys since her arrival in New York, some dissatisfaction with the arrangement may have inspired him to choose her for the assignment. And so off she sent to Europe with an advance of $125 (then a substantial sum). From England she sent Dickensian accounts of the poverty in the cities and the deplorable treatment of miners, as well as describing the perils of hiking about the rugged Scottish countryside. In France she sensed the unrest under the heel of Louis-Philippe and virtually predicted the revolution that would introduce the Second Republic. (She also became quite friendly with Sand and Chopin.)

But it was in Italy that she became a war correspondent. Indeed, her dispatches from Naples and then Rome read very much like the on-site reports we see and hear today on radio and television newscasts—Austrian weapons being burned in a plaza, royal flags being torn down and replaced with republican banners, and so on.

Meanwhile she had fallen in love with a Marchese Ossoli, her intellectual inferior but an irresistibly attractive fighter for the political freedom so dear to her heart. In September 1848 a son was born to Fuller in a mountain village outside Rome. Leaving him there in the care of a family, she returned to Rome to continue reporting on the fast-moving events, including the assassination of the unpopular papal prime minister: "Yesterday, as he descended from his carriage to enter the Chamber, the crowd howled and hissed, then pushed him, and, as he turned his head in consequence, a sure hand stabbed him in the back. He said no word, but died almost instantly in the arms of a cardinal."

Life was exciting. One day, returning to Rome from a visit to her son, she encountered some of Garibaldi's troops at an inn. A rough lot, she knew, forced by circumstances to use robbery as one means of sustenance. To avoid such an eventuality, she offered to buy lunch for everyone in a gesture that so disarmed them that afterwards they accompanied her back to her carriage most chivalrously.

In April 1849 Rome was assaulted by 12,000 French troops sent to quell the revolution, and she found herself in charge of a military hospital, assisting at surgery, tending the wounded. A representative of the U.S. State Department was there and later reported, "The dead and dying were around her in every form of pain and horror, but she never shrank from the duty she had assumed. All was done that a woman could do to comfort them in their suffering." From the hospital's balcony she could see the fighting, and of course report on it, heatedly denying the charges of republican atrocities being circulated in England and France.

As the battle seemed to be reaching its climax, she left the hospital to join her husband in the final engagement, but the expected attack didn't come. There was no need for it—the French had won the day. She retrieved her baby son, married Ossoli in Florence, and made plans for going home. The family sailed in May 1850 for the long trip. Halfway across the captain died of small-pox, and the first mate, unable to handle the ship himself, asked the captain's widow to help with the navigation. In July, in sight of land, the ship grounded on a sandbar off Fire Island, New York. Margaret Fuller was drowned, as were her husband and son.

What was that she had written about woman?—"Let them be sea captains, if you will." Equally trained, that is.

Harriet Tubman
"Conductor" of the Underground Railroad (ca. 1820–1913)

She helped the abolitionist John Brown plan his famous raid on the U.S. arsenal at Harper's Ferry in 1859, but well before that, out of admiration for her phenomenal tactical powers in rescuing and bringing north more than 300 slaves from the benighted South, Brown had taken to addressing her as "General."

She was born Aminta but was soon renamed Harriet Ross in 1820 or 21 on a plantation east of Chesapeake Bay. Her family would provide their less pigmented owners with two adult and eleven miniature chattel slaves. At seven she was drafted for housework and white-child care until she was old enough for field work. The hard field work toughened her enormously, though not enough for her to recover completely after a foreman hit her with something heavy and metallic. (She felt it without seeing it.) For the rest of her life she suffered from unpredictable blackouts several times a day. Perhaps to anyone else that would have been incapacitating. But not to Harriet Tubman.

In her twenties she settled down to plantation life and married John Tubman, a free black man. In 1849, despite her five-year marriage, she was under threat of being sold into the Deep South (as two of her older sisters had been). That provided more than enough incentive for escape, and so, with the help of the Underground Railroad, that splendid enterprise in justifiable grand larceny, she made her surreptitious way to Philadelphia. There she worked for wages (e.g., $2 a week), mostly as a maid in homes and hotels, until she had accumulated enough money to return to Maryland on a rescue mission, with the help of the Underground Railroad and those magnificent Quakers. (But not that of Congress, whose Fugitive Slave Act of 1850 had made such rescuing a criminal activity.)

Although her husband, who had remarried after her departure, wasn't interested in being rescued, many others were. After she had overcome some initial male resistance to the idea of a female "conductor" on the Railroad, she would make a total of twenty trips—return trips—to the South to bring more than 300 slaves to freedom, including her parents and most of her siblings. During that decade of the 1850s she would be feverishly pursued in the gothic South by bounty hunters inspired by large rewards, yet neither she nor any of her charges was ever captured. On one occasion she "borrowed" a fancy horse and carriage, hiding her charges in it and having a black man drive, knowing that a black driving such a rig openly would be assumed to be on his master's business. She was indeed a competent, effective general whose sympathy for the plight of slaves never degenerated into softheadedness. She was a tough disciplinarian, armed with a gun to discourage any turning back en route.

Although illiterate, she lectured in the North on abolition to antislavery groups and on women's rights to feminists of the time, earning enough money to support her parents and continue her rescue missions. When the Civil War brought those missions to an end, she volunteered for service in the Union Army, feeding and nursing white soldiers and black refugees. Her rescue experience proved invaluable when, as a scout, she led Union raids into Southern territory (freeing nearly 800 slaves on one of them) and when, as a spy, she ferreted out useful military information. Yet after the war the Union government refused to pay her, as a woman, the considerable sum of $1800 due her, which, despite her strenuous efforts throughout succeeding years, she never did collect. Not until 1890 did she get anything from the government, and then it was only a modest pension granted to her as the widow of Nelson Davis, a Civil War veteran and social activist whom she had married years before. In 1898 Congress, in a burst of generosity, raised the pension from eight dollars a month to twenty.

About forty years earlier she had settled down in Auburn, New York, where she continued working to support her parents and to take care of blacks who sought her help, as well as to contribute to a couple of schools training freed blacks in the South. She never had enough money, but she did receive some financial support from admiring, sympathetic friends. Eventually, in 1908, she had enough to establish a home for Auburn's poverty-stricken blacks.

She died there in March 1913 and was buried with full military honors—in lieu of that $1800.

Alice Eastwood
Accomplished Botanist (1859–1953)

All her long life she was fascinated by flowers—indeed, plants generally, but especially flowers. Her interest in them was by no means dreamily romantic.

It was botanical, strictly scientific. Alice Eastwood's love of flowers resulted in the addition of 340,000 specimens to the California Academy of Sciences' herbarium and in having flowers named after her, such as a desert flower, *Aliciella*, and a woodland flower, *Eastwoodia*.

Alice Eastwood was born in January 1859 in a suburb of Toronto, Canada. When her mother died six years later she and her younger sister and brother were distributed among various relatives by her grieving father, who then sought solace elsewhere for the next eight years. Alice and her sister spent a few years with a sympathetic uncle and then a few more years at a convent school. Although the nuns apparently stressed piety over education, Alice became friendly with the retired priest who cared for the convent gardens, and from him she learned a great deal, especially about flowers. Her interest was heightened and her store of knowledge increased by occasional visits to her uncle, an experimental horticulturist.

In 1873 her father, living in Denver with her brother, sent for her to join them. (The sister remained with her uncle.) On her arrival she was dismayed to find them living in a squalid hotel and was vastly relieved to hear that her father had found a place for her in the home of an affluent rancher as nursemaid to his children. The family's kindness to her included unrestricted use of their large library and summer camping trips in the nearby Rocky Mountains. The great variety of mountain wildflowers fascinated her. She learned their popular names but was eager to learn the scientific names that the priest and her uncle had often used. Unfortunately, the family library didn't have a book on botany, but she knew she'd have to get one. She had found a career.

It had to be put on hold, however. Late in 1873 she moved in with her father, brother, and recently arrived sister in her father's new store, which included rooms in the rear for the family. Despite a heavy schedule of housework and a Saturday job, she attended local schools and continued to read omnivorously. Because of her work schedule and interruptions, she was twenty on her high school graduation day. She had done well in school, but this was as far as she'd go.

Yet she hadn't forgotten botany. She had learned Latin for obvious botanical reasons and now had her own library of two books, *Flora of Colorado* and Gray's *Manual of Botany*. In the fall of 1879 she began teaching at a Denver high school—Latin, English, history, science, art—and spending her summers roughing it most indecorously in the Rockies, collecting specimens for her herbarium in town and gaining a reputation as Denver's, perhaps Colorado's, premier botanist.

That reputation brought her an introduction to Alfred Russell Wallace, a noted British botanist, when he visited Denver in 1887. Together they spent three days in the Rockies, living in a hut well above the timberline and gathering specimens by the knapsackful. Gradually she was becoming primarily a taxonomist, devoted to the scientific classification of plants by genus and species—enough of one, indeed, to publish a treatise in 1890, *A Popular Flora of Denver*. (It wasn't all that popular.)

In 1891 she paid a professional visit to the California Academy of Sciences in San Francisco. The next year she was offered a position as joint curator and then, after a timely retirement, as curator. The Academy was a highly respected institution, and this was a prestigious job for a woman of 33 without so much as an hour of college. But she would work, successfully, to make the Academy even more highly respected over the next half-century. One source of great pleasure was her teaching there—not a variety of subjects, but simply her own beloved botany.

She began roughing it again, this time throughout California, always collecting, collecting, collecting, accumulating countless items for the Academy's herbarium. Out of the thousands, she segregated some 1500 particularly rare ones, a precaution that proved downright provident when the 1906 earthquake started a fire that destroyed the Academy building, including her herbarium and all its contents except the precious 1500, which she and a friend managed to save by dint of a precariously Herculean effort. As for the loss of her specimens, her attitude was that she had enjoyed collecting them, and now she would enjoy starting all over again.

Although first she would have to earn a living, at least she could do so now as a botanist. After some years with a herbarium in Massachusetts, she worked with the National Herbarium in Washington, doing some international botanical networking that brought her invitations to visit London and Paris. Meanwhile the Academy was being rebuilt in San Francisco's Golden Gate Park. In 1912 she returned as curator, but until the rebuilding was completed, she roughed it for several months in the Yukon, gathering plants not only there but also on the way there and back.

After resuming full operations at the Academy in 1916, she spent the next three decades raising the reputation of its herbarium and its library of rare botanical books to unprecedented heights while writing and publishing hundreds of technical articles. At the age of 81 she went out roughing it again, this time in Death Valley. At 91 she flew to Sweden to be formally named honorary president of the International Botanical Congress. At her death in October 1953 she was only 94. A very sprightly 94.

Six months earlier the Academy trustees had announced plans for a new building, The Alice Eastwood Hall of Botany.

Nellie Bly
Crusading Reporter (1867–1922)

In the mid–1880s an article entitled "What Girls Are Good For" in *The Pittsburgh Dispatch*, noting the shortage of men caused by the bloody Civil

War, nonetheless decried the tendency to hire women to do men's work. Such a tendency was the work of those devil suffragettes. Anyone relegated by Divine Providence to the weaker sex had only four proper functions: nurse, teacher, wife-mother, or spinster aunt.

A day or so later the editor received a blistering reply in the mail. He'd been an editor long enough to shrug off hot replies, but this one was impressively well written—too well written, despite its viewpoint, to have been written by anyone but a man. He decided he ought to hire this feisty fellow to brighten up the editorial page. Since the letter wasn't signed, he'd have to put an ad in the paper asking him to come in, but it would be worth the effort. He did, and a couple of days later the writer arrived, a slender young girl, surely not yet twenty, stylishly dressed and graceful in motion. He glanced up at her quizzically. "You sent for me," she said.

Her name was Elizabeth Cochrane. She was born in May 1867 on a farm not far from Pittsburgh. The family was very large, providing her with plenty of rough and energetic brothers for relentless competition and character formation. An so, when the editor asked her if she'd like to try her hand at an article for the paper, she had become used enough to challenges to accept this one. What would she like to write about? he asked. Divorce, she replied. What?! That was a very delicate topic, and what could *she* know about it anyway? I'll write the article, she countered—you can always reject it.

His guess was right: she didn't know anything about divorce. But it was a subject growing in controversial popularity, and she knew there'd be plenty of material on it in the papers left behind by her late father, a county judge. They proved to be a gold mine. She wrote the article, it was published—discreetly under a pseudonym, Nellie Bly—and she was hired, incredibly, as a regular staff member. The article, stressing the miseries of family disintegration, and succeeding articles on the subject created a great deal of talk not only about the subject but also about the identity of the writer—who, it was at first generally assumed, must be a man writing under an assumed name.

After doing a series of highly provocative pieces on the atrocious plight of working girls, she was unsurprisingly transferred to the society pages, doubtless at the insistence of local factory owners. But of course she wasn't about to take *that*, and so she persuaded the editor that a series of articles on Mexico would boost circulation. But, he protested, she'd need a chaperon! All right, she'd take her mother with her. Your mother!—great protection, that. But I won't need *protection*. Well, okay, okay.

Her articles on the miserable treatment of the poor by the rich in Mexico, and on casual, widespread government corruption, of course got her kicked out of the country. The articles were widely copied in the U.S., earning her something of a national reputation. On her return in the summer of 1887 she decided that she was enough of a professional journalist now to seek her fortune in New York City, particularly on Joseph Pulitzer's *New York World*. At

World headquarters she characteristically bulldozed her way into Pulitzer's inner sanctum and daintily intimidated him into letting her get herself committed to the insane asylum on Blackwell's Island and do an investigative report on the treatment of the inmates. It was such an outlandish idea—what a story!—that he agreed. It was her funeral, after all.

It very nearly was. After convincing a judge, a court doctor, and four neurologists at Bellevue Hospital that she was suffering from "dementia with delusions of persecution," she was bundled off to the island madhouse. ("This isn't Cuba!" she complained theatrically in her role as arriving inmate.) After ten days of undergoing callous neglect and mindless abuse with the other patients, her anxiety became almost pathological. Was she going mad? Would she ever get out of here? When on the tenth day a visitor, a man, arrived and told her that he was a lawyer from the *World* and had come to get her released, she could answer only, "And none too soon."

"Behind Asylum Bars" was a sensation. Within a few weeks, after a hasty grand jury investigation and an unprecedented government appropriation, conditions on the island were vastly improved. She was now known as a "crusading" reporter. In that capacity she took up the cause of working girls again, including those on the stage (getting a job as a chorus girl). But before very long she began to get restless, and in 1889 she came up with an idea, a new challenge. One of her great-uncles had traveled around the world, but the trip had taken three years, ruined his health, and contributed to his early death. The family tradition had made Jules Verne's *Around the World in Eighty Days* one of her favorite books. Why couldn't she give it a try?

She broached the subject to her managing editor. Good idea, but not for a woman—maybe we'll send a man. You do, and I'll make the trip for another paper. And so it was that on November 14, 1889, she set sail for London, Paris, Brindisi, Cairo, Ceylon, Singapore, Hong Kong, Tokyo, San Francisco and New York with an enormous, tightly crammed satchel and a 24-hour watch. (In Paris she took time for a mutual-admiration visit with Verne.) On January 25, 1890—72 days, 6 hours, 10 minutes and 11 seconds later—she was back in New York. Her difficulties and adventures had rivaled those of Phileas Fogg and Passepartout, and she was eager to recount them in her forthcoming book, *Nellie Bly's Book: Around the World in Seventy-two Days*. (Her third book, this, the other two concerning Mexico and Blackwell's Island.)

The rest of her life was anticlimax—what else? She continued as a reporter until 1895, when she quit to marry wealthy, elderly Robert Seaman. After his death her management of his business ended in bankruptcy. When she died in 1922 she was writing for *The New York Evening Journal*, which in its obituary paid tribute to her as "the best reporter in America" without a gender-restricting adjective.

Indeed, she may simply have been born too soon—surely she would have been a smash on *60 Minutes*.

Alice Hamilton
Early Advocate for Safe Work Environments
(1869–1970)

She wasn't really interested in biology, anatomy, or other medical disciplines, nor did she seem to have any particular ability along those lines. Nevertheless, when the family finances got perilously close to the drain, she decided that a medical career promised a young single woman at least a reasonable chance at economic independence. She couldn't even guess that her decision would lead to renown as a national, indeed a world, expert in industrial medicine.

Alice Hamilton was born in February 1869 in New York but spent most of her young life on an extended-family estate in Fort Wayne, Indiana, with some fifteen young siblings and cousins. Their education was strictly a home industry until they reached their late teens. Although the atmosphere was religious (Presbyterian, with much Sunday Bible reading), it was also intellectual enough to allow the children to think their own thoughts and even to express them. The emphasis was not so much on religion as on morality, on caring for others.

She spent her late teens as a student and boarder at a school for girls which, although observing rather loose educational standards, did continue the emphasis on morality. It was there that she set her sights on medicine after her father's business failure. The scientific aspects of medicine seemed rather unattractive, yet at least doctoring involved caring for others. And it could put food on her table and clothes on her back. After getting some tutoring in chemistry and physics and taking some premed courses at a local school, she joined the meager group of women at the University of Michigan's medical school, where she was surprised to discover that she rather liked the scientific aspects after all, especially in the laboratory and at the microscope. Even more surprising, she found herself specializing in bacteriology and pathology.

Her internships in Minneapolis and Boston brought her into contact with the ailing poor, an emotionally educational experience. Urged to do some postgraduate work in pathology in Europe, she and her sister Edith (who had received like advice concerning her teaching career) spent a couple of years in Germany, where Alice apparently learned somewhat less about pathology than about jingoism, anti–Semitism, and misogyny.

Back home, in mid–1897 she was hired as an instructor in pathology by the Woman's Medical School of Northwestern University, in a northern suburb of Chicago. For living quarters she was accepted by Chicago's celebrated Hull House, famous for its residents' volunteer services to the poor in its neighborhood. There she set up a clinic for infants, tending them and offering advice to their usually young and often abused mothers. The work sharpened her interest in social justice, motivating her to promote birth control and especially to protest the sale of local pharmacies of drugs like cocaine, which were wreaking havoc among many school children.

Among the working men in the neighborhood, she learned, the most common illness was lead poisoning. She learned, further, that this was epidemic throughout the country. On a trip to Europe in 1909, to attend an International Conference on Occupational Accidents and Diseases, she met the labor commissioner in the U.S. Department of Commerce. At his request she toured England to visit factories, addressing (and in some cases solving) the lead-poisoning problem. Armed with encouraging data, she returned home, hoping to promote similar safety precautions in American industry.

On her return to Illinois she was appointed by the governor to head up a five-member medical commission to survey the state's industries and to determine the levels of various industrial poisons, especially lead. Despite bitter opposition from entrepreneurial mossbacks, the commission's report resulted in 1911 in a state law instituting financial settlements for the poisoned victims. Over the next two decades every state in the Union would pass comparable legislation.

Encouraged by the 1911 law, Alice Hamilton embarked on a similar national survey, which was intensified by munitions production during World War I. By the end of the war her expertise had become so widely recognized that she became the first woman on Harvard's faculty (ineligible, of course, for the Harvard Club or for official appearances at commencements), even though she demanded a part-time schedule so that she could continue her national survey. She did continue the survey but began adding exhortation to investigation, urging employers to eliminate the toxicity in their work environments. She was delighted to find most of them very cooperative after being made fully aware of the problems. In 1925 her book on the problem, *Industrial Poisons in the United States*, became the country's first textbook on the subject and enormously enhanced her reputation.

After retiring from Harvard in 1935 she continued her research on industrial toxins as a consultant to the Department of Labor, updated her textbook, and wrote her autobiography. She also became more political in her support of an Equal Rights Amendment, her condemnation of McCarthyism, and her demand for American withdrawal from Vietnam. She was not one for dozing on the front porch.

When she died in September 1970, in the first year of her second century, she had reason to feel proud of her contribution to society. Thirteen years earlier she had expressed her satisfaction with the vast improvement in factory conditions over the years and with the fact that "I had some part in it."

Mary McLeod Bethune
Founder of the National Council of Negro Women
(1875–1944)

She was founder and president of schools, insurance companies, and organizations. Her restless energy and conspicuous ability attracted the notice of Franklin Roosevelt, for whom she directed the activities of the Negro division of his National Youth Administration from soon after his inauguration until his death. As a young girl her liveliness and addiction to music were expressed in spirited dancing, and through all her serious activities as an adult she never entirely forsook a touch of frivolity.

She was born Mary McLeod in July 1875 in Mayesville, South Carolina, the fifteenth of an eventual seventeen children. Her parents and all of her older siblings had been slaves until freed in the Civil War, after which the family acquired a farm of their own, raising cotton and rice. Although the education of black children wasn't a primary concern of the postwar South, at least it was no longer illegal, and by a stroke of luck she was able to attend a missionary school from the age of eleven and then, on a scholarship, a college for black girls in North Carolina. After her graduation in 1893 she spent a year at Chicago's Moody Bible Institute in the hope of going on to missionary work in Africa. Told by a mission board that blacks weren't eligible for such work, she was utterly crestfallen.

And so she turned to teaching in mission schools in South Carolina, Georgia, Florida. In 1898 she married Albertus Bethune, a fellow teacher, who left her some time after the birth of their son. In 1904 she struck out on her own, founding the Daytona Normal and Industrial Institute in Florida. The name was more imposing than the school—which included only her and her son and five girls as students—but it had a sign over the door, "Enter to Learn." To support it she sold her homemade sweet potato pies and ice cream and began her lifelong habit of raising funds for worthy causes from cooperative blacks and whites alike. At first, however, her efforts brought the school no inordinate luxury: desks were upturned crates, pencils were discarded bits of charcoal, and ink was juice from mashed elderberries. When one of the children became ill and was accorded the customary rude treatment at the town's hospital, she opened a hospital for blacks—with two beds, which eventually multiplied to twenty.

Gradually, as the school became a magnet for black parents eager to improve their children's prospects, it expanded from elementary to high school status, offering moral discipline as well as education in academic and practical skills to help the young people better their lot in life. By 1923 its reputation earned it an invitation to merge with an all-male school with which, in

1929, it became a junior college and, in 1948, an accredited four-year college of liberal arts. During the 1930s and early 1940s she was its president.

By that time she was already used to being president. It would become downright habitual. In the mid–1920s she had served for two terms as president of the National Association of Colored Women, during which she raised the money for its permanent headquarters building in Washington. In her spare time she served on various Presidential commissions. In the mid 1930's she founded and presided over an umbrella organization, the National Council of Negro Women, remaining its president until 1949. In those years she was also president of a couple of insurance companies. Meanwhile, until 1951, she was president of the Association for the Study of Negro Life and History, and for fifteen years (1940–55) she was a vice-president of the NAACP and the National Urban League. When Roosevelt asked her to be director of the NYA Negro division, she readily accepted. Presumably she needed the additional activity to fill some of her idle hours.

In that job she had to persuade officials at the often benighted state level to avoid discrimination in NYA programs. She was able to hire black assistants, although not at white pay levels, and with their help she increased blacks' participation in programs in numbers approaching their percentage of the population. She also pushed for a special black college and a fund for scholarships. She led in the organization of the Federal Council on Negro Affairs to promote the rights and interests of blacks in obtaining Federal help (thwarting, for instance, an attempt in Detroit to transfer to whites a Federal housing project erected for blacks). She was grateful for the support from her friends Eleanor and Franklin Roosevelt, although she never considered it enough.

After World War II, despite a debilitating lifelong asthma, she continued with her various presidencies while receiving many honorary degrees and other awards. She died of heart failure in May 1944 in Daytona Beach, Florida.

Mary Roberts Rinehart
War Correspondent (1876–1958)

In the spring of 1915 a gaggle of war correspondents, all male of course, gathered in London to make their first trip to the war-torn Continent, where they were scheduled for a day's tour of the Belgian front. On their arrival they encountered a competitor who had already been there for the past three weeks. It was Mary Roberts Rinehart, war correspondent for the *Saturday Evening Post*, who hadn't been able to resist the tug of war.

She was born Mary Ella Roberts in August 1876 in Pittsburgh, which provided her with education through high school. Then, eager to escape from her family's respectable but uncomfortable poverty, she set her sights on nursing as one of the few career paths open to her as a woman. After completing her courses at the Pittsburgh Training School for Nurses she met and married a physician, Stanley Rinehart, by whom she would have three sons before his death in 1932.

She had hoped to go on to college, but the economic panic of 1903 so severely depleted the family's wherewithal that she had to take up another career open to her, that of writing. It proved surprisingly successful, and profitable. By the time World War I arrived, she had written ten novels and four plays (all produced), as well as countless short pieces, mainly for the *Saturday Evening Post*. By that time, indeed, she had become so valuable to the *Post* that she could demand an unprecedented assignment as war correspondent: "I don't intend to let the biggest thing in my life go by without having been a part of it." And so, provided with the necessary credentials and an expense account, she sailed for London in January 1915.

The British government was circumspectly denying reporters passage to the Continent and was wielding quite a heavy hand of censorship. At the London office of the Belgian Red Cross, however, she argued that her experience as a nurse could help her report the Belgians' plight quite vividly to her American readers. The very next day she was being vividly if ineffectively bombarded by German planes in a hotel in Dunkirk. After three weeks of feverish reporting, she joined her newly arrived male colleagues in a foray behind the lines. (It was her idea, but they horned in.) After her and their interviews of a Capuchin monk engaged in spying on the German lines, they all returned, but the men were hauled back to London by the British while she stayed on with the Belgians, to her great satisfaction.

Moving on to France, she interviewed the Allied Supreme Commander, Marshall Foch, and sent an eyewitness account of the Germans' use of poison gas to the *Post*, which nervously declined to publish it lest it compromise American neutrality. After an exclusive interview with Belgium's King Albert, she reported his accusation that the Germans were using Belgian civilians as shields, and this the *Post* did publish, arousing disappointingly little interest. She reported the atrocious conditions of neglected wounded, painfully disheartening to her as a nurse. Yet she could also file happier reports on occasion, like the story of the wounded German caught in front of the British trenches by constant heavy firing. For five long days the Tommies passed food and water out to him, and even candy, until finally they could rescue him.

Back in London, she irritated her male colleagues by obtaining exclusive interviews with the commander of the English forces, with Winston Churchill (then merely in the Cabinet), and with Queen Mary. By now she expected American entry into the war soon, and so she returned to the States in the hope of joining the Red Cross as a nurse. The kibosh was put on her application, however, by none other than General Pershing because of a War Department ruling against women as war correspondents, as well as suspicions about her noncorresponding role as nurse.

The Navy used her, nonetheless, to report on crew conditions, after which the Army competitively used her to report on doughboy conditions at various training camps around the country. Her performance earned her the admiration of the Secretary of War, who asked her to do the same service for troops overseas. Only days after her arrival in Paris the war ended with the Armistice, but General Pershing, after greeting her with uncharacteristic levity ("So you got here after all, did you?"), asked her to continue with her inspections and reports, this time for occupation troops in Germany. She did so, and their conditions were soon greatly improved. Her work was highly respected and effective, yet when she resumed her foreign-corresponding to cover the disarmament conference, she was excluded as a woman from the Press Club. That's when she became something of a feminist.

And so, back home, she returned to writing popular fiction again, churning out dozens of her celebrated books and plays almost to the day of her death in September 1958.

With the advent of World War II both the Army and the Navy asked her to do it again, to report on servicemen's and women's living conditions and morale. She could have her own plane, they said, for the purpose. But she was in her sixties, and her health wasn't up to it. She regretfully declined.

Jeanette Rankin
First U.S. Congresswoman
(1880–1973)

In April 1917, as the first Congresswoman in American history, she voted against U.S. entry into World War I. In December 1941 she did it again, this time casting the only vote in Congress against U.S. entry into World War II. Right or wrong, wise or foolish, she at least offered a note of caution amid the general frenzy

She was born in June 1880, the first of seven children, on a ranch just outside Missoula, Montana, and, after her father built it, was raised in the most elegant house in town, boasting hot and cold running water, a forced-air stove, and a zinc bathtub, all rarities in that still primitive Western community. (Montana didn't become a state until 1889.) For all its conveniences, however, she much preferred the rural delights of the ranch, including a riveting view of the nearby Bitterroot Mountains, crowned with snow. Even her burden of family responsibilities, as caretaker of six younger siblings, seemed lighter in the country. She was a take-charge, do-it sort of person, stitching up a deep gash in a horse's shoulder, amputating a ranch dog's trap-mangled foot and later fashioning a boot for it to wear.

For such a person school was mostly a bore. Assigned to read aloud from Tennyson's "The Charge of the Light Brigade," she angrily refused on the grounds, more prophetically than she knew, that it was a "hideous" piece of work. She learned much more from her father, who treated her more like an oldest son than an oldest daughter. Yet she did manage to make it through the University of Montana, graduating in 1902 with a B.S. in biology and, frustratingly, no sense of direction.

In 1904, shortly after her father's death, a visit to Boston opened her eyes to the miseries of untrammeled capitalism in the neglected squalor of workers' living conditions, so different from the life she knew. Back home four more years of irritating aimlessness propelled her into a visit with an uncle in San Francisco in late 1908, a visit that would change her life, giving it at least a sense of direction. More particularly, it was a visit to Telegraph Hill that altered her outlook. There she came across a settlement house for immigrant women and children with nowhere else to go this side of utter destitution. After four months of volunteer work there, she was hooked. As with Jane Addams of Chicago's Hull House, social reform became her credo, especially for women and children.

Half a year later she was enrolled in the New York School of Philanthropy, which included on its faculty such lights as Louis D. Brandeis (before he joined the Supreme Court) and Booker T. Washington (after he left the Tuskegee Institute). Besides courses in social reform, the curriculum required working in the police courts at night under the supervision of a probation officer. Sympathetic to the plight of the dispossessed victims of plutocratic injustice, she nevertheless carried about with her a billy club concealed in a commodious velvet bag, just in case.

After her graduation in 1909, a year in a children's home in Spokane convinced her that the social neglect of poor women and children was too widespread to be satisfactorily corrected by volunteer work, however praiseworthy. The corrective, she became convinced, would have to be social legislation, trammeling the prevailing untrammeled, predatory capitalism in the interest of social justice. That suggested getting into politics, a male bastion if ever there was one.

To that end she began taking courses in political science at the University of Washington, joined the state's Equal Suffrage Association, rose rapidly through the ranks, put up posters here, there, and everywhere (even in the window of a barber shop while the men watched in astonishment), and tasted the heady delights of victory when the legislature passed equal suffrage into law by a two-to-one margin.

On her return to Montana she was urged by the women in that state's Equal Franchise Society to address the legislature in support of a then pending equal-suffrage bill. Nervously but gamely she did so, but the bill was defeated. The issue, however, soon took on national importance when 146 working women were killed in the famous Triangle Shirtwaist Company fire in mid–Manhattan. Soon she was traveling all about the country under the aegis of the National American Woman Suffrage Association, lecturing, orating, buttonholing, earbending. She was largely responsible for a gratifying suffrage victory in North Dakota.

Meanwhile the seeds she had planted back home were sprouting: the Montana legislature passed a bill authorizing a referendum on women's right to vote. In 1914 she quit her Association job and rushed to do whatever she could to ensure her sisters' success in that referendum. Elected president of the Montana Equal Suffrage State Central Committee, she was once again here, there, and everywhere, traveling 9000 miles back and forth across the state like a restless tornado, sleeping in her car when necessary, pleading with male voters to do the right thing and urging children to ask their fathers "why they won't let your mothers vote." Ironically, the publicity attending her campaign brought her a passel of marriage proposals from admiring males, an unwanted byproduct in view of her single-mindedness. She would never marry.

Apparently she was admired even by men without marriage on their minds, for the referendum gave the state's women the vote by a less than overwhelming but nonetheless unmistakable margin. After several months' recuperative rest in New Zealand (she *did* get around), she returned to Montana in the spring of 1916 convinced that her work for the right to vote would have to be carried to the national level, even if that meant trying to run for Congress.

Trying, indeed. It was a laugh, everyone said—a *woman* running for *Congress*?!! Characteristically undaunted, and with her very political brother as her campaign manager, she filed as a Republican (anomalously, but the Democrats were better organized and loyally dedicated to their incumbent), the only woman in a field of eight candidates. Women and workers of both sexes surged to her support. She won the primary and the election, emerging as a national celebrity.

In those days politics and government were conducted at a more leisurely pace: she expected to have to go to Washington in early December 1917 for the opening of the 65th Congress. With war fever mounting against the Bloody Huns, however, President Woodrow Wilson called an emergency session for April 2. At that session he delivered what he afterwards called "a message of death for our young men," asking Congress to make the world safe for democracy by declaring war. Rankin was badgered by supporters to vote yes, including feminists who felt that a no vote would imperil the women's-vote movement, and even by her politically invaluable brother, who warned against political suicide. Yet she just couldn't bring herself to do it. She had promised Montanans that she would never vote to send American soldiers overseas. "I want to stand by my country," she announced in the hushed chamber when her turn came, "but I cannot vote for war. I vote no." Hers was only one of 56 negative votes (including six in the Senate), but it was of course hers that attracted the greatest public attention. Unfortunately.

During the rest of her stay in Congress she hardly feathered her political nest by fighting government bureaucrats and the Montana mining establishment for better working conditions. In the 1918 election, running for a Senate seat, she failed to win even the primary.

Only 23 years would elapse before the next American declaration of war. Many of those years she spent in Georgia, teaching and lecturing, but postwar disillusionment and growing antichauvinism encouraged her to return to Montana and run for the 77th Congress as a peace candidate. She did so and won, handily. Throughout 1941 she worked vigorously and persistently against precariously provocative measures like Lend-Lease support for Britain. During the previous year's campaign, after all, Franklin Roosevelt had ardently promised that "your boys are not going to be sent into any foreign wars." On the day after the Pearl Harbor attack, again she voted no. Some other Congressmen abstained rather than go on record in opposition, but she had the courage of her convictions. At the end of her term, wounded by relentless jingoistic vilification, she opted out of national politics, returning to her home in Georgia.

Indeed, she opted out of public life entirely for a while, expanding her horizons with considerable world traveling. But the Korean and Vietnam wars stimulated her into reentering the fray, speaking and demonstrating, getting involved. She was still actively engaged when she died in 1973 at the age of 92.

John F. Kennedy's book, *Profiles in Courage*, was criticized for not including any women. In response he wrote a magazine article for *McCall's* entitled "Three Women of Courage." One was Jeanette Rankin, of whom he wrote, "Few members of Congress have ever stood more alone while being true to a higher honor and loyalty."

After the famous Peace March in Washington in 1968, Coretta Scott King praised her as "the endurance symbol of the aspiration of American women—the symbol of the aspirations for peace of millions of us."

Suffrage for women, nationwide, was established by the 20th Amendment in August 1920.

Frances Perkins
First Woman U.S. Cabinet Member
(1882–1965)

At that first meeting of Franklin Roosevelt's Cabinet in the spring of 1933, Secretary of Labor Frances Perkins, first woman Cabinet member in

American history, sat opposite the Secretary of Commerce, South Carolina's crusty sexagenarian Daniel Roper, known for his sonorous misgivings over "the premature recognition of women." She appreciated the irony.

She was born Fannie Coralie Perkins in April 1882 in Boston. Her very proper New England family boasted a Revolutionary lineage, quietly of course, and she was a shy, reserved young lady except when she let herself go on national holidays like the Fourth of July. Under her usual diffidence, however, there lurked a streak of stubborn independence, which showed itself especially after her graduation from the Worcester Classical High School when she forcefully coaxed her reluctant parents to let her, despite her sex, cultivate her mind at Mount Holyoke College. Such impertinence surely would have given Secretary Roper terminal apoplexy, even though it was a girls' school.

In college she lost much of her shyness, even being dubbed "Perky" by her classmates in spite of the school autocrats' ignoring her preference for the humanities and channeling her into chemistry, biology and even advanced physics—treatment that left her little time for socializing, discouraged her, and hurt her academic record. Yet before her graduation in 1902 she managed to enter into several student activities so successfully that she was elected "permanent president" of her class. Her rather mediocre scholastic achievements didn't bother her—college, she would insist later, "is for learning afterwards."

Her learning afterwards included teaching various subjects in various schools—such as "Geology (bluff)" as she described it—although her prosperous father and her mother still preferred she stay at home and attract suitors. Her postgraduate learning also included volunteer work with girls in their early teens who worked slave-labor hours for starvation wages, work that provided her with an eye-opening learning experience. She began reading books on poverty in America, spent some time at Chicago's celebrated Hull House, and gradually reached a decision to become a social worker. In the fall of 1907, to her parents' dismay, she took a modest-paying job as general secretary of an association in Philadelphia dedicated to the care and protection of immigrants. Among her more memorable learning experiences was an attack one rainy evening by two formidable black men, pimps whose lucrative trade she was threatening. She drove them off at the point of her umbrella.

In 1909 she moved to New York to take advantage of a fellowship at a school of social work associated with Columbia University. This time her academic work earned her a master's degree. For practical experience she lived in Greenwich Village, inhabited by a wild ethnic mix of people working sixty hours a week and more for as little as employers could get away with in a labor-buyer's market. She met and worked with the young Sinclair Lewis and briefly met the gay young blade Franklin Roosevelt. She was happy with her life, helping others. She felt fulfilled.

After the notorious Triangle Shirtwaist Factory fire in New York in March 1911, in which 146 workers, chiefly young girls, died in screaming masses pressed against locked exits, she worked almost frantically in various capacities for the several organizations assembled to investigate the tragedy and to submit legislation to prevent a recurrence. While she was at it, she also buttonholed key state legislators in a successful effort to get laws enacted limiting women's and children's work schedules to a controversial 54 hours a week.

In September 1913 she married Paul Wilson, a financial statistician, but kept her maiden name. She was in her thirties now, had earned a reputation under the name of Perkins (for "nothing but agitations," a Neanderthal critic maintained) and, as the papers reported at the time, didn't want to "embarrass her husband with her political activities." He managed to interfere with her political activities, however: in January 1917 a daughter was born. Her last name would be Perkins-Wilson until she registered to vote, when the choice would be up to her.

Among the fellow investigators with whom Perkins toured the state turning over industrial rocks was a state legislator named Al Smith. In January 1919 Smith, newly elected governor of New York, appointed her a state industrial commissioner. The uproar was immediate—it was not merely that she had radical views but that she was even a *woman!* Governor Smith held firm, as of course did she, and the state senate confirmed her appointment, 36 to 14. She would keep her seat on the commission during his four terms, dealing with the geometric multiplication of immigrant labor and the bitter ethnic hostilities arising from it, making no friends among rapacious industrialists but also learning how to cooperate with their less predatory associates.

In 1928, after campaigning on Smith's behalf during his futile Presidential campaign, she was comforted at least by an honorary M.A. from her alma mater and by the election of Franklin Roosevelt to the New York governorship, a job for which she'd urged him to run. And so in January 1929 she was appointed *the* Industrial Commissioner, administrative head of the state's department of labor, with 1800 employees serving more than three million people a year and overseeing some 70,000 businesses. Over the next four years she led fights to restrict child labor, improve wages and working conditions, and promote equality for women in the workplace, although her efforts were severely hampered by the ravages of the burgeoning Great Depression and the Hoover Administration's sunny reassurances that everything was going to be all right if no one rocked the boat.

And so it was that FDR took her with him to Washington in 1933 and appointed her Secretary of Labor, the first woman member of a Presidential Cabinet, giving her an opportunity to prove herself not only an efficient administrator but an efficient radical as well. She didn't disappoint him. She drafted quite a bit of the New Deal's historic legislation, particularly the Social Security Act and the National Labor Relations Act in 1935 and the Wages and Hours Act in 1938.

Her presence in the Cabinet created some serious protocol problems.

When the men-only Gridiron Club gave a dinner for the Cabinet, for instance, she wasn't invited. To counter the slight, Eleanor Roosevelt characteristically gave a dinner in her honor that night at the White House, for women only. (Unfortunately, one of the guests was bitten by one of the Roosevelts' dogs, a male.)

Frances Perkins was Secretary of Labor for twelve years. In December 1944, after Roosevelt's fourth election to the Presidency, she wrote him a letter of resignation because "with one major exception [what we now call Medicare] all the items we discussed as 'among the practical possibilities' before you took office as President have been accomplished or begun." No, he replied, there were still things to do, and he needed her help in doing them. But a few months later, after his death, President Harry Truman accepted her resignation, reluctantly. She was in her sixties now and very tired. But she would lecture and teach until her death in 1965.

"Twelve years has been long enough," editorialized the *New York Times* magnanimously in 1945, "to prove that a woman is not out of place in the Cabinet. Frances Perkins will not be the last woman to occupy such a position."

Anna O'Hare McCormick
Pulitzer Prize Winning Journalist
(1882–1954)

Her prescient reporting and commentary between the two World Wars, among other things, brought her an extraordinary collection of honors. In 1935 Carrie Chapman Catt, premier suffragette, numbered her among her country's ten outstanding women. In 1937 she won a Pulitzer Prize, the first woman journalist to do so. She won prizes for her feature stories and her foreign correspondence, as well as several honorary degrees. But probably the *pièce de résistance* was a gift from a hosiery manufacturer during World War II, a dozen pairs of scarce, universally coveted nylon stockings. How could she rate such an accolade?

She was born Anna O'Hare in May 1882 in Yorkshire, England, during a family visit and was raised in Ohio by her American parents. Her mother, an Irish Catholic poet, writer, and editor, saw to it that she had a thoroughly Catholic education through college, after which mother and daughter collaborated in editing a Catholic weekly in Cleveland. In 1910 the daughter up and married Francis J. McCormick, an engineer engaged in an export-import business, and moved with him to Dayton, where she assumed the roles of full-time wife and part-time writer of poetry and prose.

As a journalist she was a late starter. Early in 1921, as she and her husband were planning a trip to Europe, she wrote a letter to the managing editor of the *New York Times* asking rather hesitantly if he would accept news stories from her. Partly because the *Times'* misogynist publisher was ill at home, she was told to go ahead and submit her stories on a "we'll see" arrangement. The editor discovered quite soon that her reportage was eminently publishable, such as her article in July reporting on a speech by Benito Mussolini ("one of the best political speeches I have heard, a little swaggering, but caustic, powerful and telling")—whom she identified with foresight as the dynamic leader of a rising, and menacing, political movement.

Yet she charmed him in her first interview with him, chiefly because her careful preparations had included a reading of a formidable new book on corporation law under authoritarianism. When she asked him about it, he countered by asking, rather superciliously, if she'd read it. To his astonishment, she had. He congratulated her on being probably the only person besides himself who had read it (if he had), and thereafter granted her frequent interviews until her opinion of Fascism became intolerable. Within a year, in 1922, the *Times* hired her formally as a regular contributor. She would be with the paper as reporter and featured columnist for the next 32 years.

She made a point of wandering about a country's capital city interviewing people on the street so that she could contribute some valuable information in an interview as well as ask questions. As a result her interview in Moscow with the almost pathologically reticent Josef Stalin lasted for six mutually stimulating hours. ("Lacking brilliance," this modern Cassandra wrote perceptively, "Stalin gives the impression of craft and suppleness. He is the shrewd manipulator, quietly obstinate, ruthless without passion." For all her insightfulness, little did she know.) Armed with a powerful memory, she could conduct interviews without taking notes, further disarming her victims.

Impressed with the anxiety lines in the faces of the many European leaders whom she interviewed, in the mid–1930s she predicted imminent conflict on the Continent and the isolation-intervention contention that would consequently arise in the United States. She was in Rome during Neville Chamberlain's dilatory conversation with Mussolini and in London when Chamberlain finally abandoned his efforts at appeasement. With Hitler's invasion of Poland in September 1939 she left London hastily for Romania to file grim stories on the plight of Polish refugees fleeing into that country. A little later she was even filing stories from Berlin and, as the war progressed, from the Middle East and elsewhere, following troop movements and interviewing GIs and generals. Soon after D-Day she interviewed the redoubtable General George Patton, to his considerable surprise. In March 1945 she treated Franklin Roosevelt to one of her informational interviews just a few weeks before his death.

After the war she covered the San Francisco conference that set up the

United Nations, reported on the Nuremberg trials, served as a delegate to UNESCO, and, in her late sixties, joined the guerrillas in Greece for sympathetic coverage of their losing battle to establish a socialist republic. Her constant companion through it all was her husband, who had abandoned his export-import business to accompany her on her travels as a kind of manager.

Part of her charm was her provocative Irish wit, which inspired her for example to attend the 1952 GOP national convention in a white dress imprinted with little Democratic donkeys and then the Democratic convention in a similar white dress imprinted with little Republican elephants. She had more than a nodding acquaintance with both Truman and Eisenhower.

She never did have time enough to sit down and write a book, although some of her columns have been published in two collections, *Vatican Journal* and *The World at Home*. Those columns ended with her death in May 1954, when the *Times* printed her last one bordered in black. Four years earlier she had been awarded the Roosevelt Medal of Honor with the notation that over the previous quarter-century she had "done more for the enlightenment of the American public in international affairs than most secretaries of state."

Doubtless she felt, without saying so yet quite justifiably, that this was rather small praise.

Eleanor Roosevelt
Nontraditional First Lady
(1884–1961)

After her husband Franklin died in April 1945, her response to a reporter's request for an interview was a dispirited "The story is over." Yet more than twenty years earlier, after discovering Franklin's attraction for another woman, she had decided to make an independent life of her own. Ironically, his polio attack would soon make him seriously dependent on her and her much less dependent on him. As for those seventeen years after his death, history speaks for her independence most eloquently.

Anna Eleanor Roosevelt was born in October 1884 in New York into a family of patrician affluence later made famous by her Uncle Teddy. Her childhood was largely one of affluent misery. Her incompatible parents died young, and she was raised by a grandmother with a rigidity that developed in her a need for approval and affection, evidently from a lack thereof. In an English finishing school, however, encouraged by a sympathetic headmistress, the shy young thing with an ugly-duckling complex grew into a person displaying self-confidence and even leadership qualities.

And a mind of her own. On her return to New York in 1902, she avoided the ceremonial folderol of "making her debut in society," opting instead to wait on the destitute in a local settlement house, to work with children in the ghettos, and to join an investigation into women's working conditions. Some distraction from this activity was provided during her summers by her engagingly handsome sixth cousin Franklin Roosevelt between his semesters at Harvard. In March 1905 she was married to Franklin, with Uncle Teddy filling in for her father.

Unfortunately this marriage brought her under the dominion of someone more formidable than her grandmother. Her mother-in-law, Sara, whose domestic competence and bossiness left Eleanor with little to do but give birth to her six children (one of whom died of the flu at eight months) and stifled any feeling of self-confidence. After 1910, with Franklin now a state senator, she did get somewhat away from Sara by moving with him to Albany, where she dutifully performed the social chores of a political wife. She was much happier when, as the wife of an Assistant Secretary of the Navy during World War I, she found fulfillment working for the Red Cross.

Late in 1918, while unpacking his bags after he returned home from Europe, she came across some highly compromising correspondence with her very attractive secretary, Lucy Mercer—sufficiently compromising, she felt sure, to sue him for divorce on grounds of adultery. Deeply hurt, she might have done so had not Franklin been persuaded by the indomitable Sara to give up Lucy and save his marriage, and thereby his political career. (Sara also exercised some financial clout.) The marriage was saved, although the couple's very real mutual affection thereafter was evidently platonic.

In 1921, FDR emerged from the polio attack at first completely paralyzed and then, after heroic exercising, permanently unable to walk or even to stand without braces and someone's arm for support. Eleanor had already declared her independence, becoming politically active in the Democratic Party and the League of Women Voters. Now, although her husband's illness and subsequent crippled condition intensified that independence, it also bound her more tightly than ever to him out of sympathy as well as her sense of duty. Indeed, during the 1920's, with advice and support from his and her politically savvy friend Louis Howe, and against Sara's maternally protective opposition, she helped him maintain his interest in politics and even began representing him at political gatherings—in addition to taking his place in their children's outdoor recreation. In 1926, with a couple of friends, she founded a successful furniture factory and, the next year, took over a school for girls in New York, teaching English rhetoric and literature and American history.

The year after that, 1928, Franklin crowned her efforts in therapy, as well as his own, by winning election as governor. For the next four years (he was overwhelmingly reelected in 1930) her service as First Lady and as ambulatory aide was invaluable not only to him but also to her as basic training for the impending years in the White House.

She arrived there in March 1933 and set about showing that she would be no traditional American First Lady but a woman with her own agenda. She did unprecedented things like having weekly press conferences (with women reporters), going on lecture tours, writing a regular syndicated column, holding forth on her own radio program. In the process she attracted plenty of hostile comment from dyspeptic critics like New York's Cardinal Spellman (on government aid to parish schools) and the far-righteous Westbrook Pegler (on everything). In the Administration, during the Great Depression, hers was a powerful voice for the dispossessed and, during World War II, for the dogfaces with whom she visited continually.

Her assumption that her "story was over" with Franklin's death in 1945 marked the beginning of a new and fully independent career. Quite a celebrity on her own now, she continued with her column, her radio and, later, TV appearances, her travels and meetings with world leaders for most of her remaining seventeen years. Appointed by Harry Truman in late 1945 as her country's delegate to the new United Nations, and again in 1961 by John F. Kennedy, she did much to lessen Third World hostility toward the ostensibly plutocratic United States. She continued her active support of Democratic Presidential and other candidates, especially the ill-fated Adlai Stevenson (fated to run twice against a popular war hero), and of course Jack Kennedy in 1960.

Besides her unceasing official and political activity, she had a busy personal life as matron of her prodigiously burgeoning family. On her 77th birthday in 1961 she conceded that perhaps she "should slow down." But with only another year to live she didn't really have a chance to do so.

In early 1933, after she had shown that she wasn't likely to be a conventional First Lady, the liberal columnist Heywood Broun welcomed the idea of a woman in the White House who felt that "she is before all else a human being and that she has a right to her own individual career regardless of the prominence of her husband." She didn't disappoint him.

Dorothy Thompson
Freedom Fighter (1894–1961)

She wasn't a freedom fighter in the conventional sense, literally taking up arms against an oppressive regime. Her weapon was not a sword but a mighty pen, with which she fulminated most entertainingly, for millions of newspaper readers and radio listeners, against enemies of human freedom from Adolf Hitler through Josef Stalin to Joe McCarthy. She was a strong woman with strong opinions, not much given to tolerating male condescension: when the rightist demagogue Father Charles Coughlin took to calling her Dottie, she took to calling him Chuck.

Dorothy Thompson was born in July 1894 in Lancaster, New York. Her first fighting was with her tyrannical stepmother, whom her father, a penurious Methodist clergyman, had married not long after her mother's death. The fighting became intense enough for her to be shipped off to live with a couple of aunts for greater freedom in Chicago. After a conventional education and graduation from the Lewis Institute there in 1911, she went on a kind of educational long-time spree between 1912 and 1941 that included study at Syracuse University, the University of Vienna, Tufts University, Columbia University, Dartmouth College and McGill University. After receiving her B.A. from Syracuse in 1914, she spent the next few years as a paid worker in the struggle for women's suffrage in Cincinnati.

What she really wanted was a job in journalism, and to that end in 1920 she invested her rather meager savings into a trip to Europe. In Ireland she wrote some articles on the rebellion there and, gratifyingly, sold them to the International News Service. In Italy she interviewed a prominent left-wing union leader, but she was discouraged by a general lack of interest in her reporting until the Paris bureau chief of the *Philadelphia Public Ledger* promised to look over whatever she submitted and even began to publish her dispatches on political turmoil in Hungary and Czechoslovakia. Soon she was on the *Ledger*'s payroll as its correspondent in Vienna. Her work in Hungary got her involved with a writer, Joseph Bard, whom she (among others) found devastatingly attractive, so much so that she married him at the cost of her American citizenship.

This didn't affect the quality of her reporting (often colorfully embroidered), and in 1925 she was promoted to bureau chief in Berlin not only for the *Ledger* but also for the *New York Post*. Her success was widely touted in American women's magazines, inspiring her to write an article for *The Nation* decrying their habit of publicizing women's achievements as exceptional rather than treating them as something simply to be expected.

One day in July 1927, the day on which her divorce from Bard became final, she met the brilliant and mercurial Sinclair Lewis, who thereupon embarked on a project of using his considerable literary skills in love letters to her while following her about Europe as best he could. By November it was a love match—in Moscow, where they surely needed their love to keep them warm and where she gathered information for her 1928 book, *The New Russia*. Later that year they married and returned to the U.S., where she could renew her citizenship and he could renew his heavy tippling. In 1930 she bore him a son, and he won a Nobel Prize on other grounds.

In 1931 *Cosmopolitan* magazine sent her to Germany. Her interviews with the up-and-coming ogre resulted in a book, *I Saw Hitler*. Her utter contempt for him caused her to underestimate him and him to expel her from Germany in 1934. Not long after her return to America she was hired as a columnist, alternating with none other than the paragon Walter Lippmann, by the *New York Herald Tribune*. Although the writing of columns had hitherto been strictly a male preserve, by 1937 hers was syndicated in well over a hundred papers. A journalistic celebrity, she broadened her fame with a national radio news program as her income soared to heights almost obscene in the Great Depression. Her success and busy schedule had their likely effect on her marriage with Lewis, which slowly deteriorated until their divorce in 1941.

By that time, having had her invigorating tiffs with isolationists like Charles Lindbergh and Father Coughlin, and having spent a great deal of journalistic energy inveighing against the policy of appeasement in Europe, she had visited Rome to appeal to the pope to prevent Mussolini from entering the war. (The pope suggested that, as a Protestant, she was vastly overestimating his influence.) At home she supported Wendell Willkie's Republican candidacy for the Presidency, then belatedly switched to Franklin Roosevelt as the more experienced leader, and in early 1941 her contract with the Republican *Herald Tribune* was not renewed. She transferred her allegiance to the *New York Post* and resumed her briefly canceled radio broadcasts. She was still a celebrity, receiving over a hundred personal-appearance requests per week. It was an up time for her, not only professionally: after her divorce from Lewis she married an Austrian painter, Maxim Kopf, who could handle her, and that he did, to their mutual satisfaction, until his death in 1958.

Praised by both Roosevelt and Churchill for the services that her reporting had performed, she spent the late 1940s and the 1950s concentrating on the Middle East, where, for all her pro–Semitism, she deplored the treatment of the Palestinians. She also deplored the requirement of loyalty oaths and the general McCarthyist atmosphere of the times. After Kopf's death she ended her twenty years of columns, retiring to a less frenetic lifestyle. She spent the Christmas holidays of 1960 in Lisbon, visiting her divorced daughter-in-law and her grandchildren, and died there in January.

At her request, there was no eulogy at the cemetery. Her legacy spoke for itself.

Amelia Earhart
Famous Pilot (1897–1937?)

Amelia Earhart first tried flying at the age of seven. After leaning a couple of very long planks from the roof of a shed in the family's backyard and two more at their foot propped up at the far end, she equipped a simple smaller plank with some old roller skates. After a few bruising trials, she rode giddily down the first planks and up the second and then soared into the air for a few exhilarating moments of free flight. She and a few friends enjoyed a number of delirious flights until her alarmed mother discovered the operation and had the homemade airport dismantled.

Amelia was born in July 1897 in Atchison, Kansas. Her father was a railroad lawyer who was away from home a great deal, but her mother encouraged her two daughters' tomboy tendencies, short of experimental aviation. So did their father for that matter, with purchases of boys' toys—balls, bats air rifles, sleds. A sled brought Amelia one of her more delicious thrills one winter day when she avoided colliding with a horse and cart by steering precariously but harmlessly under the trotting horse, between its legs—to her considerable relief, doubtless more than matched by the cart driver's.

Her family life was less pleasant after her father fell victim to alcohol abuse, sporadic unemployment, and the need to move from town to town in search of work. As a result she attended six high schools, graduating in 1915 from one in Chicago in time to take advantage of a break in the family's misfortunes and enroll at a girls' college in Pennsylvania. In 1917, however, during a visit to her mother and sister in Toronto, she was so moved by the sight of wounded Canadian soldiers that she left school, joined the Red Cross, and became a nurse's aide at a military hospital.

Off duty, she was invited one day by a friendly airman in the Royal Flying Corps to watch him stunt-flying at a local airfield. She did so, and again, and again. The bug was biting but not yet deeply. After the war she moved to Los Angeles with her mother and sister to rejoin their father, temporarily a teetotaler. At an air circus at Long Beach the bug began biting again, and, after she was treated to a ride in a plane, the bite penetrated to her very soul. Soon thereafter she was taking flying lessons, and early in 1921 she made her first solo flight. The next year, although licenses weren't required for flying, she made it official by acquiring an international pilot's license and buying a small plane. To prove that she deserved the license and the plane, which she could barely afford, she flew to an altitude of 14,000 feet, setting a new women's record.

Her flying career had to be put on hold, however, when her father returned to the bottle and her mother, after the divorce, decided to move to Boston. Amelia sold her plane, drove her mother to Boston, and found work there teaching English at a settlement house for immigrants. Admiringly envious of Charles Lindbergh's flight across the Atlantic in May 1927, she continued flying whenever she could, accumulating some 500 hours of time in the air and inadvertently attracting the attention of some people looking for a woman flyer experienced and dedicated and reckless enough to cross the Atlantic, including the attention of publisher George Putnam, who wanted the story. Although two men would act as pilot and navigator and she would merely keep the flight log, and although four women had died in similar projects, she agreed—eagerly. If she didn't make it, she wrote in a farewell letter to sister, "I shall be happy to pop off in the midst of such an adventure."

She made it, after nearly 21 hours of flying, including many nervous moments convinced she was off course. Indeed, because she and her crew landed in Wales instead of Southampton, England, all the welcome they received at first on landing was a friendly wave. The reporters and the cheering crowds came soon after, however. President Coolidge cabled his congratulations. In New York it was ticker tape, a key to the city, and flattering headlines for "Lady Lindy." She resented the comparison: Lindbergh had *flown* the Atlantic, she pointed out, whereas she had been about as vital to the flight "as a sack of potatoes."

At Putnam's urging she wrote a book about her adventure, a very marketable book much better written than might be expected from a sack of potatoes.

Soon she was in the air again, flying her new plane from New York to Los Angeles to visit her father and attend the air races, and then back again. Neither flight was uneventful—in 1928 this was no nonstop 747 flight. There were plenty of unanticipated stops for various repairs, including a landing on a fortunately unoccupied street in Hobbs, New Mexico. But she was the first woman to make the round trip alone without a terminal belly flop. She took a job as aviation editor with *Cosmopolitan* and toured the country in a newer, larger plane in response to a rising demand for lectures and in pursuit of air races, in which she continually set speed records. Meanwhile Putnam, after his divorce, had asked her five times to marry him, and at the sixth, in 1931, she said yes, despite misgivings as to the possible effect on her freedom and her career. As it turned out, the marriage restrained her freedom very little, and as for her career, she found that she had garnered not only a devoted husband but also a top-flight PR man.

In May 1932, confident that she was as much of a lone eagle as Lindbergh, she headed out alone across the Atlantic. Although a broken altimeter, a cracked exhaust pipe and a gas leak kept her from getting to Paris, she did make it to Ireland, the first woman to solo across that unfriendly ocean. In January 1932 she soloed from Hawaii to California, then from there to Mexico City, and then to Newark, New Jersey, where police had to protect her from the perilously admiring crowd.

In 1937 Purdue University, in connection with its new Department of Aviation, established an Amelia Earhart Research Foundation, which in turn furnished her with a magnificent new Lockheed Electra for purposes of aeronautic research. A useful as well as spectacular research project, she decided, would be a global flight of some 27,000 miles, following the equator as closely as possible. "I think I have one long-distance flight left in me," she announced, "and this is it."

Her first attempt, in March 1937, ended in near disaster. She and her copilot made it to Honolulu, but the trip from there had to be aborted after the plane was badly damaged on takeoff. Back in California for repairs, she decided to try again, in the other direction because of weather forecasts. On June 1, having stopped in Miami for final repairs, she and her navigator spent the rest of the month flying across the South Atlantic, the Sahara, India, and Australia (with refueling stops along the way) to New Guinea. The next stop was the minuscule Howland Island on the equator, a tiny target 2500 miles away without a speck of land en route.

At the island a Coast Guard cutter waited to guide the flyers in after establishing radio contact. For about two hours, roughly between 7 and 9 A.M., the cutter's radio crew heard her voice and tried frantically to establish clear two-way communications. After what seemed to be a final message from her the Navy instituted a search over a quarter million miles of ocean, but her plane was never found. It had run out of fuel, the Navy surmised, about 200 miles north of the island. Since then many other explanations for her disappearance have been posited, some assiduously researched and others quite imaginative but none conclusive.

After her death her husband's sorrow was eased somewhat by a letter that she had written to him near the end of the flight. "Women must try to do things as men have tried. When they fail, their failure must be but a challenge to others."

Margaret Chase Smith
Maverick Congresswoman
(1897–1995)

She served in Congress for more than thirty years as a Republican, although more full-blooded, doctrinaire Republicans might well dispute the party affiliation. No knee-jerk conservative, she supported quite a few of Franklin Roosevelt's initiatives and condemned virtually all of Joe McCarthy's fulminations. Ever a maverick, she was never just one of the herd.

She was born Margaret Madeline Chase in December 1897 in Skowhegan, Maine. The family of six lived in poverty but not destitution. ("We certainly didn't go hungry, but we didn't have anything.") After graduating from high school she taught elementary school for a couple of years and then took up working for a living in a series of jobs, as a telephone operator, business manager of the phone company, circulation manager for a local paper, office manager for a woolen mill, treasurer for a waste-processing firm.

The daily grind ended with her marriage in 1930 to Clyde Smith, businessman, newspaper publisher, and aspiring politician. In support of his career she joined the GOP state committee until, in 1936, he was elected to the House of Representatives and they moved to Washington for the legislative carousel, or carousal. When his career ended prematurely with his death in April 1940, she was elected in June to fill the vacancy. Two controversial Roosevelt-inspired measures were then before the Congress: The Lend-Lease compact with Great Britain and the first peacetime draft, the Selective Training and Service Act. Despite much heated Republican opposition, both measures passed, narrowly, with her support.

In 1943, having been elected to the 78th Congress in her own right, she was assigned to the Naval Affairs Committee. This gave her an opportunity to logroll for legislation promoting the status of women in auxiliary military units and of course for the 1948 Women's Armed Services Integration Act. On the domestic front after the war she inspired some conservative conniptions with her occasional support of Harry Truman, her opposition to restrictions on the right to strike, and her refusal to subscribe to permanent status for the witch-hunting Committee on Un-American Activities.

By mid–1947 she was a member of several important committees, but after Wallace White, Maine's senior Senator and the Republican majority leader, announced his forthcoming retirement that summer, the lure of a Senate seat proved irresistible. After a tough primary against the state's governor and a former governor, she easily defeated her Democratic opponent in this first of her four elections to the Senate. Although usually controversial, she would never be accused of laxity or negligence. Between June 1955 and an illness in September 1968, she piled up a total of almost three thousand consecutive votes, never missing a roll call.

Not surprisingly, she was among the first to take on the witch-hunting Senator Joe McCarthy. By June 1950 to her considerable dismay the Wisconsin demagogue was already making hay with his scattershot charges of Communist conspiracies and his feckless accusations. And so she expressed her dismay quite forcefully in a speech condemning the practice of charging people with treason from under the protective cover of Congressional immunity. The speech received a good deal of liberal applause and even the endorsement of half a dozen stalwart Republicans, although it did little or nothing to impede McCarthyism. In the 1954 Maine primary, although McCarthy had made a well-publicized point of endorsing her opponent, she won with more than 80 percent of the votes cast. That December, it need hardly be said, she joined in the Senate vote to censure the excruciatingly junior Senator from Wisconsin.

In the mid-fifties she particularly promoted greater government activity in the promotion of national health standards. In the early sixties she proved herself no peacenik, urging Jack Kennedy to convince the Soviets that he was capable of nuclear retaliation and voting against the Test Ban Treaty of 1963. On a less momentous level, she eventually overcame Senator (and Republican leader) Everett Dirksen's fondness for the marigold as the national flower, although it wasn't until 1987 that her choice, the rose, was formally named in legislation.

In 1964, alarmed at the thought of Barry Goldwater, she entered her name as a Republican candidate for the Presidency in several states, but her Party was already too keep in its suicidal primitivism to pay her any heed. During the Nixon Administration she protested against its efforts to squelch opposition while she decried the outlandish behavior of the wildly demonstrative exponents of the opposition. She herself was, of course, fairly often part of the opposition, voting against some of Nixon's military initiatives and against his nominations to the Supreme Court. (The names Haynsworth and Carswell rang many a discordant bell in those days.)

In 1972 she was 74 years old. Thus her fifth term, for which she ran in 1972, would have kept her in the Senate until she was 80. Her opponent in the primary won the election by making a big thing of her age and her inaccessibility to her constituents, based on her failure to maintain an office in the state. And so she went back home to Skowhegan and to the care and feeding of the Margaret Chase Smith Library. No regrets—she had made her mark. She died May 29, 1995.

Margaret Mead
Anthropologist (1901–1978)

Margaret Mead's father, who taught economics at the fast-growing University of Pennsylvania, had been assigned the job of establishing branches of the school, which required incessant moving about the state. As a result, in her first dozen years she lived in sixty homes. So it's hardly surprising that she could spend so much of her adult life wandering about the South Pacific.

Margaret Mead was born in December 1901 in Philadelphia. As a child she showed such great interest in the behavior of her younger brothers and sisters that her grandmother urged her to take notes. She did so, copiously, thereby establishing a lifelong habit. Her grandmother, indeed, with assists from her mother, was her teacher until she was eleven, since the family's mobility militated against formal schooling. At eleven, however, she was enrolled in a private school and, after graduation, in a public school where lack of challenge spurred her into writing dramatic sketches and starting up a school paper. In her quieter moments she read prodigiously.

While still in high school she fell in love with the brother of her science teacher. Luther Cressman was four years older than she, a college man of parts. They became secretly engaged but set no date. First she had to go to college. After an unpleasant year at DePauw in Indiana, where her Eastern ways made her something of a pariah and her good grades made her socially unacceptable among her male classmates, she transferred to Barnard, the woman's college in New York, a city where she could fit in nicely, especially since that's where Luther Cressman was living at the time.

In her senior year at Barnard she took a course in anthropology from the celebrated Frank Boaz, the "greatest mind" that she would ever encounter. Fascinated, she initiated what would prove to be a lifelong friendship with his assistant, Ruth Benedict, and made up her mind that this had to be her career. After graduating with honors in 1923, she married Luther Cressman but kept her own name because she expected to make a name for herself. Almost immediately they were separated, with him going to France to teach sociology for a year and her sailing for the South Pacific.

Boaz had wanted her to do her graduate field work among Native Americans, but she felt that the field was too crowded. (A joke at the time described a normal Native American family as consisting of the parents, a child, and an anthropologist.) With her father's moral and financial support and Boaz's reluctant agreement, she headed for American Samoa to study the behavior of adolescent girls. Petite and rather bubbly, she expected to fit right in.

After laboriously learning the Samoan language well enough to get by, and the native customs also well enough to get by, she met Edward Holt, a young naval medic, and his wife Ruth, who lived on a small island called T'au about a hundred miles away. Living with the natives on the main island meant such a lack of privacy—a single room containing all family members in steamy intimacy in the rain-soaked Samoan climate—that she jumped at the chance to go to T'au and live less aboriginally with the Holts. It was a decision that would invite criticism later from anthropological purists, but the island's modest population did include a group of fifty young ladies with whom she could make friends while observing them caring for their younger siblings, doing family chores, going fishing on weekdays and to church on Sundays, and chatting about their relatives, boys, and marriage plans. In the evenings, after joining in the dancing and merrymaking, she would work on her notes for hours.

The work resulted in 1928's *Coming of Age in Samoa*, a readable best seller that established her reputation as an anthropologist among the general literate U.S. population but would prove controversial among professionals as the years went by because of its insistence on the relative placidity of teenage life in the Samoan environment. Nonetheless, her celebrity was based on scholarly investigation. Although not the world's most celebrated personality, she was, rather suddenly, the world's most celebrated anthropologist.

During the voyage home in 1926 she had met a young New Zealander, Reo Fortune, who was en route to Cambridge University for graduate work in psychology. Although their common interests developed into a strong romantic attachment, they parted company when she returned to Luther and to a job with New York's American Museum of Natural History. Although she would never have a really permanent home, her office in one of the museum's towers would be her office for the next 52 years, Samoan decorations and all.

In October 1928, after her divorce from Luther Cressman and marriage to Reo Fortune, the newlyweds took off for Manus, an Admiralty island just north of New Guinea. There, known to the natives as Western Man and Western Woman, they studied child psychology until she was ready to go back to New York and get to work on her second book, *Growing Up in New Guinea.* After the book's publication, the couple took off again in 1931, this time for New Guinea itself, where she was interested in studying sex relationships and character differences among the several tribes (e.g., peaceable vs. warlike).

As she had on Manus, she had several attacks of malaria, and this time Reo seemed to show less sympathy. Indeed, he seemed crankier to her by the day, as did she to him. The marriage was unraveling and, after a young English anthropologist named Gregory Bateson joined them in their work, it came apart. The threesome left New Guinea in 1933. Separated and then divorced from Reo, she married Gregory in 1936, in Singapore, and then *these* newlyweds took off for Bali, an anthropological paradise full of mystery, color, grace, and ceaseless activity. There, besides snapping thousands of still pictures, they produced a film, *Trance and Dance in Bali,* an anthropological pioneer classic. Nor was that all they produced. When they sailed for New York in 1939, she was pregnant.

Little Cathy was born that December and Margaret was delighted to become a child psychologist for real. Working part-time at the museum and teaching at New York University, she worked with Gregory on a book of Bali photos. Not long thereafter they were separated by the war, which called him back to England and for which she wrote a book on Americans' attitudes toward waging war. After his return three years later, in 1946, he seemed alienated. Soon he was living three thousand miles away in California. Meanwhile she cared for Cathy (who would eventually follow her mother into anthropology), wrote, taught, gave interviews on radio and later on television, and lectured, lectured, lectured.

Her divorce in 1950 was a blow, but she had her work. In 1953 she returned to Manus to study the effects of the war on its culture and from there went to Bali. Over the next two decades she would write more than thirty books and earn even more honors of various kinds. In 1976, at 75, she was feted in an all-day affair organized by the American Association of Anthropologists. (To her great delight, Gregory was there). The museum and her publisher wished her Happy Birthday in a full-page ad in the *New York Times.* Her death in November 1978 was a worldwide news story.

She had once told a friend that what really terrified her was being bored. Evidently she almost never was.

Barbara McClintock
Winner of the Nobel Prize for Medicine
(1902–1992)

Half a century ago geneticists assumed, quite fixedly, that genes, the units of heredity, were fixed quite immovably in their positions in a chromosome. In 1951 Barbara McClintock read a paper at a symposium reporting that her study of corn chromosomes had revealed that genes move. Not that they were giddily "jumping"—that was later media hype—but that they can and do change position, thus rearranging the chromosome. The audience of specialists reacted to her proposition with stunned, stony, even hostile silence, followed later by some muttered suggestions in the lobby that maybe she'd gone bonkers. Everyone *knew* that genes don't move! It would be a quarter-century before the mossbacks caught up to her.

She was born in June 1902 in Hartford, Connecticut, but after a family move she and her two sisters and brother went to grammar and high school in Brooklyn. In the former her first love was baseball, in the latter, science. Figuring out solutions to scientific problems, she discovered, was "just pure joy." Given this addiction, she naturally wanted to go on to college, but her mother (her father was an army surgeon overseas) could neither afford nor countenance sending a girl to college, even after one of her sisters earned a scholarship to Vassar.

She resorted to working, with evenings spent at the local public library, until her father returned and took her side, finding her a place as a biology major at Cornell's College of Agriculture. She had a surprising amount of company, for women, newly enfranchised, were eager for college training. Of her class on graduation day in 1923, a quarter were women. Not many of them, however, had her interest in genetics, which had captivated her in her junior year and now led her into postgraduate study. Although women unaccountably weren't allowed in the plant-breeding program, she found a cytologist on the faculty broad-minded enough to overlook her sex and support her study of plant genetics, especially with reference to corn, or maize, which was then all the rage at the college as a topic of investigation and conversation. She received her doctorate in 1927 and was invited to continue at Cornell as a teacher and researcher.

She continued her study of corn chromosomes (which, unlike genes, could be seen with a microscope). Her frequent articles rapidly earned her a reputation as a geneticist worth reading, but she nevertheless felt herself stymied at Cornell, where, with the exception of home economics, women faculty members were generally confined to the instructor level. Her frustration was diminished considerably in 1931 by the award of a fellowship from the National

Research Council, which expanded her research to the University of Missouri and the California Institute of Technology, and, in 1933, by a Guggenheim fellowship for a year in Germany—where she was distracted by horror at the rising Brown Shirt movement.

After her return and a couple more years at Cornell, a friend who was starting a program in genetics at the University of Missouri asked her to join him. Her few years there, however, proved unsatisfactory in part, at least because her insistence on independence and noninterference convinced the front office that she was hard to get along with. (What's more, she played jazz banjo, and she wore *trousers!*) So it was with some relief that she found work at the Cold Spring Harbor Laboratory on Long Island, especially after a friend was appointed director of the genetics department and in 1941 offered her a temporary position that quickly became extremely permanent. She would have her office there for the next half-century.

It was her observation of anomalous, inexplicable color characteristics of leaves on some of her corn that spurred her into formulating an hypothesis to explain the inexplicable. She called it "transposition," the ability of a chromosome to rearrange itself, as it were, with some of its genes moving from one location to another. When her 1951 report on this met with much disdainful rejection by the genetics community, which was then seething with competitive interest in explaining the mysteries of DNA, she simply went back to further research and patient waiting. Or perhaps impatient waiting.

She had had her share of recognition, such as her election in 1944 to the National Academy of Sciences and her presidency in 1945 of the Genetics Society of America. But after the 1951 debacle it wasn't until 1970 that she won the National Medal of Science. By that time many geneticists, unable to explain some mutations in their favorite bacterium, the *E. coli*, had decided that maybe she wasn't all that bonkers after all. Also by that time she had elaborated on her theory, reporting that gene mobility led to differences in function, permitting plants to adapt to external stresses like excessive heat or cold or lack of moisture.

Thereafter she received plenty of recognition, including an honorary doctorate from Harvard in 1979 and the initial McArthur Laureate Award in 1981, coupled with the very practical gift of a tax-free sixty thousand a year for the rest of her life. And finally, in 1983, the Nobel Prize for Medicine or Physiology.

A photograph accompanying the story in several newspapers showed her happily beaming and holding in her hands, rather affectionately, an ear of Indian corn.

She died September 2, 1992, in Huntington, New York.

Clare Booth Luce
Powerful Politician (1903–1987)

She had several careers—society matron, journalist, novelist, playwright, war correspondent, politician, legislator, diplomat—none lifetime, but all at least reasonably successful. She was also a celebrity.

She was born Clare Booth in April 1903 in New York. Her father barely managed to support her ex-chorine mother and their two children with his meager earnings from playing an instrument in theater orchestra pits until he gave it all up in 1911 and vanished into the shadows of nonsupport, leaving her mother with a young son and daughter. Her mother, however, proved a great deal more responsible and resourceful, teaching her daughter, encouraging her to read (which she did, voraciously), and even sending her, as resources permitted, to a couple of good private schools. Her conscientious efforts were eventually rewarded by her marriage to a wealthy and appreciative physician.

Not long after her mother's marriage, Clare, having graduated from high school in 1919, herself married an even more affluent though less appreciative millionaire, providing him with a daughter before her divorce in 1929 on the customary grounds of mental cruelty. Although now independently well-off, and having resumed her maiden name, she went to work, at first for a book publisher and then for the magazine *Vanity Fair*. After a stint as editor and then managing editor, and some playwriting in her off hours, in 1934 she quit to devote all her time and talent to her plays. She had already published a novel in 1931, *Stuffed Shirts*, satirizing New York's brittle elite, but now the theater beckoned. Her most famous play, *The Women*, was produced in 1936 and was so successful that it was readily converted into a hit movie only three years later.

This was no woman to be married to a milquetoast, and Henry R. Luce, cofounder and colorful, forceful honcho of the nascent *Time* empire, was anything but that. This was a man of her mettle, and so she not only married him but also joined him in planning for a new, groundbreaking picture magazine, *Life*. His passionate interest in politics proved infectious, as did his staunch Republicanism, to this until now lifelong Democrat, to the extent of supporting Wendell Willkie against Franklin Roosevelt in the 1940 Presidential campaign.

By that time *Life* had reached a wide and profitable circulation, giving her an opportunity to visit Europe during the early part of World War II and, on her return, consolidating her war reports into a popular book, *Europe in the Spring*. (Her nemesis Dorothy Parker remarked that the title should have been *All Clare on the Western Front*, but then her attitude toward Clare is perhaps best illustrated in the doubtless apocryphal story of the two women encountering each other at the door of a hotel, with Clare stepping aside and saying,

"Age before beauty," and Dorothy sweeping into the hotel while retorting, "Pearls before swine.")

Meanwhile her stepfather had served a term in the U.S. House of Representatives. By the time his death in 1941 left the seat vacant, her reputation had grown to the point that she was invited to campaign for it in the 1942 election. She won the Republican primary handily and the election narrowly. Neither her marital connection nor her considerable charisma did her any harm at all.

Using her Congressional opportunity and her noted eloquence to castigate Franklin Roosevelt for "lying us into war" (despite her affection for Eleanor), in a sense she talked her way into being the first woman to be chosen, in 1944, as keynote speaker at a national convention. Her speech was a rabble-rouser, the rabble being mainly the zealots of the GOP's dyspeptic right wing.

She won reelection, though closely, in 1944, and soon thereafter was appointed to a Congressional delegation that embarked on a tour of Europe, including the horrors of Buchenwald. In the House she inveighed against America's passive role in the partition of Poland and expressed her growing alarm over the Soviet threat. Still firmly conservative, she nonetheless offered bills promoting equal treatment of minorities in the armed forces and better housing for veterans. Her interest in the logrolling environment waned, however, and in 1946 she decided that two terms were quite enough.

That didn't mean that she'd had enough of politics. She tirelessly promoted the G.N.P. in articles and speeches and campaigned actively for Dwight Eisenhower in 1952. When the following year President Eisenhower offered her a post as Secretary of Labor, she understandably declined, but she did agree to become ambassador to Italy. After five years there, notable for her political maneuverings against that country's Communist Party—and for the debilitating arsenic poisoning that plagued her because her bed in the embassy lay below a ceiling raining down invisible particles of arsenic-loaded paint—she retired to private life only to be offered, in 1959, the post of ambassador to Brazil. She accepted but then declined when her Senate confirmation was jeopardized by Oregon's feisty Wayne Morse, who acidly reminded the Senate of her vigorous denunciations of Roosevelt during the war. When he also nastily referred to her visits to a psychiatrist more than thirty years earlier, she replied that he'd been voting left ever since he was kicked by a horse on the right side of his head. This didn't endear her to his fellow Senators.

Her withdrawal still didn't mean that she'd had enough of politics. But after 1964, when she campaigned enthusiastically for Barry Goldwater, his overwhelming defeat and her own lack of success as the Conservative Party's candidate for the Senate finally persuaded her that she'd had enough of politics after all.

In 1967, after her husband's death, she moved to Hawaii, returning to Washington only after the accession of Reagan & Co. The doctors discovered a brain tumor twenty years later, and she knew that the end was near. And so, one evening a few days before her death in October 1987, she threw a good-bye party.

Margaret Bourke-White
Photojournalist (1904–1971)

Although not notably in the conventional libidinous sense, Margaret Bourke-White had a roving eye. It was her camera, which roved with her all over the world and made her reputation as one of the world's great photojournalists.

Margaret Bourke White was born in June 1904 in New York. (She added the hyphen to her mother's maiden name of Bourke in her twenties for a note of distinction, but she was Maggie White to almost everyone and Peggy to her close friends.) Her father's interest in snakes took the edge off any latent childish fears: as a child her special pets were a young boa constrictor and an aged puff adder presumably too long in the fang to be lethal. But it was the paternal interest in the behavior of light and therefore in cameras and film that gave a sharp edge to her latent fascination with photography and to its development into a lifelong addiction.

In her sophomore year at the University of Michigan she precipitously married an engineering student but, after his belatedly possessive mother announced that she never wanted to see her again, as precipitously divorced him. For her senior year she transferred to Cornell University, paying part of her tuition by selling pictures of campus goings-on. After graduation, living with her mother in Cleveland, she submitted some photos in a contest at the Museum of Art and won the first of the many prizes that would come her way.

Her father had invented the first Braille printing press, and her visits to the factory manufacturing it had piqued her interest in mechanical and industrial operations. With that interest now revived, she began visiting mills and factories and, sometimes on retainer, photographing the often beautiful complexity of their various functions. Somehow her pictures got to the desk of Henry R. Luce, who at the time (1929) was contemplating the introduction of a new magazine for business executives called *Fortune*. Wiring her to come to New York, he offered her an irresistible thousand a month for a half-time work schedule.

Sent to Berlin to photograph factory operations (artfully, Luce insisted superfluously), she got the idea that a visit to take pictures of the Soviet Union's new and burgeoning industry would be a spectacular journalistic coup. It took five weeks of making a nuisance of herself at the Soviet embassy, but she finally extracted a visa and was soon traipsing about Russia with her cumbersome equipment and her interpreter-guide, who might have been a hindrance but proved an invaluable help. She'd end up with some 800 film plates and, after the inevitable (but on this occasion innocuous) censorship, she brought them home after receiving a Russian invitation to return. She did indeed return, this time also making a couple of brief documentary movies which eventually became world classics. Back home again, she wrote her first book, *Eyes on Russia*. Illustrated.

Meanwhile Erskine Caldwell of *Tobacco Road* fame needed someone to provide pictures for a projected book. Some literary colleagues suggested her. Although he resisted working with a woman at first, perhaps because he was precariously married, he succumbed in the face first of her talent and then of her charm. In the Soviet Union she had turned increasingly from factories to faces, and in their first book, a treatise on the South entitled *You Have Seen Their Faces*, she used this new talent to great effect. Her work in this and another book with Caldwell evidently convinced Luce that she had abilities beyond the demands of *Fortune*. With his introduction of *Life* magazine in November 1936, he confidently assigned the first issue's cover photograph and the cover story to her.

When she was sent to Europe to cover Hitler's predations in 1939, Caldwell accompanied her and joined her in producing their third book, *North of the Danube*. Back in America, they formalized their relationship with a wedding before returning to Moscow in May 1941, just before the German invasion. Eluding Russian building wardens, they stayed in their apartment rather than going to a bomb shelter so that she could take some characteristically exciting pictures of the city under a night brightly streaked by the air attack and the antiaircraft artillery. As the only foreign photographer in the country she wangled her way to the front, or close to it, until the Soviets issued a general prohibition against such perilous and perhaps too revealing activity. But of course by then she had her pictures.

In the spring of 1942, in the wake of Pearl Harbor, the War Department made her America's first accredited woman war correspondent, with uniform and all, when it requested her to photograph the Air Force in operation in England (with her pictures promised to *Life* after their initial, official use). Although she feared that the separation would endanger her marriage, she accepted the assignment, and within a year Caldwell had indeed divorced and remarried. She was devastated but, transferred to Italy, she found some brief surcease there with an army officer who shortly thereafter was killed in action.

Her official status got her some official assistance such as GIs to help her tote about her heavy and rather primitive equipment and sometimes to join her in taking simultaneous shots with several cameras from different angles ("Load! Ready!—Fire!!"). Because of her official status she also had to submit all her pictures to the military, which culled them carefully to depict war's exhilarating, patriotic aspects. It wasn't until she reached Buchenwald with the Third Army that her pictures of human inhumanity reached a wide public. After the war, another aspect of that inhumanity was caught by her cameras in India, where she covered the Hindu-Moslem battles over Pakistan and the funeral of the assassinated Gandhi. When the Japanese rioted violently in Tokyo in June 1952, she was there, clicking away. Not long thereafter she was doing the same from a bunker on a mile-high mountain in Korea, in the thick of it within a hundred yards of enemy riflemen. She covered the bloody fighting, but she also covered the release of an enemy guerrilla and his moving reunion with his mother.

It was in Tokyo that she first noticed some muscular weakness, the first symptom of the Parkinson's disease that would bring her active career to an untimely end. Yet before she died in August 1971 she would publish six books and receive many awards, as well as having her work displayed in prestigious galleries, including those of the Museum of Modern Art, the Brooklyn Museum, and the Library of Congress.

Maria Goeppert-Mayer
Winner of the Nobel Prize for Physics
(1906–1972)

Prompted by Enrico Fermi, she demonstrated mathematically the hypothesis of spin-orbit coupling to explain the nuclear stability of certain elements (lead, tin, the noble gases, etc.) and even the structural behavior of nuclear particles (protons, neutrons). She was also something of a party girl, an enthusiastic hostess who loved dancing. And so, to explain her theory to her daughter, she suggested imagining a hall filled with couples waltzing around it in concentric circles. So it was with the atomic nucleus, its particles whirling around in concentric spheres and spinning in various directions and attitudes. Of course that's not quite how she explained it in the professional publications that eventually led to her sharing the 1963 Nobel Prize in physics.

She was born Maria Goeppert in June 1906 in Kattowitz, Germany, and grew up in Gottingen, where her father taught pediatrics at the university and, as Herr Professor, supported his family quite handsomely. Her mother entertained rather lavishly, giving parties at which the dancing may have implanted the seminal simile in the child's mind for later use. As the only child of a pediatrician, Maria received a great deal of paternal attention, joining her father in country walks for botanical, geological, and other lessons until she was eight. Then, with the coming of World War I, the entertaining gradually ceased, life became more stringent, and papa grew preoccupied, less readily available.

After the war the intellectual activity at the university shifted considerably from its specialty, mathematics, to the emerging discipline of atomic physics. Maria, on enrolling, chose mathematics as her major at first, but after attending a seminar led by Max Born and hearing his stimulating lectures on quantum mechanics and atomic structure, she switched to physics. She also met a fellow student, Joseph Mayer, an American whose specialty was experimental chemistry. By now her father was dead and her mother was taking in boarders, including Mayer. He promptly fell in love with the attractive blond daughter, whom he later described as "a terrible flirt" but also "brighter than any girl I'd ever met." As for her, the flirting slowly grew into something more serious, and they were married even before she received her doctorate. She had understandable misgivings about moving with him to America but hoped that her chances of a university teaching job would be better there than they were in misogynist Germany.

They weren't, at least at first. With Joe teaching chemistry at Johns Hopkins, the best she could extract from the administration was a tiny office and a tiny salary as a German translator for correspondence in the Department of Physics (where interest in atomic physics was minimal). The couple used their spare time teaching each other quantum mechanics and physical chemistry and producing daughter Marianne. After a while the university assigned her to teach physics to graduate students. Without pay.

With the Nazis coming into power in Germany in the early 1930's she was happy that she had become an American citizen but was saddened by the flight of so many refugee intellectuals, not a few of whom were given temporary shelter in the Mayer home. One of the refugees was a creative young physicist from Hungary, teaching at George Washington University, named Edward Teller. With Washington so close to Baltimore, he began visiting Johns Hopkins, and before long he and she were an item—a professional item, that is, for their mutually attractive minds were fully engaged with the complexities of nuclear physics, with the exchange of views and insights. Eventually their relationship became more personal as he began confiding in her his hopes and dreams, his shortcomings and failures, as he might to an older sister. (He was a couple of years younger than she.)

In 1939, after the birth of son Peter, Joe took a post with Columbia University, where the couple collaborated on a textbook, *Statistical Mechanics*. Although they shared the work, he received most of the credit, to his chagrin as well as hers. But after all he was a male associate professor and she was a mere female lecturer. Yet this also was the year in which she met Enrico Fermi, who was on the verge of playing a major role in the Manhattan Project for the development of an atom bomb.

World War II brought separation each week after Joe was enlisted for weapons work at the Aberdeen Proving Grounds in Maryland. She was doing some part-time teaching at Sarah Lawrence College when, in early 1942, she was hired by Harold Urey (who had won the Nobel Prize in chemistry in 1934 and was now involved in the Manhattan Project) to join a research team at Columbia working on ways to separate fissionable uranium–235 from ordinary uranium–238. The top-secret work was challenging, and she met the challenge. At first she had two assistants, but eventually she headed up a group of more than fifty technicians. The strain, however, affected her health: she had to have gall bladder and thyroid surgery and contracted pneumonia. And she was smoking too much.

The atomic destruction of two Japanese cities did nothing for her morale, but it ended the war and brought Joe an offer to join Teller, Urey, and Fermi, among others, as a full professor at the University of Chicago, which also urged Maria to join the faculty as associate professor, without pay but with a respectable office of her own and complete professional recognition. For the first time in her life "I wasn't considered a nuisance but was greeted with open arms," if not an open purse. Not long thereafter she was offered a salaried job as senior physicist at the university's Argonne National Laboratory. Participating in Joe's weekly seminars on nuclear physics, and working especially with Teller and Fermi, she came up with her idea of concentric shells of orbiting, spinning particles—only to read a paper in *The Physical Review* describing a dismayingly similar concept proposed by one Hans Jensen of Heidelberg.

On a visit to Germany, however, she found Jensen anything but aggressively competitive. He was also anything but energetically industrious. They decided to write a book together on their mutual specialty, but it took four years to finish largely because she was saddled with most of it. But it brought her a full professorship, with Joe, at the University of California in San Diego and, one morning in November 1963, a phone call from Stockholm to her home in La Jolla.

Until her death nine years later she would often remember the next morning's headline in the local paper, "La Jolla Mother Wins Nobel Prize."

Rachel Carson
Pioneer Environmental Advocate
(1907–1964)

There was a story told during a debate in the early 1960s in England's House of Lords about a cannibal tribal chief who forbade his people to eat

Americans because of the 11 parts per million of DDT in their bodies. It was a story that Rachel Carson, implacable foe of DDT, could appreciate.

She was born in May 1907 in Springdale, Pennsylvania, and spent her childhood not on a farm but in a suburban rural setting with her parents and her older sister and brother, as well as with the family's small collection of livestock. There was plenty of wildlife in the surrounding woods to fascinate her. After she learned to read and write, reading and writing became her favorite pastimes. She read much and wrote well—well enough to have stories published in a highly respected national magazine for children and to win an occasional prize. A writing career beckoned invitingly.

By the time she entered college (the Pennsylvania College for Women, later renamed Chatham College), she was sure enough of herself to choose English for her major, to join the literary club, and to start writing for the college paper. In her second year, however, a course in biology, utterly intriguing, gave rise to some doubts. In her third year her doubts grew into a conviction, and she switched her major to zoology, which didn't seem all that incompatible with writing. Her conversion was so complete that as a senior she was elected president of the school's science club.

That made it pretty official. After graduating at the top of her class in 1928, she went on to graduate work at Johns Hopkins, earned a master's degree, and then taught zoology there and at the University of Maryland. During summers at the Woods Hole Biological Laboratory her interest became focused on life in the sea. After all, her master's thesis had been on nothing less than "The Development of the Pronephros During the Embryonic and Early Larval Life of the Catfish."

She could write better than that, much better, and she was developing an expertise in a subject that interested her and might well interest others. It did, in articles on fish life that she began writing for *The Baltimore Sunday Sun*. Her prose was lucid, graceful, engaging, and it gave her a bit of a reputation. Consequently, when her father died in 1935, in the middle of the Great Depression, and she suddenly needed a reliable job to earn a living for her mother and herself, she was able to take advantage of a lucky break. The biology department of the Bureau of Fisheries, then planning a series of radio programs on fish life colorfully entitled "Romance Under the Waters," needed a scriptwriter. It was a lock made for her key. She was hired unhesitatingly, though only for a part-time job. (Even government money was scarce.)

She could get by on the rather meager salary—she was anything but goods-acquisitive—but her sister died the following year and left two school-age girls in her care, and so she needed something more dependable and lucrative. As though in answer to her need and doubtless her prayers, the Bureau conveniently required a full-time "Junior Aquatic Biologist" to fill an unexpected vacancy. She took the civil service exam, the only woman and the highest scorer. The job was hers, the salary was respectable, and she had found her niche.

She continued writing scripts for the radio project until the last program of the series was completed, after which she was asked to write an introduction. She did so, but her boss rejected it as too beautifully written—the series would pale embarrassingly by comparison. Write another, more prosaic, and submit this to a magazine—say, *The Atlantic Monthly*. It was indeed published in that prestigious magazine in September 1937, titled simply "Undersea." Encouraged by enthusiastic reactions to it, she began writing her first book, *Under the Sea Wind*.

It was published in 1941, a month before the American entry into World War II. Perhaps on this occasion her timing wasn't so fortunate. Whatever the reason, the book's sales were very discouraging—fewer than 1600 copies in its first six years—although the admiring reviews offered considerable compensation, especially those by scientists who welcomed a pleasantly written and accurate popular book on science. (The actual popularity would come later.)

Her next book, written after the war, was a best-seller, *The Sea Around Us*, published in July 1930. She first submitted chapters as articles to a number of magazines only to have them continually rejected until *The Yale Review* finally bought one and published it. After the article won several awards for scientific writing, the book was published. It soon made the best-seller list, as did a reissue of *Under the Sea Wind*. She was making good money now and began receiving honorary doctorates and other awards by the carload. She started her next best-seller, *The Edge of the Sea*, and, although she was now Biologist and Chief Editor for the Bureau, resigned in 1952 to focus on her writing. In 1958 she was saddened but not deterred by the death of her greatest fan and booster, her mother.

Many of her friends had serious misgivings about her next book subject. She had grown ever more troubled about the damage to wildlife from the unrestrained use of pesticides and was ever more determined to write a book about it. Despite a more personal worry about an accelerating cancer, she did so. *Silent Spring* was published in 1962, to the consternation of agricultural, chemical, and medical industries. She was branded a bird lover, a nature freak. She was called to testify before Congressional committees to justify the need for laws to protect the environment, and she did so quite forcefully. Meanwhile the book was being published all over the world, in many languages, and she was being invited to lecture here, there, and everywhere. She received countless honors, among them election to the exclusive American Academy of Arts and Sciences.

Sixteen years after her death from cancer in April 1964 she was awarded the Presidential Medal of Freedom. Her eloquence, the accompanying tribute explained, had "fed a spring of awareness across America and beyond."

Miriam Rothschild
English Scientist (1908–)

Parasitology, entomology, zoology, marine biology, chemistry, pharmacology, neurophysiology, horticulture—all have been grist for her omnivorous scientific mill. Although she had no formal education until she was seventeen and very little thereafter, she managed to write so many impressively scholarly articles (300-plus), in addition to a dozen similarly impressive books, that six universities, including Oxford, awarded her honorary scientific doctorates. In 1985 she was inducted into the Royal Society.

She was born Miriam Louisa Rothschild in August 1908 at her famous family's vast estate near Peterborough, England. Her father was, not surprisingly, a banker, and her mother, a former lawn tennis champion, devoted herself not only to her two girls and two boys but also, quite effectively, to her husband's business affairs and charitable activities. Much of Miriam's childhood, into her teens, was spent with her family at another large, arcadian Rothschild estate called Tring Park, where her grandfather vigorously engaged in experimental agriculture and where her father dedicated his spare time to entomology. In addition, her uncle's enormous lifetime collection of animals, "from starfish to gorillas," were housed in a museum that made Tring Park's reputation as a place to visit.

She was surrounded by animals, insects, and flowers, and she was utterly captivated. At four she was breeding caterpillars and beetles and delightedly doing farm chores suitable to her tender age. Her father, impressed by her natural curiosity and not wanting to do anything to stifle it, refused to subject her to the rigidities of formal education and granted her the freedom of self-education under the gentle guidance of a governess, seasoned with recreation in a variety of sports. It wasn't until after her father's death in 1924 that she tentatively took a few courses at a local polytechnic institute.

After doing some research on mollusks for the British Natural History Museum in the Mediterranean in the late 1920s, in the early 1930s she took a job as a student researcher at a marine biological establishment, discovered an unknown and unusual specimen of flatworm, and, as she wrote later, her "fate was sealed. I was completely hooked." She spent the next seven years in assiduous study of those parasitic flatworms (known also as trematodes or flukes), accumulating specimens and associated paraphernalia, but in November 1939 a Nazi air attack destroyed all this—all her notes and drawings and equipment, everything.

But the disaster proved to be a "liberating" experience, freeing her from the thralldom of parasitic flatworms and releasing her for service in the famous Enigma project that cracked the German military code, as well as for housing and feeding war refugees and for overseeing the conversion of Ashton

Wold, the family estate, into a hospital and airfield. There among the many airmen whom she tended was a devilishly attractive commando named George Lane. They were married in 1943 and amicably divorced in 1957 after producing five children. During their marriage she was forced to indulge her addiction to scientific study only after the children's bedtime, "falling into the microscope with sleep at about one o'clock."

At the turn of the century her father had made a hobby-inspired trip to the Sudan, where he identified the flea that transmits bubonic plague. This had inspired him into a study of the flea—some 1600 species ranging in size from the microscopic to one a quarter-inch long, which, to paraphrase John Donne, are not homicidal but do all the harm they can. During the trip he collected about 30,000 specimens and donated them to the British Natural History Museum. Her fascination with them resulted in a six-volume catalog that took her twenty years to complete. She also published, in less exhaustive but much more readable form, 1952's *Fleas, Flukes and Cuckoos*.

The lifestyles of parasites especially intrigued her, such as that of "the worm which lives exclusively under the eyelids of the hippopotamus and feeds upon its tears," and of the flea that can reproduce only when attached to a pregnant rabbit. She offered new and important data on resilin, a remarkable protein that enables a flea to use its vestigial flight muscles in performing the astounding leaps for which it is celebrated. "If you were a flea," she explained to interviewer David McCullough, "you could jump to the height of Rockefeller Center ... about 30,000 times without stopping." (The acceleration force is twenty times that on an astronaut during takeoff.) Small wonder that she has written more than 200,000 words on the little buggers.

She has done pioneering study on caterpillars as well, particularly on the ability of monarch caterpillars to absorb plant poisons that make them unpalatable to predators, however hungry. Her enchantment with butterflies resulted in 1983's *The Butterfly Gardener*, offering tips on the design of gardens to attract the colorful creatures. In 1991 her *Butterfly Cooing Like a Dove* used them to lure the reader into a wide-ranging discussion of just about everything under her sunbonnet. On the side she supported herself, à la her doughty grandfather, with her profitable farming.

In the mid–1990s, Rothschild was still living in the ivy-envelope manor at Ashton Wold, sleeping securely in the room in which she was born. The Hon. Miriam Rothschild (a.k.a. Mrs. Lane) actively carries on with her charitable and social activities, including the promotion of wildflowers and hedgerows to preserve the beauty of the English countryside. Yet none of this is at the expense of "burning the midnight oil, enthralled, while reading about other people's observations and discoveries." In her mid-eighties, she finds "everything interesting."

Rita Levi-Montalcini
Italian Scientific Researcher
(1909–)

She was a fully credentialed medical doctor, a future Nobel Prize winner, but she couldn't practice her profession nor do any research at the university in her city of Turin. It was 1939. Il Duce had joined Der Führer to form their notorious Axis, and Jewish doctors in Italy were no longer permitted to practice or teach or do research in the universities.

But she had become engrossed in her research on nerve fibers. To carry it on under these circumstances, with family help she converted a small room in their home into a usable laboratory with mostly homemade equipment. When Allied bombing in 1943 became intolerable and she fled with her family from the city, she resolutely continued her research on the kitchen table of their little country cottage. Only after the Nazis invaded from the north and the family had to flee south to Florence for precarious refuge, and only after the American occupation troops accepted her volunteered services there as a doctor—only then was her laboratory research interrupted for a while. She was a pretty determined woman.

Rita Levi-Montalcini was born in 1909 in Turin to Adamo Levi, an electrical engineer, and Adele Montalcini, a role-model mother. Unlike her older brother and sister and her twin sister, she was almost pathologically diffident—unlike them, afraid of her father, for instance, who, despite his quick temper and formidable mustache, apparently was a perfectly gentle gentleman. And so it was a severe ordeal for her when, after graduating from high school and after tearfully watching a devoted family servant die of cancer, she had to tell her father of her decision to become a doctor instead of getting married as he imperiously expected. He warned her of the arduous course of study involved but, seeing her determination, reluctantly gave his consent. In the fall of 1930, having passed her entrance exams with a gratifying score, she enrolled at the University of Turin's medical school. Her father unfortunately wouldn't live to see her receive her medical degree, with honors, in 1936.

After three more years of study in neurology and psychiatry, she began her practice at the university's neurological clinic, treating indigents who elicited her sympathy so strongly that she was tempted to forsake research for doctoring. The decision was made for her by the Fascist Authorities' ban on Jews' doing either. She did get some formal research done during a visit to Belgium in 1939, but on her return to Turin she was limited to the domestic research described above.

Assisted by one of her professors similarly limited by official bigotry, she buried herself in her study of cell growth, partly for distraction amid the enveloping terror but chiefly for a greater understanding of the enigmatic element, the "trophic factor" that encouraged the growth and activity of nerve cells, a phenomenon hitherto unknown. The flight to Florence, where the family was protected by a sympathetic landlady, and her work there as a doctor (as well as her romantic attachment to an old friend, now a partisan soldier) interrupted her research. Indeed, on her return to Turin in the spring of 1945 she forsook it in favor of taking some biology courses at the university. But only for a while.

Her work during the war had largely been inspired by and based on reports of studies of nerve-cell behavior in chick embryos conducted by Viktor Hamburger, a German refugee and head of the zoology department at Washington University in St. Louis. Surprisingly, the war hadn't prevented her from getting an article published in a Belgian journal, which Hamburger had read. Impressed, he sent her a letter in mid–1946 inviting her to join him in his investigations. She did, and he proved a splendid collaborator. When a former student of his sent him a report on the behavior of nerve cells in mice with cancerous tumors, she got the student's permission to carry his research further and discovered that the tumors were the source of a fluid that diffused and encouraged the growth of nerve cells. Professional skepticism forced her to make a brief visit to Brazil, where a very special laboratory unit included equipment for intensive in vitro research and where, in the isolation of the glass dish, the proliferation of nerve fibers about the cancerous tissue was readily observable. She was so relieved that she spent her last week or so in Brazil enjoying the carnival in Rio de Janeiro.

Back home, with the invaluable help of a new assistant—an industrious and resourceful young biochemist named Stanley Cohen—and a year or so of intensive work, she identified the mysterious "nerve growth factor" as a protein, a very special protein also puzzlingly extractable from snake venom and the saliva of male mice. This time the reaction was not so much professional skepticism as professional neglect—"My name was entirely omitted from the literature," for example. Thoroughly disheartened, she began focusing her research work on insect nerve cells. She conducted her research in St. Louis and in the small laboratory that she founded in Rome. This was only temporary, however. Unable to resist her fascination with the mysteries of nerve growth, she returned to it in 1972.

It would be fourteen years before she and Stanley Cohen would share the Nobel Prize for Physiology or Medicine. Since then professional neglect has been no problem. Quite the contrary.

Jacqueline Cochran
Outstanding Pilot (1910–1980)

At the age of six she did volunteer work. Just for a day, for a traveling circus which she hoped would take her away from "all that" the next morning. She even spent the night, unobtrusively but hopefully. When she awoke in the morning the circus had already departed. She was devastated.

Born in 1910 in Florida under rather obscure circumstances, Jacqueline Cochran was an unwanted little girl farmed out to a destitute couple who couldn't adequately feed, clothe, or shelter the two boys and two girls they already had, although the father and the boys all worked endless hours at the local lumber sawmill. She had little to eat, slept on the floor, wore a flour-sack dress, and no shoes. It was all that, of course, that she wanted the circus to take her away from.

During her third grade all that became a little more bearable when a new teacher from up north took her under her wing, bought her a dress and shoes, got her interested in reading, and generally mothered her. But only for that year, after which, to Jackie's utter dismay, she returned to her home in Ohio. Without her, Jackie decided, there wasn't any point in going back to school. Reading, however, was another matter: *that* she continued to do.

In 1918 the sawmill closed, and suddenly there wasn't even enough money for grinding poverty. The family moved to Columbus, Georgia, where the cotton mills needed workers—even Jackie, who at eight was paid 6 cents an hour for a 72-hour week. Although most of her earnings were confiscated by her foster mother, her remaining $1.50 a week proved to be enough for some simple clothes and even a pair of incongruous yet precious high-heeled shoes.

When the mill was closed down by a strike, she found work in a beauty shop owned by a woman who not only paid her $1.50 a week, but also offered her room and board and virtually membership in her family, giving the waif a new feeling of belonging in a tolerable, even comfortable, environment. By the time Jackie was 13 she was earning $35 a week as a full-fledged beauty operator, sending money home, and even saving some—several hundred dollars by her fourteenth birthday.

She was good at her job, good enough to be offered another job in a department-store beauty shop in Montgomery, Alabama. There she stayed for a couple of years until a customer suggested that she could do better for herself as a nurse. After three years of training and about a year of nursing for a poor doctor in a small Florida mill town, she decided that she was doing no good for herself and little good for others. She gave up nursing, tried her hand at several jobs, and in 1930 wound up in a New York beauty salon, quite a ritzy establishment where she quickly accumulated a list of very satisfied customers and a reassuring bank account.

She also became a fun-loving as well as pretty party girl, and it was at a party that she met a rich businessman named Floyd Odlum. When she told him that she'd like a job touring the country selling cosmetics, he remarked that she'd have to do a lot of flying. That caught her fancy, although in those days it meant that she'd probably have to learn to fly. A few months later she made her first solo flight, which ended in a dead-stick landing after the engine failed. Yet soon thereafter, encouraged by Odlum, she obtained her pilot's license.

By this time she had decided to start her own cosmetic business, and to this end she spent the next couple of years flying about the country making contacts. She learned a great deal about cosmetics and business but even more about flying—the instruments, repair procedures, Morse code—indeed, she became the first woman to make a fully blind bad-weather landing. By 1934 she felt, and was, skillful enough to enter an air race, her first, from London to Melbourne, but the plane wasn't up to it, and she and her copilot made it no farther than Bucharest.

With Odlum's continued encouragement, she entered the important Bendix Transcontinental Air Race from Los Angeles to Cleveland. Or tried to, but was told that it was for men only. After getting her fellow flyers to sign a paper agreeing to her entry, she did indeed enter, opening the Race to women from that time on. An electrical storm over the Grand Canyon, however, turned her back to California. This time, in May 1936, Floyd Odlum, instead of merely encouraging her, asked her to marry him. She accepted, eagerly, thankfully. The marriage would last for forty years, till his death did them part.

She entered the Bendix race again in 1937 and ruefully came in third. She entered again in 1938, but this time she won, to the riotous applause of 200,000 welcoming admirers. She continued entering various races, usually testing experimental products—instruments, propellers, engines, lubricants, fuels, clothing, goggles, helmets—sometimes at considerable risk, to accumulate important data. During World War II, before the U.S. entry, she was asked to fly an American bomber to England, which she did, and then to collect a group of American women for noncombat flying there. After Pearl Harbor she organized the Women's Air Force Service Pilots—the WASPs, eventually 1800 of them. She had plenty of problems, including, after a few crashes, the discovery of sugar in the fuel tanks of a number of planes, contributed by an enemy agent. But her work earned her the Distinguished Service Medal by war's end.

After the war she returned to her languishing cosmetics business, rejuvenated it, and eventually sold it to concentrate on the Odlums' charitable activities on behalf of poor children (she remembered) and also on her test flying, especially with the new jets. In 1952 she took a Sabre Jet F-86 up to 45,000 feet, pointed its nose down, and became, precariously, the first woman to break the sound barrier. Over the next ten years or so she also became the first woman to reach Mach 2, to land a jet on a carrier, and to pilot a jet across the Atlantic. She was awarded, among other things, the International Flying Organization's gold medal "for outstanding accomplishment by any pilot, man or woman, during 1935," as well as the Distinguished Flying Cross, the Legion of Merit, the Harmon trophy for outstanding woman pilot of the year (14 times), and election (twice) as Business Woman of the Year. At the time of her death in August 1980 she held more records for altitude, speed, and distance than any man or woman pilot in history.

Millicent Fenwick
Legislator (1910–1992)

She was sixty, approaching a time for getting down to some serious leisure. Instead, she was in her first term in the New Jersey state assembly, and she had just finished speaking in favor of an equal rights amendment for women. A male colleague, as she has told the story, "rose and with real anguish in his voice—you could tell he was addressing a subject close to this heart—said, 'I just don't like this amendment. I've always thought of women as kissable, cuddly, and smelling good.'" Restraining a perfectly reasonable homicidal impulse, Millicent Fenwick replied, "That's the way I feel about men, too. I only hope for your sake that you haven't been disappointed as often as I have."

She was born Millicent Vernon Hammond in New York in February 1910. She and her brother and sister lived in elite comfort, fruit of a flourishing family tree with roots in the American Revolution and branches in the rarified atmosphere of New York high society. In true noblesse oblige tradition, her mother was on her way across the Atlantic in May 1915 to set up a hospital for war victims when her ship, the *Lusitania*, was sunk by a German torpedo. She died, although her husband, also on board, was rescued by a fishing vessel. He remarried some thirty months later.

In 1925 the young girl left her tony school in Virginia to accompany the new ambassador to Spain, her father, to Madrid. Thereafter her formal education was limited to a brief encounter with European convent discipline, yet her informal education continued apace, with extensive reading and training in languages that rendered her fluent in French and Italian and passable in Spanish. Women, after all, weren't designed by God to meet the demands of formal academic study. (Or, to put it another way, they weren't designed, by God, to meet the demands of formal academic study.) After their return in 1929 to the family home in New Jersey, however, she did take some college extension courses at Columbia University, even dipping into the murky depths of philosophy under the tutelage of Bertrand Russell.

As the family affluence slowly dissipated during the Great Depression of the 1930s, she began earning some money as a model for *Harper's Bazaar*. This clothes-horse period came to a close with her marriage to Hugh Fenwick in 1934, but when the marriage ended in divorce four years later she was left with two children to support. To that end she took a job as associate editor for Conde Nast Publications and began writing for that firm's magazine *Vogue*. She would do so for the next fourteen years, authoring countless articles as well as the magazine's *Book of Etiquette* in 1948, in connection with which she did much touring and lecturing. In 1952 a maternal legacy, until then entangled in bureaucratic gridlock, enabled her to quit working and devote herself to the local and state politics in which she had grown interested as a source of distraction outside the eight-hour day.

A fairly typical northeastern moderate Republican who distrusted Democrats' trust in government, she volunteered in the 1954 campaign for the GOP candidate for the U.S. Senate. She served in the local legal aid society and, for six years, on the town council. For fourteen years, from 1958 to 1972, as vice-chair of the New Jersey advisory committee to the U.S. Commission on Civil Rights, she learned a great deal about how precariously and deplorably the other half lives and how helpful government can be. She had been thinking about getting into elective politics but hesitated out of a timidity en-gendered by a sexist society: women were taught, "You have to be *invited* to the dance."

In 1969 she invited herself to an election for a seat in the New Jersey General Assembly, and won. She won again in 1971. She didn't complete her second term, however, because the governor, impressed with her display of social conscience in the legislature, asked her to head up the state's new Division of Consumer Affairs. The job not only enabled her to empower the powerless but also brought her enough favorable public notice to achieve what the *New York Times* called a "geriatric triumph" when in her mid-sixties she ran for Congress in 1974, defeating a 37-year-old youngster.

Despite her ingrained Republicanism, her record in Congress over the next eight years generally earned her the approval of liberal and disapproval of conservative rating organizations. Indeed, during her first term she voted against the GOP positions more often than for them. She didn't strive to be the Ford Administration's favorite legislator, on occasion helping to override Presidential vetoes. Accused of being too liberal, she retorted that many so-called "liberal" positions, such as her strict interpretation of the Bill of Rights, actually are quite conservative. In 1982 she left the Congress and spent the next five years in Rome as the U.S. representative with the United Nations Food and Agriculture Organization. She died at home in New Jersey in 1992.

During her years in Congress, what Norman Cousins (a neighbor) described as her "combination of intelligence, fairness, openness, good will, and good humor" earned her the respect of her fellow legislators. She was opinionated, even feisty, especially about Congressional corruption and profligacy

("It is obvious that the *system* is hideously wrong") but she could work well with others. During campaigns she gave up her incumbent's privilege of postage-free newsletters to her constituents as a gesture of fairness to her opponent. In her later years one of her eccentricities was smoking a pipe. But it was a pipe of peace.

Dorothy Crowfoot Hodgkin
Winner of the Nobel Prize for Chemistry (1910–1994)

A nonchemist may find it difficult or impossible to comprehend the significance of her crystallographic analyses, but the Swedish Royal Academy of Sciences, in awarding her the 1964 Nobel Prize in Chemistry, praised her for her solution of "a large number of structural problems, the majority of great importance in biochemistry and medicine," and especially for "two landmarks which stand out. The first is the determination of the structure of penicillin, which has been described as a magnificent start to a new era of crystallography. The second, the determination of the structure of vitamin B_{12} [foe of pernicious anemia], has been considered the crowning triumph of X ray crystallographic analysis, both in respect of the chemical and biological importance of the results and the vast complexity of the structure." Most of us will simply have to take the Academy's word for it.

She was born Dorothy Mary Crowfoot in May 1910 in Cairo, Egypt, where her father, a learned archeologist, was at the time an inspector in the Ministry of Education. (The surname was quite British, whatever the Native American overtones.) She and her two younger sisters spent the war years with a grandmother in England. When her mother joined them in the fourth and last year with a fourth newborn daughter, she introduced the girls to some very intense educational activity to make up for grandmotherly leniency.

After the war, in school and now in her eleventh year, Dorothy developed an exceptional interest in chemistry, especially in the growth of crystals, whose orderly, latticed, symmetrical beauty fascinated her. In 1923, during a visit to her wandering scholar of a father in Khartoum, she met a chemist who not only conducted experiments with her but also gave her a going-away present of a rather sophisticated chemistry set. She brought it home to use as the nucleus of an attic laboratory. There in 1925 she encountered the new discipline of X ray crystallography, which was to become the scientific love of her life.

She was distracted briefly in 1927 during a long visit with her peripatetic parents, now in Jerusalem, where her father's dedication to archeology proved highly contagious and very nearly lured her away from her crystals. After her return to England and enrollment at Oxford, however, she gradually became engrossed in chemistry again, especially in X ray crystallographic research despite its demanding mathematics and exhausting every-single-angle photography. (A crystalline structure has to be determined, in effect, by examining the shadows that it casts under radiation.)

A research fellowship in 1933 provided her with a couple of years of analytical investigation divided between Cambridge and Oxford, after which she was hired to teach chemistry at the latter's colleges for women. As an instructor in mineralogy and crystallography, she wangled a grant for more sophisticated equipment than she could afford on her very limited budget. The year 1937 proved a memorable one, including the granting of her doctorate and her marriage to historian-teacher Thomas Hodgkin. Although the newlyweds were often separated by their respective teaching jobs until 1945, when he came to Oxford as Director of Extramural Studies, they managed to produce their two sons and daughter by 1946.

The pressing need for penicillin during World War II prompted intense research for an artificial, mass-producible chemical version, to which her chief contribution at Oxford seems to have been her persistence and, if we can excuse the expression, her woman's intuition. Colleagues noticed her habit of doggedly following through on her initial hunch until she reached *the* solution of a problem and could explain it to them, patiently. After penicillin came the vitamin B_{12}, whose structural secrets her group managed to unlock during the 1950s.

That decade included much separating travel for the Hodgkins as his teaching took him to Illinois, Montreal, Ghana, and her various professional trips took her to the United States, China, the Soviet Union, during which she was kept busy inspecting laboratories, attending conferences, and collecting honorary degrees and other awards. (In 1958, to her delight, Oxford gave her father, then 85, an honorary doctorate.)

In 1962 her husband became Director of African Studies at the University of Ghana, and it was there that she happened to be working in the school's lab on crystals when she received the news in 1964 of her Nobel Prize. In Stockholm she and Thomas were joined by their daughter from Zambia and their son from India, though their other son couldn't get away from his teaching at the University of Algiers, and her sister was busy with her geographer husband at the North Pole. It wasn't a stick-in-the-mud kind of family.

On the happy couple's return the University of Ghana threw a spectacular party to celebrate her award with much exotic dancing and native merriment. But the next day, after giving her Nobel lecture, "The X Ray Analysis of Complicated Matter," she was back in her lab, radiating crystals to discover the molecular structure of a vital substance. This time it was insulin.

She died July 29, 1994, in Warwickshire, England.

Mother Teresa
Missionary to the Poor
(1910–)

When she established her Congregation of the Missionaries of Charity in 1950, it consisted of one community with about a dozen members. Today it has hundreds of members, men and women, scattered throughout the world in scores of communities. Mother Teresa is a rarity: a capable yet selfless executive.

She was born Agnes Gonxha Bojaxhiu in the Balkan town of Skopje in August 1910, daughter of a grocer in a happy and very religious home. Twelve years later, having learned of foreign missionary work in sodality meetings, she felt sure that she "had a vocation to help the poor" as a missionary—particularly the poor in India, the poorest of the poor. At 18 she joined a community of Irish missionary nuns with a school in Calcutta and spent many gratifying years there as a teacher and then as principal. As she became increasingly aware of the miserably poor slum dwellers outside the school and convent walls—the penniless homeless, the hopelessly ill, the outcast lepers—she became also increasingly aware of a call beyond her calling. The poor needed more than her help; they needed her to be among them. In 1946 she asked permission to leave the convent and fill this need. In 1948 the mills of the Vatican gods ground out her permission, making her answerable only to the archbishop of Calcutta.

She left the convent with five rupees, gave four to beggars and her last one to a priest soliciting donations. Soon thereafter the priest returned to her with an envelope given him by a man aware of her intention. She opened it and found fifty rupees. She was on her way. For the rest of her life she would never ask for money and indeed would "never think of it. It always comes. The Lord sends it. We do his work, he provides the means. If he doesn't give us the means, that shows he doesn't want the work. So why worry?" Her communities decline any church "maintenance," for example. Yet, she insists, never has anyone been refused help for lack of wherewithal.

After a few months of intensive training in practical medicine, she started with an open-air school and clinic for slum children. Her combination of selfless determination and competence attracted not only financial support but also volunteers and, in 1950, official recognition from the archdiocese. Two years later she established a Home for Dying Destitutes in a hall given to her by city officials, a dormitory where the mortally ill and utterly neglected could spend their final hours in some comfort and an environment of loving care. The accommodations weren't fancy, but then everything is relative.

There was never too much money of course, yet in 1957 the community was able to introduce a program of care designed particularly for lepers. Seven years later the shortage of funds was alleviated somewhat when the inordinately male papal establishment decided to bestow on India the exhilarating honor of a visit. Paul VI, impressed with her work and probably going further than the establishment intended, impulsively gave her the white Lincoln Continental limousine that he used for ceremonial transportation. She immediately put it to much better use, auctioning it off and using the money to establish a separate colony for lepers under the direction of a physician. Not just a few lepers—eventually about 20,000 in Calcutta, 60,000 throughout India.

Meanwhile she had been less expensively setting up a number of schools and orphanages in Calcutta, had expanded operations to a score of Indian cities, and had begun to travel, establishing small communities in the Far East, South America, Europe (including Skopje, to her great satisfaction), Africa, the Middle East, New York's Harlem. In interviews she made it clear that caring for the poor was her business, and that she knew how to mind her own business. Government welfare? The more the better, but her business was more personal, more involved. Catholic social activists? Splendid, but that's their business, not mine. When she was awarded the Pope John XXIII Peace Prize in 1971, she used the papal affluence once again to found a leper colony, then hurried back to the Far East to organize a place to stay for Bangladesh victims of rape by Pakistani soldiers and another for handicapped Indians. The next year, after a trip to Northern Ireland in the forlorn hope of bringing peace to that troubled land, she hurried back to the slums of Calcutta to care for the victims of a devastating flood. She is a tiny wisp of a woman, frail as a steel girder, an inexhaustible dynamo, undaunted by the irreversible.

In 1979 she was awarded the Nobel Peace Prize, by then worth a couple of hundred thousand dollars, plus what she received instead of the costly banquet she didn't want. She would know what to do with the money.

Babe Didrikson Zaharias
Athlete Phenomenon (1911–1956)

That's what the celebrated sports writer Grantland Rice called her, "the athlete phenomenon of our time." It's almost untrue that she "played" golf. She worked at it, excelled in it, as she did in just about every other sport she tried, including various track and field events, basketball, football, baseball, boxing

and wrestling, archery and skeet shooting, swimming and diving, horseman-
ship, pool and billiards, etc., etc.

She was born Mildred Didrikson in June 1911 (she later held out for 1914)
in Port Arthur, Texas, but would be known as Babe throughout her life. (The
"Didrik*son*," she thought incongruously, made her sound Norwegian rather
than Swedish.) She was the third of four children born to immigrant parents.
After a devastating hurricane demolished their home in 1915, the family moved
guardedly to another oil town a few miles away. There, once they were settled
in their new home, her father built a very complete wooden gym set, ironically, for the two boys. She used it, a lot.

It was a very poor, very busy family. Besides chipping in on household
chores, everyone worked, furiously. Seventh-grader Babe packed figs at one
local plant and then stitched potato sacks at another. In her spare time she
mowed lawns and accumulated enough uncommitted money to spend 35 cents
for a harmonica, which would ever thereafter be a source of enjoyment as well
as therapy for discouragement. Another source of enjoyment was provided by
a series of hedges in the neighborhood, which, as she grew older, she used as
hurdles in her incessant running. By then she had settled on her ambition, to
be the greatest athlete ever. She would add intensity to the word "competitive."

In high school she entered every sport open to her (football was exclusively male). Her coach, who had trained some 12,000 young ladies, said she
had never seen such perfect "neuromuscular coordination." At first rejected by
the basketball team on grounds of inadequate size and weight, she practiced
exhaustively until she was allowed to join and to make local headlines with
her spectacular play. The headlines attracted the notice of an executive of a
Dallas-based insurance company that prided itself on its girls' basketball team.
She accepted his offer of a good job, moved to Dallas, and eagerly set about
leading the team to successive victories. Voted an all–American forward in
1930, she began receiving other offers but stuck with the insurance company
in order to organize a track and field team. In her first meet she entered four
events and won them all, setting national records in javelin throwing and baseball pitching. Since she was too fiercely competitive to be a good team player,
track and field events were just her ticket, as golf would be later.

In 1932, after winning six gold medals and setting four world records in
the American Athletic Union Nationals, she entered that year's Olympics in
Los Angeles. Setting two more world records and winning two gold medals,
she inspired Grantland Rice into a giddy encomium, describing her as "the
most flawless section of muscle harmony, of complete mental and physical
coordination the world of sport has ever known." The Associated Press named
her Woman Athlete of the Year, for the first of five such years. Her home-
coming in Texas was worthy of—well, Texas.

Impatient with AAU supervision of amateur athletics, she turned professional only to discover that making money in sports was a man's game. She had no reason to feel overwhelmingly welcome: one sportswriter, arguing that women had no business in sports, recommended that it would be better if athletes of "her ilk stayed home, got themselves prettied up, and waited for the phone to ring." For about a year she earned a living with exhibition performances and even in vaudeville, but in March 1933 she moved to Los Angeles with her mother and sister, determined to take up golf—championship golf, of course.

In contrast with the misogynist sportswriter, a young golf pro named Stan Kertes trained her for six months free of charge. When her grocery money ran out, however, the three women had to return to Beaumont. To pay her father's medical bills she joined first a touring basketball team and then a touring baseball team, sending money home from her now more than modest income and spending her off hours assiduously practicing her golf at driving ranges. In late 1934 she quit touring to enter the Fort Worth Women's Invitational, won a medal, and took aim at 1935's Texas Women's Amateur Championship Tournament.

She practiced and practiced, and then practiced some more. She won the tournament, narrowly but so spectacularly (she could play to the crowd) that the U.S. Golf Association formally classified her as a professional. And so she practiced professionally, lengthening her powerful drives routinely to an impudently masculine 300 yards, one to 336 yards, and signing up with the Wilson Sporting Goods Company for promotion of its products.

Despite help from a few lucid men like champion golfer Gene Sarazen, with whom she teamed up in lucrative exhibition matches against some other, less helpful champions, she met with gender-engendered hostility—she just wasn't *feminine* enough. And so before entering 1938's Los Angeles Open, she let her hair grow longer and began wearing dresses on appropriate occasions. It may have been just as well, for in the Open's first round she had two partners, one of whom was a good-natured, good-looking, and comfortably rich professional wrestler named George Zaharias. Perhaps because of mutual distraction, neither played very good golf that day.

About a year later they were married. The honeymoon was in Australia, where he exhibited his wrestling and she her golf. On their return to California in late 1939, he quit wrestling to manage her career. Professional exhibitions were pleasantly profitable, they decided, but they didn't need the money, and for recognition as a top-flight golfer she really should regain her amateur status. This required a 36-month waiting period of noncommercial impatience, which she assuaged with endless practice not only in golf but also in tennis. This was a new game for her, but soon she was skillful enough to enter the U.S. Lawn Tennis Association's Southwest championship tournament—only to be informed that anyone who had played any sport professionally was forever ineligible. So much for tennis. She turned to bowling, developing not only expertise but also considerable renown in and around their hometown of Los Angeles.

Indeed, she was a celebrity now, displaying her skills at golf to sell war bonds. She was a gallery-titillating trickster who could drive five balls off so fast that she hit the fifth before the first touched ground and who could hit two balls at once, one down the fairway and the other into her pocket. In 1944, her amateur standing restored, she won the Western Women's Open, and she did so again in June 1945, despite the shock of her widowed mother's death. Later that year the Associated Press named her Woman Athlete of the Year for the second time, in 1946 for the third time, and in 1947 for the fourth time.

By the summer of '47 she had amassed a record of 15 consecutive tournament victories, more than any man or other woman. Her sixteenth was in Scotland, birthplace of golf, where she won the British Women's Amateur against formidable competition and then danced a triumphant if unconventional version of the Highland fling to the vast amusement of the gallery. She had proved to be, a sportswriter lamented, "a crushing and heartbreaking opponent." Her 17th victory, in Colorado Springs, marked the end of her second amateur career but only after she had announced that she was going to enter the U.S. Open for men and then learned that the USGA had hastily passed a rule barring women from it.

She returned to the profitable professional routine, becoming president in 1950 of the newly formed Ladies Professional Golf Association. That was also the year in which the Associated Press named her the Outstanding Woman Athlete of the Half Century. In 1952, in the film *Pat and Mike*, she gave Katharine Hepburn a golf lesson. In 1954, despite a cancer that doctors insisted would keep her from playing at anything, she won five tournaments and spent a few hours at the White House discussing the President's favorite pastime with Ike himself.

Two years later, after she had finally succumbed to the cancer, he paid her a warm and touching tribute. But it was another friend who perhaps had the best last word. Life, she said, was never dull with Babe. She "loved living. She loved every minute, more than anyone I've ever known."

Eva Crane
Leading Apiculturist (1912–)

From King's College at the University of London she received a bachelor's degree in mathematics and physics, a master's in quantum mechanics, and a doctorate in nuclear physics. Then she taught mathematics and physics at a number of colleges for a decade or so. Only because fate intervened, rather peculiarly, in the 1940s did she become a world authority, if not *the* world authority, on the subject of bees.

She was born Eva Widdowson in June 1912 in Wallington, Surrey. Her stationer father and dressmaker mother encouraged her and her older sister to satisfy their curiosity through reading and conscientious school work. This she did, soon finding herself attracted more strongly to science than to the arts. Her attraction became absorption, which in turn became a learning ability that earned her scholarships for both preparatory school and college. At King's College, in spite or because of her being the only woman in her physics class, she wasn't subjected to any gender discrimination, at least so far as she can recall. Certainly none that impeded her learning.

In 1942 she married James Alfred Crane, a naval reserve officer, and settled into a home with enough land attached to accommodate their most remarkable wedding present. Because the war had created a sugar shortage, honey was in great demand, and an increasingly frequent gift was a swarm of bees to the adventurous. Thus the time after their wedding was a honeymoon in more than the conventional sense, since she had to undertake some self-education in apiculture. Her omnivorous reading on the subject soon had her hooked on it partly because she was naturally inquisitive but largely because she found the bee business to be in a rather inchoate state, a condition crying out for an orderly mind to set it straight.

There was, for instance, no scientific periodical devoted to the subject, although there was a Research Committee attached to the British Beekeepers' Association. She joined the Association and in 1949 was asked to head up its new Bee Research Association, founded to keep apiculturists apprised of recent developments in research. She was given the title of director, which she considered "much too pompous," but she wasn't too shy to take over as editor of the unique international journal *Bee World* and make it, as the Association's official voice, a less precious and much more scientific publication presenting serious technical articles from experts all over the globe. She also reported, quite enchantingly to judge from the reactions, on her own visits to her experts at home and abroad. Later she added a regular feature giving abstracts of scientific papers on apiculture, which still later became a separate periodical. Bee science thus gradually attained not only greater respectability but also a kind of community spirit as a result of the improved communications.

By the mid–1970s the Association had grown into a formally international organization able to fund her world travels, which eventually amounted to nearly a hundred trips, with visits to every continent except the beeless one at the South Pole. Besides attending and addressing conferences, she kept on researching, investigating apicultural techniques such as the Third World's surprisingly sophisticated practices.

From her visits she garnered a vast amount of information, the kind of information appropriate to encyclopedic books. One day in 1965 a book editor happened to ask her if any particular kind of books were needed in her field, and she jumped eagerly at the opportunity. By then scientific books on bees and beekeeping were being published, but, she told him, there wasn't a one specifically about the busy ones' product, honey. And so she wound up soliciting chapters, and writing some herself, for just such a book, which, after its publication in 1975 under the title *Honey: A Comprehensive Survey*, rapidly became the world's apicultural bible.

That wasn't enough. In 1980 she brought out *A Book of Honey*, which among other things described exotic meals based on honey and included such historical tidbits as the ancient Greek use of honey for embalming. In 1983, having earlier been inspired by the sight of some prehistoric cave paintings in Zimbabwe picturing honey gatherers, she offered a third book, *The Archeology of Beekeeping*, with some misgivings that proved unfounded when it was welcomed enthusiastically by the world's antiquarians. Between 1980 and 1990 she compiled her fourth work of eccentric scholarship, a description of contemporary apicultural techniques comprehensive enough to be valuable to entomologists generally.

For her contributions, Ohio State University, which is something of a bee-research mecca, awarded her an honorary Ph.D. in 1985, an honor more specific and significant than her earlier royal elevation to the status of Officer in the Order of the British Empire.

From the standpoint of work schedules, her formal retirement in 1983 had involved a barely noticeable transition.

Rosa Parks
Civil Rights Leader (1913–)

In good ol' Montgomery, Alabam', in the 1950s the Southern policy of chattel slavery had been replaced by a Southern policy of chronic statutory abuse of the ex-chattel. Besides the fastidious contumely of "colored" restrooms and drinking fountains, of whites-only restaurants and movie-theater sections, et savage cetera, there was the legally imposed racial segregation on the city buses.

In every bus the front section (five rows, ten seats) was for whites only. The back section was for blacks—but not only. Although the city's population was only 42 percent black, bus passengers were 70 percent black, significantly, and often there were more than could fit in the black section. In such cases the overflow passengers would have to stand rather than pollute even an empty white section with their pigmented presence, including weary black women burdened with packages and holding precariously onto support posts and bars.

Conversely, on the rarer occasions when too many whites boarded a bus than could fit in the white section, blacks in the front rows of their rear section would have to yield their rows (not just the seats) to the white newcomers and, if necessary, stand. The rules were enforced by the gun-toting drivers—all white, of course, and imposingly male.

To add insult to insult, black customers naturally had to wait until all the whites had boarded the bus, enter by the front door and pay the fare, and then get out and walk to the back door and enter there, since they couldn't be permitted to pollute the white section by passing through it. A favorite sport of some drivers was to close the back door then and drive away. Injury also could be added to insult when an uppity black was subjected to corrective discipline by an irascible driver.

All this was perfectly legal. Any show of resistance would result in arrest, a prejudicial hearing, and punishment. And any such rebellious behavior would require a plentiful supply of spunk, to put it mildly. Yet this whole noisome system of racial abuse was brought to an end, quite abruptly by historical standards, by the exasperation not of a strapping young man but of a mild, weary little woman named Rosa Parks.

She was born Rosa McCauley in Tuskegee, Alabama, in February 1913. Her father was a carpenter, her mother a teacher; she and her younger brother spent much of their childhood on their grandparents' farm, pleasant during the day but sometimes terrifying at night during Klan festivities. In her teens, after a family move to Montgomery, she was trained at an "industrial school for girls" and later took some courses at the local branch of the state college (courtesy of *Brown v. Board of Education*). In 1932 she married Raymond Parks, a politically active (and courageous) barber, and became politically and socially active herself, particularly in the National Association for the Advancement of Colored People. In 1943 she was elected secretary of the NAACP's Montgomery branch, handling cases, as she described them later, of "flogging, peonage, murder and rape." The job also brought her plenty of abusive phone calls. Legal victories were rare, since there wasn't all that much difference between judges and bus drivers, but the legal activity was better than spineless, obsequious inactivity.

To earn a living she had sold insurance and had taken housekeeping jobs, but most of her work was as a seamstress in a job that required her reluctant use of the Montgomery bus system. And so it was that on Thursday, December 1, 1955, she and three other black riders, sitting in the front row of the black section, were told by the driver to vacate it for a white man. (The driver, she noticed, was a man who had ordered her out of his bus years earlier for boarding it through the front door.) Her three row-mates stood up and dutifully found seats elsewhere, but she was dead tired from a long day with the needle at the department store where she worked. Well, challenged the driver, are you gonna get up? When she refused, he threatened to get the police. Go ahead, she replied, you just do that. And so, still sitting, she was arrested, hauled off to jail, booked, put in a cell, and fined ($14) after an appearance in something called a court.

She was rescued by three people, a white couple (he a lawyer, she a civil-rights activist by whom she'd been employed) and a black man active in the NAACP. Back home, she was asked if she'd be willing to appeal the judgment. Yes, she answered, if you think it'll do some good. No, no, exclaimed her husband and mother, for safety's sake. The white folks, warned others, will kill you. But she was used to living with fear, and she refused to change her mind. A black lawyer took up her appeal.

Her decision was the spark for some tinder that had been gathered over the preceding months. The local Women's Political Council, reacting to *Brown v. Board of Education* and to the city's refusal to do anything about the bus line's seating arrangements, had been making tentative plans for a city-wide black boycott of the bus system. The Council's president, Jo Ann Robinson, felt that the mistreatment of Rosa Parks would prove ideal as justification for the boycott: Rosa had a good reputation in her community, was "quiet, unassuming, and pleasant in manner and appearance; dignified and reserved; of high morals and strong character." Strong character indeed.

The Council wasted no time. On Friday, December 2, the day after her arrest, a rain of its leaflets descended on Montgomery's black neighborhoods urging black citizens to join a boycott of city buses beginning the following Monday, the 5th. Over the weekend the community's ministers, including Ralph Abernathy and Martin Luther King, Jr., added their calls for cooperation, and the rest is history. The boycott lasted through 382 days of intimidation and brutality against blacks' attempts to use alternative transportation (mostly walking) until the Supreme Court's order, upholding a lower court's decision that public bus segregation is unconstitutional, arrived in the Montgomery mayor's office on December 20, 1956. As for Rosa, who had lost her job and whose family had been plagued with obscene and threatening phone calls, she felt some satisfaction, of course, but no great exhilaration, especially during the homicidal redneck violence that followed the Court's decision. There was still so much more to do.

Indeed there was. In August 1957 she and her husband moved to Detroit only to suffer through eight years of poverty and illness until, in 1965, she was hired to handle the Detroit office of Congressman John Conyers, Jr., a black political activist if ever there was one. The job has given her untold opportunities to promote blacks' civil and other rights, as well as permitting her time for her countless speeches and participation in social programs—and to accept her many honors and awards. In the late 1970s her mother, brother, and husband died but left her with a large family for great consolation.

Asked often if she had felt great fear during the bus-seating incident, she has said no, not really. She had lived with fear all her life, so that whatever fear she may have felt that day was no big deal.

Katharine Graham
Newspaper Publisher (1917–)

As she has always seen it, the way to promote freedom with the press through freedom of the press is with freedom *in* the press—the freedom of editors and reporters to disagree among themselves and with their publisher. As publisher of the *Washington Post* she paraphrased Groucho Marx's celebrated comment on club membership, insisting that she couldn't respect anyone who respected an advisory from her office as a morally binding edict.

She was born Katharine Meyer in June 1917 in New York. The five Meyer children were raised in an atmosphere of noblesse oblige cultivated by a financier father and philanthropist mother. They were rich but not idle: of *course* everyone would have to work, not for a living but for a worthwhile life. In 1936, after a couple of years of patrician tutelage at Vassar, she transferred to the intellectually more galvanic University of Chicago, spending her summers working for the *Post* in Washington—her father had bought the money-starved paper three years earlier at auction. After graduation she moved to San Francisco and worked as a reporter covering the waterfront, where the longshoremen generally treated her with more respect than did her male colleagues.

But she worked there for only a year, after which her doting father came and got her, took her back home, and installed her in an editorial job at the *Post*. The job lasted through World War II, from 1939 until 1945, with only brief interruptions to marry Supreme Court law clerk Philip Graham and then to follow Army Air Corps trainee Philip Graham about the country until he flew off to the Pacific theater of operations. She continued working until Major Graham returned from the war in 1945.

To her great delight, husband and father proved compatible. She immediately became the wife of an associate publisher of the *Post* and, six months later, of its publisher. By 1948 the Grahams owned the paper, essentially a gift from admiring parents. Phil took increasing charge, and he took over entirely after the old man's death in 1959. He expanded the holdings and operations of The Washington Post Company, acquiring another paper (the *Washington Times-Herald*), a newsmagazine (*Newsweek*), a news service, some broadcasting companies, and, sagaciously, a paper mill.

The pressure may have been too much for the brilliant but unstable Phil Graham, who tragically committed suicide in 1963. Katharine, wife and homemaker, society matron and mother of four, was devastated. Phil, despite some extramarital tomfoolery and masculine disdain for her opinions, had been and would continue to be *the* man in her life. Yet she was soon signing her name with "Katharine" instead of "Mrs. Philip." Further, she had never completely lost touch with the family business. Suddenly, as controlling stockholder, she was president of the company, inexperienced, timid, but determined to maintain family control. She sought profits, yes, but only through serving the public good (as, of course, one sees the public good). To that end she hired journalists of noted competence and various viewpoints within a respectable range (no fanatics invited), including *Newsweek*'s live-wire Washington bureau chief Ben Bradlee as managing editor and then executive editor of the *Post*. For the business end of the business she relied chiefly on the advertising and cost-cutting, anti-union expertise of a longtime employee noted for company loyalty. With their help she gradually overcame most of the male resistance among staff and workers to female assertiveness, improved editorial quality, and increased revenues. By the end of the decade she had taken over formally as publisher, had raised salaries, had radically modernized the pressroom equipment, and could take satisfaction in heading up a reputable, influential, and quite profitable enterprise.

And a feisty one. When Richard Nixon, whom she supported despite her dead husband's distaste for the man, named Spiro Agnew as his running mate in the 1968 election, the *Post* likened the nomination to the mad Roman emperor Caligula's appointment of his horse as proconsul. In 1971 the *Post* and the *New York Times* carried their battle to publish parts of the classified "Pentagon papers" on the Vietnam imbroglio to the Supreme Court, and won. The *Post*'s gritty, implacable "Deep Throat" investigation of the Nixon Administration's felonies in the notorious Watergate cover-up, immortalized in a celebrated book and movie, *All the President's Men*, earned the paper a Pulitzer for distinguished public service. It also earned her the reputation of being one of the most powerful people in the country—as Richard Nixon ruefully conceded.

Helen Thomas
First Woman UPI White House Bureau Chief
(1920–)

A housekeeper helps to keep a house clean, and a major part of Helen Thomas's job as senior White House correspondent (ending briefings with the traditional "Thank you, Mr. President") is helping to keep the political White House clean by holding it open for public inspection. Jack Kennedy, evidently in a mood of political rue, once remarked that she'd "be a nice girl if she ever got rid of her pad and pencil." Yet during the Watergate cover-up Martha Mitchell, her primary lowdown source, came to admire the pad and pencil's owner as "fair and square and trustworthy," and Liz Carpenter, Lady Bird Johnson's press secretary, described her as a Washington rarity, someone with "warm blood in her veins." Her own feeling was one of pride in her role as doyenne of White House correspondents, keeping "an eye on the Presidency [and thereby] helping to keep an eye on democracy—to keep it alive."

She was born in August 1920 in Winchester, Kentucky. Four years later her Lebanese parents moved with their nine children to Detroit, where her father, ever a grocer, opened a store and established a happy household in which animated discussion was the order of each day and from which he managed to send both sons and all seven daughters to college. Helen, inspired by a byline in her high school paper, opted for a career in the man's world of journalism. At Wayne (now Wayne State) University she majored in English and worked on the school paper and in the library, graduating in 1942.

She wasted no time in getting to Washington and finding a job on a newspaper, the late *Washington Daily News*, as copy girl and general coffee-and-rolls factotum amid the prevailing male hubris and condescension. She was happy just being there anywhere on the totem pole until a cost-cutting reorganization cost her the job. After much submitting of resumes she was hired by the United Press office to handle local news items, mostly of interest to women, for its radio wire service. Although the job required her to work 12-, 14-, 16-hour days, she generally enjoyed it for the next dozen years, especially after it was expanded to include celebrity interviews and a column of her own. In a 1955 promotion, she was transferred as a correspondent to cover Capitol Hill and various executive departments.

In November 1960 President-elect John F. Kennedy was vacationing in Miami Beach, Florida, and she was dispatched to cover the colorful Kennedy entourage at work and play. Although she paid them much closer attention than they found comfortable—Jackie reportedly once asked Jack if that harpy couldn't somehow be exiled—they couldn't shake her after moving into the White House, where she began attending briefings and press conferences and asking the same kind of sharply pointed and usually unwelcome questions that had characterized her celebrity interviews. Although her interrogatory talents weren't especially appreciated by Kennedy, Johnson or Nixon, her targets were by no means unfriendly, and those talents impressed her bosses at what was now United Press International. In 1970 she was promoted to chief White House correspondent, and in 1974 she became the first woman to be named White House bureau chief.

In her fifty years as UPI reporter and her 32 years covering the White House she has consistently maintained a grueling schedule, popping out of a bush early in the morning to toss a question at the jogging Bill Clinton, traveling countless miles all over the world with junketing politicians (with Nixon to China in 1972, for instance), and assiduously trying to hold the voters' preeminent hireling accountable. She'd be happier if only paragons of honesty and integrity could be elected to the Presidency, but she knows from experience that, to coin a phrase, eternal vigilance is the price of liberty.

In 1971, despite a longtime vow against mixing career and family, she married a colleague, Douglas B. Cornell, who had been covering the White House, for the Associated Press, even longer than she had. Their marriage was a stimulating, gratifying experience but regretfully brief. He died eleven years later.

Over the years she has received nearly a score of honorary doctorates, a dozen or so various journalism awards, and unceasing invitations to lecture. The first woman to hold office in the National Press Club, in 1975 she became the first woman member of the prestigious Gridiron Club, which in 1993 elected her its president. She expects, of course, "to die with my boots on, with pen and notebook in hand."

Marguerite Higgins
War Correspondent (1920–1966)

She was a lovely woman, very feminine, not above using her loveliness to inveigle men into bemused cooperation. She was also courageous, tough, armed with steely determination, aggressively competitive. Some of these qualities appear in a story of her persuading a fellow correspondent, a male, to take her in his jeep to the fighting in Korea and in his later explanation that "the front is no place for a woman, but it's all right for Maggie Higgins."

Marguerite Higgins was born in September 1920 in Hong Kong, where her father, a fighter pilot, had brought his French bride shortly after World War I. The daughter lived a much more prosaic childhood, however, in a rather boring suburb of Oakland, California, especially after her father took up drinking and her mother hypochondria, marked by convenient fainting spells. To compensate, she focused her interest and energy on her school work, including sports and other activities. A loner eager for acceptance, she entered the University of California at Berkeley with high hopes of being pledged by a sorority. Crushed by a rejection, she sought solace in self-sufficiency, and to a large extent found it.

By the time she graduated cum laude in 1941, her work on the school paper had given her a journalistic itch. New York, that hotbed of journalism, beckoned, and soon she was there, complete with seven bucks and a suitcase. After a number of futile attempts to find newspaper work, she decided that what she needed was a graduate degree in journalism from Columbia University. Rejected there also at first, she got herself enrolled by dint of a herculean effort to collect and submit the necessary records and affidavits within the time limit. With a classmate's help she found a job with the *New York Herald Tribune* as campus reporter, enabling her to afford the tuition. After graduation and a

marriage consisting of a brief honeymoon before her husband was drafted and
sent overseas, she got a job on the *Herald Tribune*'s city staff that made the
separation quite tolerable, especially after she began seeing her name in bylines.

That heady experience inspired her to think about war correspondence
and to apply for an assignment overseas. The inevitable rejection inevitably
spurred her determination. By the fall of 1944, after a direct appeal to the publisher's feminist wife, she was working for the paper's Paris bureau. With the
German collapse she persuaded a *Stars and Stripes* reporter to jeep her into
Germany to cover the liberation of the Dachau concentration camp (she could
speak both French and German), and she arrived there just ahead of the American forces. With an SS tower machine gun trained on her, she identified herself and her companion as American and invited the 22 tower guards to sur-
render to her, and they did. When the Americans arrived, their apprehensive
German prisoners rioted, and her efforts in calming them down won her an
Army campaign ribbon from a general who before this had vainly ordered her
to leave the premises. They also earned her a later award from the New York
Newspaper Women's Club. During the subsequent liberation of Buchenwald,
after coming upon a large group of GIs brutalizing a half-dozen young German soldiers, she made a point of reporting the incident, suggesting that the
difference between Germans and Americans might lie not so much in their
personal characters as in their political traditions.

After a hazardous tour of what would soon become East Germany and
of Poland, in 1947 she was appointed chief of the *Herald Tribune*'s Berlin
bureau, just in time for 1948's journalistically exciting blockade of Berlin by
the Soviets and the even more exciting airlift employed to counter it. The
appointment, however, was a foolish one, for she had never been noted for getting along well with others, and handling a crew of variously envious male correspondents required more diplomatic tact than she could muster. The bureau
was soon in such turmoil—one male colleague described her as "a dangerous,
venomous bitch and a bad reporter"—that in 1950 she was summarily transferred to Tokyo.

This was a form of exile that she wasn't likely to tolerate. So it was off to
Korea despite an Army ban on women correspondents there ("No facilities").
Imperiously returned to Tokyo, she appealed through the paper's publisher to
Douglas MacArthur, who overruled the field commander. Back in Korea, when
the war erupted she again was imperiously ordered back to Tokyo, this time
by the paper's senior correspondent in Korea. She refused, appealed to New
York, was told to stay, and spent the rest of her time there in aggressive junior-
senior competition. It was this competition that motivated her into that jeep
ride to the fighting where it was "all right for Maggie Higgins."

She covered the back-door Inchon landing, coming ashore in a Marine
landing craft and hitting the beach with the assault troops, lugging her
typewriter through thick and thin. In spite of Navy restrictions on women

correspondents, she did some of the war's best reporting and was one of the six correspondents in Korea to be awarded a Pulitzer Prize—and was, of course, the only woman.

Back home in 1952, she married Lt. Gen. William Hall, whom she had met romantically in Tokyo despite his wife and four children back home, and with whom she eventually had two children. This interfered only moderately with her career. In the mid–1950s she covered the French defeat in Vietnam and the early stages of American involvement there. She traveled about the world interviewing prominent political figures and in her spare time wrote her six books. In 1961, dissatisfied with some assignments, or lack thereof, she left the *Herald Tribune* and became a columnist for *Newsday*, which sent her to Vietnam in 1963. It was her ninth trip there, and she was becoming known as something of a Pentagon mouthpiece. When the Chinese had entered the Korean War, she had urged using the atom bomb, and now she was urging the practically impossible, a military victory in Vietnam.

Her tenth visit there, in 1965, was her last. From the bite of a sand fly she developed leishmaniasis, a rare and painful tropical disease. In January 1966 it killed her. Significantly, she was buried in the Arlington National Cemetery.

After her death a *Herald Tribune* colleague, John Rogers, wrote an obituary acknowledging her venomous temper and her talent for arousing resentment among male competitors for whom, at the front, "it was like encountering a woman in a crowded men's room." Yet, he continued, all she asked for was "the chance to ply her formidable energy in the battle for news beats."

Rosalyn Yalow
Developer of Radioimmunoassay
(1921–)

Her measuring technique, called radioimmunoassay, or RIA, is sensitive enough to detect a gram of salt in a thousand tons of water, for instance, or a teaspoonful of it in a freshwater lake as big as New Jersey. More to the point, it can measure previously undetectable traces of harmful substances in human blood. It earned her a share in a Nobel Prize in 1977 for its "revolutionary" contribution to medical research, the most important since the introduction of X rays.

She was born Rosalyn Sussman in July 1921 in the South Bronx, not America's most luxurious neighborhood. But her parent were models of patient industry who managed to keep the family's bodies and souls together even

during the Great Depression. And they were respectably ambitious. Having
had no chance to attend high school themselves, they were determined that
Rosalyn and her brother would go to college.

The children showed an aptitude for it. Rosalyn was only five when she
and her brother started their weekly visits to the local library. She learned to
read before she entered kindergarten and graduated from high school before
she was sixteen. Hunter College, which offered tuition-free schooling to academically gifted young female New Yorkers, accepted her application. After
a sophomore course in physics, and after reading a biography of Marie Curie,
she knew that physics was the career for her. This would require a doctorate,
and although her parents' hearts were set on her becoming a grammar school
teacher, she was determined to get it. The Hunter College administration
cooperated by establishing, for her in her senior year, a physics major program.

After graduation, magna cum laude and Phi Beta Kappa, gender raised
its ugly head. Unable to find a graduate school open to her as a teaching assistant, she took a friend's suggestion, accepting a job as secretary to a biochemist
at Columbia University. The job made her eligible for tuition-free classes, but
fortuitously she didn't need them, or the job. The war in Europe had brought
Selective Service into the lives of America's young men, and suddenly there
were openings for young women as graduate assistants. Early in 1941 she
received a letter from the University of Illinois at Urbana accepting her as such
at $70 a month in its College of Engineering. Her exhilaration was only
slightly diminished when she discovered that she was the only woman on its
faculty of 400. But the 400 included the compatibly intellectual Aaron Yalow,
headed for a Ph.D. in physics. They were married in the summer of '43.

In spite of a frantic schedule she managed to earn A's in all her courses
except lab, where her A-minus inspired the department chairman to pontificate
that this simply proved that women were incapable of doing good laboratory
work. During her orals, when this oaf contradicted one of her answers, she
replied that two of the teachers in his department had taught her this, "so if
there's anything wrong you'd better talk to them about it." He stamped out in
a huff, and she passed. Throughout her life, among certain people she would
be considered hard to get along with. Yet one of her professors would later recall
her as "a cheerful little person, not at all imposing."

Armed with their doctorates, the loving couple found jobs as engineers,
with Aaron doing sideline work in medical physics. At his suggestion she talked
to a medical physicist at Columbia, who recommended her to the Bronx's VA
hospital as someone who might be able to organize their projected radioiso-
tope service. This she did, from scratch and with little scratch, but before long
she realized that she needed someone to work with, someone trained in internal medicine, from whom she could learn functional anatomy and to whom she
could teach radioactive physics. At her request the VA's medical director sent
her someone, a young internist named Solomon Berson. Their collaboration

would occupy the next 22 years, until his death in 1972, even though she had to concede that he was something of a male chauvinist pig. He edited what she wrote, for instance, but resented it when she edited what he wrote. Yet she so admired his energy and his intellectual acuity, and incidentally his chess and violin playing, that his rougher edges were easy to overlook.

She wasn't exactly indolent. For the birth of each of her two children she took off a week from work. Aware of working-mother syndromes, she made a point of going home for lunch with the children each day and spending weekend time with them, at the lab when necessary. (They could play with the laboratory animals.) Meanwhile her work with Berson focused on the radiological detection of antibodies, heretofore undetectable. Finding that they had devised a method for detecting such elusive microorganisms, they wrote it up and submitted their article to several journals. After a disheartening number of rejections it was finally published in 1956. An expanded, more comprehensive version, published in 1959, inaugurated a long period of traveling and publicity as she and Berson talked it up in lectures and seminars. Soon RIA was being used in studies of infertility and steroids, in screening blood supplies for viruses and drugs. Honors and awards were heaped on the partners. When he died she arranged for her lab to be named the Solomon A. Berson Research Laboratory so that his name would appear in all its publications. (Unlike a Nobel Prize, this honor could be granted posthumously.)

She continued researching, publishing, and receiving awards, among them the very special Albert Lasker Prize for Basic Medical Research. By this time, understandably, visions of a Nobel Prize were dancing in her head. The phone call came early one October morning in 1977. Half the Prize in Physiology or Medicine was hers, the other half going to a couple of men for their hormone research. One headline greeted her that afternoon with "She Cooks, She Cleans, She Wins Nobel Prizes." All true enough, as her family could testify.

Although by now RIA had spawned a highly lucrative industry, she had never taken out a patent. So the Nobel Prize money was appreciated. But not all that important.

Flora Lewis
New York Times Paris Bureau Chief
(1923–)

That description, "She's one hell of a newspaperman," wasn't a tribute to her professional competence as a journalist. On the contrary, it was an expression of bitter resentment from a male rival over her appointment as chief of the Paris bureau for the *New York Times*. Indeed, it was only one comment amid a chorus of tenor, bass, and baritone complaints. But for that kind of music she has a tin ear. As for tributes, she had the appointment.

Flora Lewis was born in Los Angeles around 1923. (Her *Who's Who* entry shyly omits any date.) Her father was a lawyer, her mother a housewife. Her academic talents got her through high school by the time she was fifteen and through the University of California by the time she was eighteen (B.A., summa cum laude). With her career sights set on journalism, she gave her ambition a preliminary test in a job as cub reporter for the *Los Angeles Times* and then, encouraged by the experience, crossed the country and enrolled in the Graduate School of Journalism at New York's Columbia University for her master's degree.

With that degree in hand at nineteen, she was hired by the Associated Press, sent to Washington to cover the Departments of State and Navy, and in 1945 assigned to the London bureau in war-torn Britain. That summer she married a foreign correspondent for the *New York Times* whom she had met at Columbia. He was Sydney Gruson, who would be the father of her son and two daughters as well as a serious professional competitor in later years. The marriage would end in divorce in 1973.

When he was assigned to Poland in 1946, the devoted wife gave up her AP job and accompanied him, filling her spare time over the next ten years with journalistic writing, freelance and on contract, for various papers and journals in New York, London, and Paris. But in 1956 the *Washington Post* hired her as its first female foreign correspondent. She met the competition and eventually was appointed chief of its bureaus in Bonn and London. In 1965, after the paper opened a New York bureau, it assigned her to head it up. The grueling details of managing a large city bureau soon proved a poor alternative to the joys of writing, however, and in January 1967 she left the *Post* to take up writing three-a-week columns for the *New York Post*, *Newsday*, and a few foreign papers. Over the next five years preparing the column proved no sedentary task what with her frequent trips to Vietnam to report on futile battle strategies, to the Middle East for 1967's Six-Day War, and to Chicago and Miami for 1968's hostilities during the national political conventions.

In July 1972 an offer too good to refuse came her way when the *New York Times* asked her to be chief of its Paris bureau, one of journalism's most prestigious jobs. This was the assignment that provoked the heavily ironic expressions of rueful masculinity. Indeed, it proved an enviable one, at least in the sense that it burst out of its French seams so that she found herself, as she has put it, on assignments "as far as Tokyo, Havana, Cape Town" while "traveling two-thirds of the time." It may have been in recognition of this aspect of the job that, in 1976, she was made European diplomatic correspondent as well as bureau chief.

But in 1980 an opportunity arose to return to writing full time as the *Times'* foreign-affairs columnist, giving her an outlet for what she has called her "rock-ribbed, hard-nosed, knee-jerk, bleeding-heart moderate" political opinions. Suspicious of ideological certitudes, she could defend the American government against the implications in the 1982 film *Missing* that it had instigated the overthrow of the Allende government in 1973, while attacking Ronald Reagan's expensive and provocative military tumescence and his "gross mismanagement" of U.S. policy toward the nations of Central America.

Her countless articles and four books have earned her numerous awards for her "distinguished reporting," for her "equanimity, precision, resourcefulness and courage," and for her "lifetime of contributions to American Journalism." From the French government (she lives in Paris) she received the esteemed Cross of the Chevalier of the Legion of Honor.

After all those countless articles on European developments, there's some irony in the fact that her latest book, 1987's *Europe: A Tapestry of Nations*, opens with this disclaimer: "Writing about Europe is so vast and ambitious a project that the first problem is deciding what to leave out."

Elena Bonner
Soviet Human Rights Advocate
(1923–)

Her health problems, particularly the heart trouble and the aggravated glaucoma, were alone enough to daunt the dauntless, but to her they were merely major inconveniences that seriously interfered with the exercise of her irrepressible talent for confrontation.

She was born in Moscow in 1923. As the elder of the two children of parents of exalted status in the Comintern, she lived a very comfortable, even cosseted life as part of the collectivist elite. Prosperity in the old Soviet Union, however, could be a very sometime thing. In the summer of 1937 her parents were unaccountably arrested during a Stalinist purge, and life no longer was comfortable. With her father executed and her mother imprisoned for seventeen years, she and brother Igor were shipped off to Leningrad to live with an aunt and uncle and, after they also were purged, with her grandmother, a strong-minded woman who somehow kept right on surviving despite her stubborn refusal to go along with all that trashy communism. Her influence on Elena must have been enormous, at least eventually.

Elena completed her schooling while working as a cleaning woman and then file clerk in a factory. In 1940, while taking night courses at a teachers' college, she joined Party youth organizations, with some misgivings. After the Nazi invasion she enlisted in the army, and was severely wounded in October 1941. She suffered several wounds, but it was the concussion that left her virtually with vision in only one eye, and that one failing. Yet she recovered sufficiently to work in a hospital train for the rest of the war and to celebrate the victory in 1945 as a lieutenant.

The next two years were devoted to successive efforts to halt the deterioration of her eyesight. With it apparently stabilized, in 1947 she enrolled at Leningrad's medical institute, fell in love, married, started a family (girl, boy), and in 1953 received her medical degree. This led to work as a general practitioner and pediatrician in Leningrad and, for a while, as a health specialist in Iraq. In her spare time she wrote for and edited professional journals. (The marriage ended amicably.)

Her political reservations kept her from actually joining the Party until 1965, when it finally got around to denouncing the Stalin regime. Amid the pious rhetoric her reservations nevertheless lived on within her and were fully revived by the imperialist invasion of Czechoslovakia in 1968. Soon she was on the ramparts of dissent, writing for underground publications. Her disenchantment was completed during the trial of a comrade dissident in 1970, especially after she met the downright rebellious Andrei Sakharov, immediately recognizable as a political soulmate. They were married in 1971, and in 1972 she quit the Party.

Although by now they were subjected to relentless surveillance by the KGB and other equally intrusive police agencies, Sakharov's international reputation as a nuclear physicist and former weapons specialist gave him some measure of clout, both within the country and outside it. When she was called to report at police headquarters five times within a couple of weeks in November 1973, he complained directly to Yuri Andropov, then the Party's top dog, and announced to the press that, at his urging, she would not so report again. The harassing ceased.

His clout also was needed to save her vision. With her eyesight failing again and Soviet medicine unable to help her, he spent four nerve-racking months in 1975 pestering the bureaucrats to give her a visa permitting her to travel to an Italian eye clinic. His nomination that year for a Nobel Peace Prize fortunately enhanced his reputation further, so that he was able to get her visas for two more visits to the eye clinic during the next five years.

However enhanced his reputation, he was nevertheless refused permission to go to Oslo for the prize-awarding ceremony. And so she went and accepted the prize for him. Since it amounted to $143,000, she didn't bring it back with her but instead judiciously left it in a Western bank for untroubled accumulation of interest.

Meanwhile the Soviet Union had incongruously signed the Helsinki accords, and in 1976 Andrei and Elena joined seven other Moscow irrepressibles in forming a committee to keep an eye on the government's faithfulness to its new commitment to respect human rights. This brought them unwelcome attention for four cat-and-mouse years until, in January 1980, exasperated autocrats packed Andrei off to internal exile in Gorky, a factory city some 250 miles away in the direction of Siberia. Astonishingly they left Elena free to travel between that city and Moscow and thus to provide some communication from his grimly exclusive club, doubtless as a result of bureaucratic imbecility.

Meanwhile her son, now living in welcome exile in Boston with her mother and daughter, had been trying fruitlessly for years to get an exit visa for his wife to join him in America, and in November 1981 his mother and stepfather, despite their poor health, embarked on a hunger strike in Gorky to call attention to this example of Soviet disdain for human rights. Although they were force-fed, often brutally, in a Gorky hospital, they remained doggedly uncooperative until the visa was finally granted. The harassment continued in Gorky and in Moscow, where in September 1982 she had to announce the end of the Helsinki watchdog committee, since all sixteen members had been imprisoned or exiled.

The strain was too much for her heart, and in November she suffered an attack of angina pectoris. She was helped so little by Soviet medicine, unsurprisingly, that the couple asked for permission to emigrate, only to be turned down of course because of his classified nuclear expertise. In May 1984 they began another hunger strike in a desperate effort to extract an exit visa from the bureaucracy so that she could get some twentieth-century medical treatment in the West for her failing heart and eyesight. The bureaucracy responded by charging her with anti–Soviet behavior and, after a secret trial, committing her also to internal exile in Gorky. But it failed to recognize her, and their, incorrigibility. She *had* to have that visa, and so the next several months were filled with hunger-striking and forced feeding until at last, in October 1985, the visa was grudgingly issued. Her arrival in Boston in December was a media event, although she had promised the bureaucracy in writing not to talk to the press.

After a sextuple bypass operation, with complications, she recovered swiftly and, although obviously a prime candidate for asylum, returned home, by way of London and Paris (Thatcher and Mitterand) and Italy (her eye specialist). Back in Moscow, she made it clear that she wouldn't have returned but for her husband. She failed to mention that she had smuggled out and left behind in the U.S. manuscripts of his memoirs as well as hers.

Meanwhile—Gorbachev. One day late in December 1986 the harried couple were astonished to have an unexpected telephone installed in their apartment in Gorky and even more astonished the next day to hear Mikhail Gorbachev inviting them back to Moscow to enjoy the new policy of *glasnost*. They wasted no time. Within about a week they were back in Moscow. No KGB, no police, no restrictions on associating with friends and even on talking to the press.

It would take some getting used to, but she felt sure that they could handle it.

Patricia Roberts Harris
Secretary of Housing and Urban Development
(1924–1985)

The discrimination against blacks today is bad enough, but half a century ago and more it was worse. When, during a Congressional hearing in 1976, Patricia Roberts Harris was asked if she, a prosperous lawyer, could really be sympathetic with the plight of minorities, she pointed out that, as the daughter of a railroad dining-car waiter, she had been too poor to go to college without a scholarship and too black to choose an apartment freely. "If you think I've forgotten that, you're wrong."

She was born Patricia Roberts in May 1924 in Matoon, in central Illinois, and not long thereafter she and her mother and brother were left by her father to their own devices. She learned to read quite early and did read a great deal. At her mother's urging, she conscientiously attended school in spite of being called "nigger" by children carefully taught. A small minority in the town, blacks hadn't even the safety of numbers, although in this respect things were better after the family moved to Chicago, where Patricia hit the books so vigorously that in her senior year she received scholarship offers from five universities.

She chose liberal arts at Howard University in Washington, D.C., graduating summa cum laude in 1945. While there, as vice-chair of the school's NAACP student group, she was active in student protests against racial discrimination, joining, for instance, a sit-in at a whites-only cafeteria. Armed with a Phi Beta Kappa key, she spent the next dozen years pursuing graduate studies in industrial and social relations at the University of Chicago and American University, and working for the YWCA. In 1953 she became executive director of Delta Sigma Theta, a national black sorority, serving until 1959.

In 1955 she met an interesting and interested lawyer, William Beasely Harris. At his suggestion she entered George Washington University's Law School and in 1960 again graduated with top honors. After about a year with the Justice Department's criminal division, she was hired as a lecturer in law and as associate dean of students by her Howard alma mater. Within a couple of years she was teaching law full time as an associate professor. Meanwhile her social activism had attracted the notice of the Kennedy Administration, for which she served as cochair of the National Women's Committee for Civil Rights, representing about a hundred women's groups throughout the country.

In 1965, as the first black woman ambassador in U.S. history, she was appointed by Lyndon Johnson to represent her country in Luxembourg. She was there for two years, departing with the Order of the Oaken Crown and returning to Howard University as professor and its first woman law-school dean. Her term as dean proved quite short-lived after some internecine turmoil among both students and faculty. She departed quietly, having accepted employment with a prestigious law firm in the District, and spent the next ten years practicing corporation law and sitting on the boards of several major companies—token black, no doubt, but an outspoken and influential one.

In 1977 she left private practice to join the Carter Administration as Secretary of Housing and Urban Development. After three years of promoting racial equality in housing and more generous funding for inner cities, and hearing herself described by Carter as "a fine Cabinet officer, sensitive to the needs of others, and an able administrator," she had to leave HUD to its fate under Reagan & Co.

In 1982 she ran for mayor of Washington against Marion Barry of later notoriety but lost the Democratic primary to him, decisively. (Discrimination is not unknown within the black communities.) The next year, however, she was offered a full professorship by the George Washington University Law School, but taught there only briefly. A couple of years later her husband died, and soon thereafter, in March 1985, she died of cancer.

All her life she had looked forward to hearing "the Speaker of the House addressed as Madam Speaker ... as she introduces Madam President to the Congress assembled for the State of the Union."

Shirley Chisholm
First Black U.S. Congresswoman
(1924–)

When Shirley Chisholm was elected to Congress from Brooklyn in 1968 she became the first black woman ever to occupy a seat in that more or less august assemblage. The news of her election brought forth many headlines in papers throughout the country. Her favorite was "Black Woman Will Sock It to Congress." She would be in Congress for the next fourteen years, socking away.

She was born Shirley Anita St. Hill in November 1924 in Brooklyn, the first of three girls. Her parents, immigrants from the island of Barbados in the West Indies, although hardworking and responsible, were barely able to provide the family with necessities and became concerned over the effects that poverty and an education in New York's ghetto schools might have on their children. Life on their grandmother's farm on Barbados would at least expose them to the relative serenity of rural life, to a better education in the island's

British Commonwealth schools (99 percent literacy), and to the child-rearing talents of the grandmother, a stately woman of imposing presence whom the adult Shirley would remember as a person of uncontested authority. And love.

And so she spent her early childhood there. What with Granny and aunts and cousins, it was a family of ten on the farm, but there were plenty of chores to keep the children busy (and, especially in rapscallion Shirley's case, more or less out of mischief). She had the intelligence and enough idle moments, nonetheless, to learn to read and write by the time she was four and thus to take full advantage of her British schooling.

Meanwhile back in Brooklyn her parents grew ever more discouraged over their chances of emerging from poverty, and whatever small hopes they had were dashed with the onset of the Great Depression. But early in 1934, desperate to have their children with them whatever their financial situation, they decided that they simply had to bring them back. And so, after six years on the island, Shirley and her sisters were brought back by their mother to Brooklyn, where the unfamiliar winter cold was countered at least by the warmth of their father's welcome.

It was her father, indeed, who now became the strongest influence on the young girl's life. Although he had received only a partial elementary school education on Barbados and was mired in a job as a baker's helper, he was an avid reader of three newspapers a day and a perceptive observer of current events, especially as they affected the "last hired, first-fired" predicament of blacks in America. Listening to his lively conversations with friends on politics and social conditions, she concluded that he was nothing less than brilliant. (Her own IQ was 170.) He became her hero.

In the Brownsville section of Brooklyn, where white (mostly Jewish) residents outnumbered the blacks about four to one, there was little racial tension. But when the family moved to the Bedford-Stuyvesant section, where the mix was about fifty-fifty, Shirley encountered reciprocal racial hostility, hearing for the first time casually hateful expressions like "nigger" and "kike." She also encountered some sex discrimination in junior high school, where her standout scholastic performance failed to protect her from being "only a girl." This problem disappeared with her attendance at an all-girls high school, where, in a student body half black and half white, she won a prize in French and was elected to the vice presidency of an honor society. Her incessant reading meanwhile turned increasingly to black history and biography. She had lots of time to read because her social life was rather restricted. Although she learned to play the piano and dance and did both at school parties, under her mother's strict supervision she lived through four years of high school without ever having what the other girls would call a real date.

Since the family's relentless poverty kept her from accepting scholarship offers from both Vassar and Oberlin, in 1942 she rather ruefully enrolled at the city's tuition-free Brooklyn College, majoring in sociology. After four years of hard study and increasing volunteer social work, she graduated cum laude, and after being turned down for many teaching jobs chiefly because her diminutive size made her seem younger than some of her prospective charges, she was hired by a child care center on a trial basis. Deciding that she would have to add to her stature as a teacher with a master's degree, she started taking night courses at Columbia University.

There, freed somewhat from maternal supervision, she finally began dating, met an irresistible man and nearly married him before, to her painful shock, he was charged with fraud and deported back home to Jamaica, where he already had a wife. Not long thereafter, when Conrad Chisholm, a private detective, met her and became fascinated with her brainy sparkle, he overcame that painful shock only through gentle persistence. They were married in 1949.

Afterward he was persistently tolerant of his wife's role as tireless party worker, envelope-stuffer, doorbell-ringer, obstreperous member of the 17th Assembly District Club, and major factor in the election of the first black to join Brooklyn's panel of 49 civil judges. This was of course in addition to pursuing her own career as teacher, which led to her being hired as director of a large child care center in Manhattan with a clientele of 130 young children and a staff of 24—who found that she took some getting used to but who eventually shared her principles of child care—mixing firm control with tender loving care—principles that she had learned from her grandmother more than from her classes at Columbia. (After two miscarriages, she'd decided to devote herself to the care of others' children.)

In 1959 she accepted a job as consultant to the City Division of Day Care, responsible for overall management of ten day-care agencies. It kept her busy, but within a few years she was irresistibly back in politics again, a leader in the new Unity Democratic Club, a black political organization that ended the "plantation politics" of the lily-white political establishment in Bedford-Stuyvesant with the election in 1962 of blacks as district leader and state assemblyman.

Two years later, with the loyal support of her husband (but not that of her equally loyal father, who had died the previous year), she herself ran for the state assembly and, amid a great deal of talk about a woman's place, won more than comfortably and soon found herself on the assembly's Committee on Education, an astonishingly sensible appointment. She shepherded bills increasing funds for schools and day-care centers, providing scholarships for deserving black students, extending unemployment insurance to domestic workers (her mother had worked as a maid for a while). Although continually refusing to go along just to get along, she managed to build enough of a record and reputation to be ready for her next challenge, which came with the creation of a new Congressional district in Bedford-Stuyvesant, the Twelfth.

She campaigned for the new Congressional seat without organization support but with a provocative bumper-sticker slogan, "Fighting Shirley

Chisholm: Unbought and Unbossed." She won the primary adequately if not comfortably, and, despite the Republicans' bringing in nonresident but noted black activist James Farmer to run against her (very masculinely), despite surgery to remove a benign but threatening pelvic tumor, and despite her selection as a delegate to the notorious 1968 Democratic Convention, the support of the district's women and Hispanics (to whom she spoke Spanish) netted her a two-to-one victory in the election.

One thing that pleased her as a brand new Congresswoman was that the many black people working in the Capitol as guards and elevator operators seemed eager to help her find her way around in the labyrinth, at least physically. Although learning the political ropes was something else again, she followed a characteristic course in dealing with them. No new member of Congress would *ever* protest a committee assignment, but when this representative of the utterly urban district of Bedford-Stuyvesant was appointed to the Agriculture Committee and its subcommittees on rural development and forestry, her protest took the unprecedented but thoroughly American form of marching up to the front of the House, insisting on recognition, and confronting Speaker John McCormack with the idiocy of such an assignment. After being shifted to the Veterans' Affairs Committee, she conceded that, although it certainly wasn't an ideal alternative, at least there were "a lot more veterans in my district than trees." Two years later she'd be ensconced in the Education and Labor Committee where she belonged.

During her 14-year stay in Congress she accumulated seniority, learned the ropes, made friends and deals, cultivated compromise to get her way, became a forceful proponent of the liberal agenda. In January 1972 she announced her candidacy for the Presidency chiefly just to see what would happen and, well, to make a statement. After a grueling campaign, what happened was what she expected. Thereafter, with the Republicans in the White House, her work in Congress would keep her busier than ever—busier, but also increasingly discouraged. In 1982, with super–Republicans in the White House, she resigned, pleading her "inability to effect change in a conservative atmosphere." To the neo–Democratic Convention in 1992, she wasn't even invited.

She continued lecturing and conducting seminars. But, she observed, her day had passed.

Felice Schwartz
CEO of Catalyst (1925–)

A catalyst, according to the Merriam-Webster dictionary, is "an agent that provokes or speeds significant change or action." As CEO of Catalyst, a nonprofit enterprise that she founded in 1962 to provoke or speed change in the acceptance and treatment of women by "policies and practices of male-led corporations," she's been praised both by businessmen and by feminists. The changes that she proposes, she has argued, benefit the corporations as well as the women.

She was born Felice Nierenberg in January 1925 in New York to a businessman, owner of an engraving firm, and his homemaker wife. After a conventional elementary and high school education, she entered Smith College as a premed student whose father had visions of her as a physician. At Smith, however, she met the chairman of the college's department of religion and under his influence developed a social conscience. After her graduation in 1945, impressed with the proportion of black students at Smith (1 to 400) and other depressing statistics, she took a job with the NAACP in the hope of provoking some change yet quit within a year out of impatience with its bureaucratic pace. Impatiently, she set up her own agency, the National Scholarship Service and Fund for Negro Students.

During the next five years she devoted the agency's efforts to enrolling blacks in institutions of higher learning, for instance publishing a list of "interracial colleges" and of scholarships available to students of any pigmentation. In 1951, although she had helped hundreds of black students enter college and had received a *Mademoiselle* Merit Award for her work, her father's death brought a call from her brother to help save the family business. She quit to become vice-president in charge of production, supervising the firm's 750 employees.

She was subjected to sexist put-downs, especially from the shop stewards, but as a response she chose disarming laughter instead of expensive and time-consuming litigation. Although this wasn't what she wanted to do with her life, she handled the job well. By 1955 the business was prosperous enough to be profitably sold.

By 1955, too, she had been married for ten years to a physician, Irving Schwartz, was awaiting the birth of the second of their three children, and had decided to devote herself full time to home and family. In that process during the next eight years she met many women who would soon complete their most burdensome family responsibilities and whose abilities would then be spent on largely meaningless activity. Finding the situation thoroughly frustrating, she "became consumed with wanting to do something about this terrible waste of talent." And that gave her the idea for Catalyst.

In 1962, her youngest now ensconced in nursery school, she took off on a trip around the country to visit college presidents, persuading nine of them to sign on as board members of the firm she was starting in order "to bring to our country's needs the unused abilities of intelligent women who want to combine family and work." Soon she was busily producing dozens of pamphlets to help such women do so, as well as setting up more than two hundred resource centers and a central library for their information. She described the firm as "a facilitating rather than a confrontational organization," dedicated not to upbraiding employers or preaching to them about their responsibilities to women but rather to making it easier, and even more profitable, for them to discharge those responsibilities.

Concentrating first on the practicality of hiring women for part-time work and on public organizations as being more vulnerable to her approach, in 1963 she talked Boston's Department of Public Welfare into advertising for 50 part-time caseworkers for 25 full-time jobs. The overwhelming response permitted the delighted department managers to choose the best from a very large group of applicants. The continued success of her efforts inspired her first book, published in 1968 and titled, significantly if somewhat garrulously, *How to Go to Work When Your Husband Is Against It, Your Children Aren't Old Enough and There's Nothing You Can Do Anyhow.*

In the 1970s an economic recession, aggravated by inflation from OPEC oil price increases, forced even more women to leave home for work, and this in turn prompted Catalyst to turn increasingly to the private sector, advising corporations on ways to handle the problems of child care, parental leave, and benefits, as well as the advantages of promoting women into positions of responsibility and leadership consonant with their education and ability. Although she had to fight off criticism, such as that spawned in 1989 by an article of hers in the *Harvard Business Review* and the *New York Times*'s acid criticism of her concept of a working mother's career as "the mommy track," she continued to insist that a corporation choosing talent from an exclusively male population would be hobbling itself in competition with one choosing talent from a much larger male-female population.

Her persuasion of corporations failed to persuade some feminists, who evidently considered male-female equality to be male-female identity. Her response was obvious: men do not, for example, have problems of maternity leave and child care. Women do, as she stressed in her second book, published in 1992 and titled *Breaking with Tradition*. Profits from the book's sales, after her retirement from Catalyst in 1993, have gone to the Felice N. Schwartz Fund for the Advancement of Women in Business and the Professions.

Recipient of many honors and awards, she has continued writing and lecturing. She fully accepts the celebrated French shibboleth of "Viva la différence!" but sticks to her goal, "to make gender no longer an issue in the workplace."

Margaret Thatcher
First Woman Prime Minister of the United Kingdom (1925–)

In 1975 she became the first woman leader of a major English political party, and four years later she became England's first woman prime minister.

She was born Margaret Hilda Roberts in October 1925 in a little town north of London, in the family's respectable but quite unpretentious digs above their grocery store. Only ten years later she was active in politics, an eager envelope-stuffer and errand-runner for the local Tory organization. The eagerness was partly to please her father, who was variously alderman, justice, and town mayor but who also was a caring father devoted to his two daughters' education, the man to whom the prime minister years later would say she owed everything—"I really do."

In school she skipped a grade, won scholarships, led teams in sports (including hockey), and reveled in public speaking, sometimes inconsiderately. At home, besides helping out in the family grocery stores (her father had two now), she pored over books on politics, took lessons in dramatic piano and in elocution, and watched her father solemnly meting out justice in court. She spent much of World War II at Oxford University on a scholarship, concentrating on chemistry and X ray crystallography and emerging in 1947 with an M.A. and a B.S. in natural science. (At Oxford, ironically, she was barred from the all male debating society.) For the next four years she worked as a research chemist while devoting her spare time to the stimulus of Tory politicking. (The fact that she was paid less in her job than her male peers intensified her extracurricular incentive.) Encouraged by the local party boss and by her dashing fiancé and then loving, supportive husband Denis Thatcher, a fellow Tory and affluent businessman, she even ran twice for Parliament—unsuccessfully, for she did so in a district controlled by Labor, although her vote-gathering was impressive. Such male chauvinism as she encountered was never a match for her impatience with it.

After the birth of boy-girl twins in 1953, she might well have relaxed into comfortable domesticity. Instead, having studied law in her leisure time, she practiced law for a few years; for her specialty she chose tax law, notoriously a male preserve. In 1957 her political itch could be ignored no longer, and she returned to the hustings, this time in a district populated by upper-middle-class constituents. Having impressed the voters with her charm, adhesive memory and Cro-Magnon viewpoints, in October 1959 she joined Prime Minister Harold Macmillan's Tory majority in Parliament, where she became that body's resident whirlwind and soon its chief authority on insurance, pension plans, the national budget, energy, and whatever else she was asked to look into during her twenty-hour workdays.

Labor's return to parliamentary power in 1964 gave her an opportunity to put her elocution lessons and her natural combativeness to work in opposition—condemning, for instance, Labor's proposal to eliminate elitism in the grammar schools. This stance, after the return of the Tories under Prime Minister Edward Heath in 1970, doubtless accounted for her appointment to the Cabinet as Minister of Education, despite some nose-wrinkling in the old-boy ranks. She lost no time in turning back to educational elitism and inviting accusations of "sabotage" from the teachers' union. In response she argued for "a place for select schools of excellence" and added, "I have sometimes thought that some extreme advocates of equality would be happy if all the children were in bad schools as long as they were all equally bad."

In October 1970 the government, with characteristic Tory benevolence, decided to cancel free milk rations for 3.5 million schoolchildren. Although originally opposed to the decision, Thatcher became its strong advocate and implementer, earning her the appreciative sobriquet of "Thatcher the Milk Snatcher." Rising to the occasion, and adding financial insult to nutritional injury, she also raised the price of school lunches by about a third. Lest the colleges feel neglected, she cut government funding of higher education as well. She did manage, however, to obtain more money for her department, which she spent on building and repairing elementary schools and on teacher improvement.

She got along pretty well with some of her colleagues, especially in her charming mode, and not at all with others. During Cabinet meetings she usually was uncharacteristically subdued, but on occasion she couldn't resist needling the assembled stallions. When Prime Minister Heath rejected a proposed candidate for an office because he had "much too high an opinion of himself," she offered her unsolicited opinion that "most men do." A few chuckles, but no applause.

After the Tories lost Parliament in February 1974 she became the opposition's acidulous spokesperson, arguing tirelessly for much less public spending, severe budget-balancing and "sound" financial policies. As for unemployment, she was for "the workers, not the shirkers." The Tories, she insisted, had lost political power because they had failed "to stand for anything distinctive and positive"—and, she might have added, *right*. Within a year, in February 1975, she was elected party leader over Edward Heath, who would thereafter refer to her only as "that woman." (But the Tories' Carlton Club suddenly was no longer for males only.) Her shadow cabinet proved to be much more carefully balanced ideologically than might have been expected after her comment on taking over the leadership: "I am not a consensus politician, I am a conviction politician." The Soviet press, among others, agreed with her: after her strident denunciation of communism in 1976, it bestowed on her the soon famous title of Iron Lady. She was delighted.

With the return of the Tories to power, in May 1979 she became the prime minister to preside, with her all-male Cabinet (her "spayed Cabinet," one critic charged), over a defanging of the intimidating labor unions, a return of much nationalized industry into private hands, a reduction of taxes and of inflation, and a restoration of middle-class affluence and values. This was accompanied by a rapid rise in unemployment (especially in the industrial north) and a greater tolerance of poverty, but also, in 1982, a faint resurgence of imperial pride in repelling the Argentine invasion of the Falkland Islands. In this connection she was described by her defense minister as "the toughest man we've got," and doubtless was smiled on from above by Boedicea, the warrior queen of the ancient Britons who fought so stubbornly against the Romans.

The Falklands exhilaration lasted long enough for her to win a second term in June 1983. By the end of that term stock ownership had increased 300 percent, home ownership 27 percent, and income—for the employed—15 percent while the budget deficit dropped from 5 percent of GNP to 1 percent and the economy was growing at a heartening rate of 3 percent per year. After an unsuccessful year-long mine-workers strike, the unions, hampered by new anti-union legislation and intimidated by her stubborn belligerence, lost a quarter of their membership, to the chilling dismay of the Labor Party. In the 1980s unemployment dropped form 11 percent to 6 percent.

Unsurprisingly, she launched into a policy of upgrading Britain's nuclear weaponry while dealing with Soviet President Mikhail Gorbachev in a spirit of cordial intransigence. In return for the support of her ideological buddy Ronald Reagan in the Falklands war, she allowed American aircraft to attack Libya from British bases. She repeatedly called for international cooperation against terrorism and was almost eliminated by a terrorist bomb that destroyed her bathroom in a Brighton hotel.

Despite some signs of a Labor revival in 1987, that June she won an unheard-of third term and intimated that she was looking forward to her fourth and fifth. But those were not to be. A declining British economy, a failing educational system, and especially her imposition of an utterly regressive poll tax in March 1990, followed by riotous protests, so weakened the Tories politically that she found herself facing an irreversible party revolt. There was also a personality problem. "She's reached the point," one Tory M.P. complained, "where everyone else is wrong and she's right. None of us wants it, but there comes a point when we simply have to say, 'Enough!'" Many of her fellow citizens had taken to carrying a small "Thatchcard" in their pockets, reading, "I do not wish to be visited in the hospital by the prime minister."

And so her tenure as prime minister, the longest in 160 years, came to an end in November 1990. She would emerge, as Lady Thatcher, from relative obscurity in the spring of 1992, characteristically calling for more aggressive international military action in the Balkans.

Jeane Kirkpatrick
Ambassador to the United Nations
(1926–)

Jeane Kirkpatrick—the first woman to regularly attend meetings of her country's National Security Council—has become enough of a tradition on the American political stage to have established a reputation as a liberal on domestic issues and a hard-line conservative on foreign policy. Indeed, she was an active Democrat for most of her adult life, formally becoming a Republican only after leaving her United Nations post in April 1985.

Yet in her celebrated article in the November 1979 *Commentary* ("Dictatorship and Double Standards")—the article that came to the attention of Presidential candidate Ronald Reagan and earned her the UN appointment—she revealed a thoroughly Republican attitude toward the fundamental issue of social responsibility. Defending the U.S. foreign-policy support of rightwing dictators and avaricious oligarchies, she wrote that although "traditional autocrats" do indeed "favor the affluent few and maintain masses in poverty," this is tolerable "because the miseries of traditional life are familiar, they are bearable to ordinary people." To *those* ordinary people of course.

She was born Jeane Duane Jordan in November 1926 in Duncan, Oklahoma. Because her father was a roving wildcatter, her early education was peripatetic, but eventually, in 1950, she earned a master's degree in political science from Columbia University, fortifying it in 1952–53 with graduate work at the University of Paris, courtesy of a French governmental grant, and embellishing it with fluency in French and Spanish. After returning home and working in a couple of academic research jobs, she took a job, also in research, at the State Department, married her boss, Dr. Evron M. Kirkpatrick, in 1955, and settled down in Washington, D.C., to raise a family (three sons) while doggedly pursuing her academic career. In 1973, after spending the intervening years teaching political science and earning her doctorate from Columbia with a dissertation on Argentina under Juan Peron, she was made a full professor at Georgetown University.

Although teaching was the main course, it left her with time for horsd'oeuvre consulting and writing—lots of writing. She published articles in both academic and popular periodicals, scholarly monographs, and a book on Argentina derived from her dissertation. In 1971 her book *Political Woman*, based on interviews with fifty women serving in state assemblies, achieved a somewhat wider circulation with its general theme that their lack of opportunities for higher office made them better, more responsible legislators than their male counterparts.

The next year she piloted a study of the delegates to the political party conventions. It comprised an analysis of responses to questions addressed or mailed to some 1300 "of the effective elite of the Presidential parties." Besides concluding that men and women delegates differed little in their political opinions, she expressed some alarm at the strong ideological element in the McGovern campaign as perilous to the two-party system. That campaign's antagonism to the Vietnam adventure and to American materialism disturbed her deeply, so deeply that she threw her public support to the Johnson-encumbered Hubert Humphery.

Despite McGovern's nomination she stuck with the Democratic Party, although she joined in organizing a Coalition for a Democratic Majority with the aim (according to an interview published in the *New York Times*) of rescuing the party from the "antiwar, antigrowth, antibusiness, antilabor activists." Richard Nixon couldn't have put it better.

She continued actively participating in Democratic Party politics, but it's small wonder that in 1977 she was engaged as a resident scholar by the American Enterprise Institute for Public Policy, best known for its dedication to the social ideals of Calvin Coolidge and the foreign-policy principles of William Randolph Hearst. Two years later her *Commentary* article condemned the Carter Administration's lack of enthusiasm for right-wing "authoritarians" and its tolerant attitude toward left-wing totalitarians. Its behavior in foreign policy, she suggested, bordered on the masochistic.

Such criticism obviously brought a delightful tingle to Ronald Reagan's political nerve endings. So, surely, did her remarks in the *Washington Star* in November 1980 that his political skills should enable him to gather together a political coalition of varied elements and perhaps "to restore the consensus and confidence that has been missing in this country for more than a decade." After his election she was invited to join his shadow advisers on foreign policy. In December he named her as the nation's new Permanent Representative, a.k.a. Ambassador, to the United Nations. The next month the Senate confirmed her appointment, unanimously.

She made a difference, despite bureaucratic antagonism from the State Department on this side and the UN on that. Even her aides, furnished of course by State as part of the regular UN delegation, seemed unsympathetic to her view of her responsibility to assert U.S. views and interests, as she saw them, forcefully and even provocatively. She felt isolated, according to her counsel Allen Gerson, and reluctant to trust anyone. Yet during her four lively years at the UN, against Soviet intransigence and Third World hostility and European apathy, she managed to raise attitudes toward the U.S. at least to a level of grudging respect. When she left in 1985, to return to teaching and writing and at last to join the GOP, her fellow delegates honored her with several dinners and countless toasts. She had, she felt, at any rate taken that sign off the door to the office of her country's ambassador to the UN—the sign reading "Kick Me."

Her entry in *Who's Who in America* includes at the end a statement of her opinion on women's roles: "My experience demonstrates to my satisfaction that it is both possible and feasible for women in our times to successfully combine traditional and professional roles, that it is not necessary to ape men's career pattern—starting early and keeping one's nose to a particular grindstone, but that, instead, one can do quite different things at different stages of one's life. All that is required is a little luck and a lot of work."

Lina Wertmuller
Film Director (1927–)

For movie goers bored with conventional cinematic fare, Lina Wertmuller ranks high on the list of directors who can be relied on to offer something different. If nothing else, her titles often are challenging in themselves. An early film was *Swept Away by an Unusual Destiny in the Blue Sea of August* and a very late one was *The End of the World in Our Usual Bed in a Night Full of Rain.*

Born in Rome around 1927 (she is diffidently vague about the date), she was baptized with a name worthy of her movie titles: Arcangela Felice Assunta Wertmuller von Elgg Spanol von Braucich, a name also worthy of her noble Swiss ancestry. The family was brought to Italy generations ago by a baron reluctant to account to the Swiss authorities for a moment of homicidal passion. She has little doubt as to who eventually inherited his temperament.

That temperament was channeled into angry rebellion against authority by a despotic father and by despotic nuns in school (she was expelled fifteen times by successively exasperated principals but left the church only once, and for all). A major source of relief from the rigors of education was provided by illicit viewing, whenever possible, of American movies. There was a certain advantage to the oppressiveness of her immediate environment, for it overrode any awareness she may have had of the widespread oppressiveness of Italy's Fascist regime.

When it came time for college after the war, her father imperatively recommended the Academy of Law (he was a lawyer, of course), and an actress friend pointed her toward the Academy of Theater. She enrolled at both schools, only to discover with a few hours at the Academy of Theater that a career in law could never be more than second best, at best. She was hooked on show biz.

After graduation in 1951 and a brief fling in vanguard experimental theater, she took off on a tour of Europe with a band of puppeteers who also were vanguard experimentalists, using impressionist and surreal hand puppets to present socially significant tales based on Franz Kafka and musical plays based on Manuel de Falla. She reveled of course in the company's unconventional approach to children's theater—no big bad wolves, no fairy godmothers—especially when it provoked parental indignation, as it almost invariable did, sometimes even involving stimulating attention from the police.

Seeking broader horizons, she spent the rest of the 1950s in various theatrical pursuits, including acting, set designing, stage managing, publicity, and writing for stage, radio and TV until, in 1962, an actress friend, wife of screen idol Marcello Mastroianni, brought her to the attention of noted movie director Federico Fellini, whose *La Strada* and *La Dolce Vita* had already given him icon status. Mastroianni would be starring in his next movie, *8 1/2*, he told her. Would she like to hire on as his assistant? Would she ever!

Working with Fellini opened her eyes, she has said, to "new dimensions of life." Not new dimensions of *art*, but of life in the sense that his liberated spirit, his lack of inhibition gave his art an originality, a freedom from restraints imposed by conventional cinematic proprieties. She fit into the project so well that her decision to try some film directing on her own received the enthusiastic support of cast and crew and even of Fellini, who helped her get funds for her first attempt.

That first attempt, for which she hired most of the crew of *8 1/2*, resulted in a grimly comic picture of aimless living in the Italian south. Although *The Lizards* never reached U.S. audiences, it won a prize for its neophyte director at the Locarno Film Festival in 1963. Three years later her second feature film, *Let's Talk About Men*, offered four short tales involving sexual abuse, also grimly comic. It did reach U.S. audiences, but ten years later, earning somewhat better box-office returns than critical reviews.

Problems in money-raising forced her back to the stage and TV for a while. In 1966 the problems proved less acute when, significantly as "George Brown," she directed the emerging idol Giancarlo Giannini, whom she'd met three years earlier, and became, inadvertently but not unwillingly, hitched to his star. In 1968 she married Enrico Job, a sculptor who thereafter served as art director for her films. In that year also Giannini became interested in a play she had written, *Two and Two Are No Longer Four*, and brought it to the notice of the talented Franco Zeffirelli, who had recently directed Richard Burton and Elizabeth Taylor in his splendid *The Taming of the Shrew*. With him as producer and Giannini prominently featured, the play earned good reviews and gratifyingly huge revenues at the box office.

Thus encouraged, in 1971 she directed Giannini in *Mimi the Metalworker, His Honor Betrayed*, a risible satire for which she also wrote the script and which brought her a Best Director prize at Cannes in 1972. The following year it was Giannini's turn when he was awarded the Best Actor prize for his depiction of a maladroit wanna-be assassin of Mussolini in her *Love and Anarchy*. Both movies were given American release, received rave reviews, and rewarded her with a burgeoning celebrity among literate moviegoers.

Her next movie, 1975's *Swept Away*, offered those literate moviegoers a witty script but broadened its appeal with a kind of slapstick at which Giannini proved very adept. It burnished her reputation all the more rightly, even to the extent that one of her early movies was demothballed and distributed in the U.S. under an American title, *All Screwed Up*. Any harm it might have done to her reputation was soon overwhelmed by the enthusiasm of critics in 1976 over her *Seven Beauties*. Like her other films, it seemed rather disorderly—"An imposed order," she explained in an interview, "is stifling"—but the admiring consensus hailed it as a harrowing tale of survival, splendidly done. She was even compared favorably with all those splendid foreign male directors.

Althea Gibson
Tennis Champion (1927–)

She had "always wanted to be somebody," she said, and so she became a somebody with a reputation as one of the greatest athletes of her day. As a child she showed not only a competitive nature but also a remarkable ability at stick ball, basketball, and paddle tennis. As an adult she concentrated on her championship tennis, and in later life she became a professional golfer.

Althea Gibson was born in August 1927 in Silver, North Carolina (sans silver spoon), but grew up in a crowded tenement in Harlem. With a great deal of her time spent in movie theaters instead of classrooms, her graduation from junior high school was a pleasant surprise. This was followed by a disappointment, however, when she was told that her grades weren't good enough to qualify her for one of the better high schools, where most of her classmates were going. And so she forsook education for work, including a job at the New York School of Social Work, where her indulgence of an addiction to the movies and stage shows at the Paramount Theater quickly brought a dismissal notice.

At the School of Social Work she encountered the Robinsons, Sugar Ray and his wife Edna, who urged her to finish high school, get a decent job and stick with it. Later they would help hone her tennis skill, which they had a chance to observe and found very promising. But for the time being she returned rather uneasily and aimlessly to work, ricocheting from workaday pillar to post. Her loafing and lolling between jobs attracted the notice of the New York Welfare Department, which helped her to move to better living quarters and to look for more satisfying employment. Under its auspices she began participating in games sponsored by the local Police Athletic League.

A summertime city recreation counselor became so impressed with her skill at paddle tennis that he bought her a secondhand conventional tennis racket and introduced her to its use at his park's handball court. As soon as the court's walls were clearly no longer providing enough competition for improvement, he arranged for her to play some sets against a tennis pro at the New York Cosmopolitan Club. Her competitive energy and native talent for the game led some observant members of the club to enter her as a junior member and underwrite her lessons and practice time. Less than a year later she entered 1942's New York State Open Championship matches and won the girls' singles.

This inspired the club members to increase their financial support and dispatch her to Pennsylvania, where Lincoln University was hosting the national girls' championship matches, mostly for blacks, for the American Tennis Association. She made it to the finals but lost the crucial match, perhaps because she was distracted by a boy in the stands who was laughing at her, or so she thought. Still a bit rough at the edges for genteel tennis, she threatened unceremoniously to come up into the stands and throw him out bodily.

During the Association's cancellation of its tournaments during most of World War II, she continued with vigorous practice play at the club and as a result was victorious in the girls' singles when the matches were resumed in 1944 and again in 1945. The next year two black tennis enthusiasts, both prosperous surgeons and prominent members of the Association, were so taken by the performance of the 18-year-old in some matches in Ohio that they offered to provide her with food, shelter, clothing, and an education if she'd give tennis her otherwise undivided attention. She agreed and lived with one of the men's family while being strenuously trained by the other on his private court (since no public court was open to blacks) and occasionally visiting tournaments with him. She practiced faithfully, out of gratitude as much as ambition.

In her senior year in high school she was offered a tennis scholarship by the Florida Agricultural and Mechanical College in Tallahassee. She accepted with understandable alacrity and spent the summer of 1950 practicing on the college's courts. She also entered minor tournaments while hoping for overtures from the U.S. Lawn Tennis Association, since she yearned to play in its celebrated Forest Hills grass court tournament. It ignored her, however, and this so infuriated tennis champion Alice Marble (also celebrated) that she inveighed against "the injustices perpetrated by our policymakers." In the ensuing uproar some racial walls began to crumble, and soon Althea was playing in some of the more prestigious tournaments, both lawn and clay. Toward the end of the 1950s she had won victories in 16 out of 18 tournaments on the Continent, as well as two straight victories at Wimbledon. Finally, in 1958, she took the American championship at Forest Hills. Nineteen fifty-eight was her year: she was named Woman Athlete of the Year in the Associated Press poll, appeared in a movie, *The Horse Soldiers*, and published her biography, *I Always Wanted to Be Somebody*.

Having achieved her goal, she retired. Although she had a degree in physical education from Florida A&M and had taught it for a couple of years, she tried her hand at a number of things, including nightclub singing, before taking up professional golf for a reasonably lucrative livelihood. (This was before tennis stars could earn enough for a comfortable retirement.) Over the next quarter century she would finally get married, in 1983 to Sidney Llewellyn, and would be named to several athletic halls of fame—and would be crowned a beauty queen of Harlem.

Sarah Caldwell
First Woman Conductor at the Metropolitan Opera (1928–)

She has been dogged, daring, and dauntless in her promotion of opera. One of the great singers of the world, Joan Sutherland, has called her "one of the great producers of the world."

Sarah Caldwell was born in Maryville, Missouri, in March 1928 but was raised in Fayetteville, Arkansas, where her father taught at the state university. Her mother, a skilled pianist and music teacher with an M.A. in music from Columbia University, encouraged an extraordinary musicianship in her daughter, who began giving violin recitals at the age of ten. Mother and daughter regularly attended both stage plays and concerts, treating the child to a combination of words and music that may have given rise to her lifelong addiction to opera.

After high school and a couple of years at the University of Arkansas (she was also prodigiously talented in mathematics), she transferred to the New England Conservatory of Music in Boston for further study of the violin as well as for training in orchestra conducting, stagecraft, and opera production. After graduation she declined offers to join the Indianapolis and Minneapolis symphonies as a violinist, choosing instead to work as an assistant to the celebrated Boris Goldovsky, director of the New England Opera Theater (and regular commentator for the Metropolitan Opera's Saturday radio broadcasts). She would spend the next eleven years as his busy factotum, handling props, preparing librettos, directing the chorus, supervising the staging, conducting the orchestra.

This left her summers free, and so she spent them mostly as a student and then as a teacher at the Berkshire Music Center at Tanglewood. Her transition from student to teacher occurred at the instance of conductor Serge Koussevitsky after her first staging of a complete opera, Ralph Vaughn Williams' *Riders to the Sea*, while still in her teens.

The 1950s were to be among her most productive years. As department head of Boston University's Opera Workshop she put her students through their musical paces in a great variety of operas from the obscure to the familiar, including works of composers from Bohuslav Martinů and Robert Middleton through Stravinsky and Hindemith to Bizet and Puccini. She would never be accused of confining herself to a narrow repertoire.

In 1957 she led a covey of fellow "opera addicts" in a fund-raising project that eventually resulted in the founding of the Opera Company of Boston. In her spare time she devoted herself to musical research, which enabled her to produce neglected works of, again, a wide variety of composers—Rameau, Mussorgsky, Verdi, Offenbach. Indeed, her production of Offenbach's *Voyage to the Moon* proved notable and popular enough to survive a national tour of fourteen weeks in 1960 and to be presented at the Kennedy White House to an audience of space-age celebrities.

The 1960s rivaled, perhaps surpassed, the 1950s in productivity. She would not neglect the neglected—Kurka, Charpentier, Schuller, Smetana—nor disdain the familiar—Mozart, Verdi, Puccini. She offered Berg's controversial, R-rated *Lulu* and staged Stravinski's *The Rake's Progress* with a panoply of boot, whips, and motorcycles. She received special praise from critics for her production of Schoenberg's intimidating *Moses and Aron* and a full-flower version of Berlioz's *The Trojans*. Critics also praised her founding of the American National Opera Company, although it lasted for only a single season before succumbing to bankruptcy. Her faith in the sophistication of American opera goers wasn't exactly bolstered by the experience.

Critical praise was by no means limited to her role as producer. "Not only is she a great director," commented a *New Yorker* critic in the late 1960s; "one must also place her among the finest operatic conductors currently before the public." Characteristically, she conducted vigorously, often with her fists clenched and her generously proportioned body swaying precariously, as in her performance as the first woman to conduct at the Metropolitan.

She has become famous for her absent-mindedness. She lost hats, gloves, purses, even royalty checks—so many items that she took to carrying things about in paper bags ("I don't relate well to possessions."). Once she conducted in an outfit made up by panicky aides from a set of drapes as an alternative to her state of casual dishabille. Although her chronic lack of adequate funds may have been subtly gender-engendered, her career seems surprisingly free of instances of severe, overt sex discrimination. But that may well be because she was too preoccupied to notice.

Violeta Chamorro
President of Nicaragua (1929–)

"Some are born great," reads Malvolio from a letter in *Twelfth Night*, "some achieve greatness, and some have greatness thrust upon them." Violeta Chamorro, among others, would dispute the degree of greatness, but certainly it was thrust upon her, uninvited.

Violeta Barrios de Chamorro was born in Rivas, Nicaragua, in November 1929. The family was large (seven children) and affluent (rich in land and cattle), enabling the children to be educated abroad. Enrolled at a Catholic high school in Texas and then at college in Virginia, she returned home after her freshman year following her father's death. Although the country was in the political grip of the notorious Somoza family, she had every reason to look forward to a long life of simple aristocratic luxury.

But in December 1950 she married Pedro Joaquin Chamorro Cardenal, whose family owned *La Prensa*, the country's major newspaper, and who, on the death of his father in 1952, became its publisher. Under his direction it developed into the principal organ of popular dissent against the infamous Somoza regime, which relied on terror and U.S. support to maintain itself in power. As a result he spent much of the mid–1950s in jail until, in 1957, after he had led a revolt against the embedded despots, he was summarily dispatched to a judiciously distant town in the south, where she joined him, leaving their four children with his redoubtable mother. From there they soon escaped to exceptionally democratic Costa Rica, where he took to writing books against the regime and planning a rebellious return. That return landed him in a Nicaraguan jail again in 1959.

He was released during a period of brief amnesty in June 1960. He resumed his journalistic and other rebellious activities, again spending much of his time in jail over the next seventeen years. As for her, she stuck with him through thick and distressingly thin. Although she had none of her husband's political intensity, she had married him for better or for worse. She took care of home and children, stayed with him when possible on his travels about the country, and visited him faithfully in prison until, in January 1978, he finally, inevitably, was assassinated.

His death was followed, and indeed was the spark for, a revolt that lasted over the next year and a half. During this time she, as owner and publisher of *La Prensa*, continued its nettlesome opposition to their majesties, despite bomb threats, and began supporting, journalistically and financially, the Sandinista guerrilla rebels. In July 1979, after their majesties had fled the country with heaps of ill-gotten gains and the Sandinistas had victoriously entered Managua, the capital, she was asked to be one of the five members of the junta

formed to administer the new "Government of National Reconstruction."
Reluctantly, patriotically, she consented.

The new government found itself in a situation not unlike that of President Bill Clinton & Co. fourteen years later, but *in extremus*: a country had been impoverished by years of misrule. The destitution facilitated the imposition of a Marxist ideology favored by the Sandinistas and by their friend and mentor Fidel Castro. Within a year she found herself very uncomfortable with the Cuban connection, the increasing police-state atmosphere, and the encroachments on freedom, especially freedom of speech and press. And so she left the junta, and soon *La Prensa* was vigorously opposing *this* government. Her apostasy split the very political Chamorro family into two unhappily contentious factions. She was not fazed.

Instead of bomb threats she was subjected to graffiti threats on the walls of her home, and in 1986 President Daniel Ortega Saavedra threatened her with thirty years in prison on a charge of treason—to which she replied, in effect, okay, come and get me. He didn't. What he and his cabal did do, of course, was to close down *La Prensa* for the umpteenth time, but this time indefinitely. She was disappointed, infuriated, but not fazed.

In the meantime the dogged effort of Costa Rica's President Arias to bring some peace to Nicaragua was bearing fruit. His first offer in 1987, in the name of his own and other Central American countries, was rejected by Ortega, who tried to make up for the poor PR impression this created by proposing to his distaff adversary that she resume publication, but under government censorship. Her response was the Hispanic equivalent of Not on Your Tintype, Buster—freedom of *la prensa*, or no *La Prensa*. Oh, well, he answered in effect, go ahead anyway. And so she resumed publication, with annoying harassment but no censorship.

Arias persisted, and in February 1989 he and his fellow Central American leaders pressured Ortega & Co. into agreeing to hold free elections within a year. (These elections were to be monitored, by Jimmy Carter et al., unlike those held five year earlier.) Unsurprisingly, Ortega became a presidential candidate, and the Union of National Opposition chose his journalistic nemesis to run against him. Although inexperienced and rather inept in the glad-handing and name-remembering department, she campaigned vigorously. Her celebrated integrity and genuine religious fervor impressed voters so deeply that one supporter remarked that really all she had to do was "lead the procession." And so she won, with a 15 percent lead. She even had coattails: in the National Assembly, Union candidates wound up with a 57 percent majority.

Being President, she found, required at least as much diplomacy as courage. She was on a tightrope between the Sandinistas, still a powerful political and military force, and the anti–Sandinista "contra" rebels, still a powerful military force. With the advice and support of her chief minister (and son-in-law) Antonio Lacayo, she decided on a conciliatory yet firm middle course, for example leaving the Sandinista army chief in place but appointing herself Minister of Defense. She would make up for her lack of political experience, a foreign observer remarked, "with common sense."

Indeed, she ended the civil war if not all the violence. She stabilized the economy, although at a level of abysmal poverty. Meanwhile the people waited for her, despite attacks from zealots right and left and a new element of U.S. indifference, to perform miracles. She still led the opposition, but it was growing ever more unruly. And Ortega announced his candidacy for the 1996 election—in early 1992!

Her family remains politically divided. Her four children visit her frequently, however, and the conversation is kept strictly apolitical.

Barbara Harris
First Woman Bishop (1930–)

Every ten years Anglican bishops from around the world solemnly gather in Canterbury, England, to discuss church problems and to issue such episcopal, if not pontifical, proclamations as may seem inescapable. In 1988 a pressing problem confronted the conference, that of ordination of women to the priesthood, already in effect in some dioceses of the associated "national churches." Beyond this there was another, similar problem, not yet in effect but looming large on the ecclesiastical horizon, the harrowing possibility of consecrating a woman to the episcopate, to the exalted office of bishop. With most American bishops favoring such consecrations, a decision, to approve or disapprove, seem unavoidable.

Their decision, sufficiently indecisive to be passed by an overwhelming vote, requested that each Anglican province "respect the decisions and attitudes of other provinces in the ordination and consecration of women to the episcopate, without such respect necessarily indicating acceptance of the principles involved." In short, please mind your own business.

And so, the following year, Barbara Harris of Massachusetts was consecrated the first woman bishop in the history of Anglicanism and was appointed suffragan (assistant) bishop of the Massachusetts diocese. Addicts of the men-only tradition of clerical and episcopal appointments—a tradition based chiefly on the New Testament account of Jesus Christ's appointment of men only as apostles in an obscure milieu 2000 years ago—were shocked and appalled, and, of course, they did not mind their own business.

She was born Barbara Clementine Harris in 1930 in Philadelphia. Her father, a steelworker, and her mother, homemaker and church organist, were second-generation Episcopalians who raised her and her brother and sister accordingly. After her graduation from a local girls' high school, she took a job with a public relations firm owned by blacks and representing blacks' interests in the business community. In her spare time she earned a degree from a Philadelphia school of advertising and journalism. Her rather unchurchly course of studies would later provide convenient ammunition for her adversaries, as would her ten years (1958–68) as president of the public relations firm.

Her next job, in the community relations department of the Sun Oil Company, was similar, and similarly remote from her eventual destination, especially after she became department manager in 1973.

During the sixties and early seventies, however, she spent many an off-hour as a civil-rights activist, picketing for the NAACP, encouraging blacks to vote in Mississippi, joining in freedom marches, including the famous one in 1965 from Selma to Montgomery in Alabama. After learning of a predominantly black North Philadelphia Episcopal parish of the Church of the Advocate, a section characterized as the cradle of Philadelphia's black movement, she dedicated her efforts not only to caring for its poor residents but also engaging in more radical activity, as when she played host to a spectacularly well attended gathering of Black Panthers. (Her marriage during this time apparently couldn't compete with the activism; it lasted only three years.)

She also participated in more liturgical sorts of activity. When eleven women were impertinently ordained by three bishops in the Church of the Advocate in July 1974, she carried the crucifix at the head of the procession in the ceremony. Ordination, she decided, was a worthwhile goal, and to achieve it she turned to dedicating her off-hours to getting qualified. Between 1976 and 1979 she took courses at Philadelphia's Metropolitan Collegiate Center, at Villanova University, and at the Episcopal Divinity School in Cambridge, Massachusetts, as well as receiving some theological training at a school in England and some more practical training at the Pennsylvania Foundation for Pastoral Counseling.

In October 1980, having left her Sun Oil job and having been made a deacon a year earlier, she was ordained priest and assigned to pastoral duties, including those of chaplain in Philadelphia County's prisons. In 1984, her prison assignment completed, she was appointed executive director of the Episcopal Publishing Company, which issued an unofficial, socially conscious journal significantly titled *Witness*. Soon she was writing a regular column for it, inveighing in cheerily provocative language against the injustices perpetrated on blacks in Angola and South Africa, as well as in her own country's slums and prisons. She protested against mistreatment of minorities generally, including gays and lesbians, and didn't hesitate to censure an Episcopal doctrine or activity that she considered socially unjust.

Small wonder that the consecration of a black woman, especially *this* black woman, as bishop in February 1989 brought heated accusations of heresy, Marxism, even terrorism from the rigidly righteous, as well as strictures on her lack of conventional indoctrination and her unprecedented gender. Her consecration was an act of insolent defiance against "the God-given order of the church," and so on. A priest ordained by a woman bishop, it was claimed, wouldn't be recognized as such by half of the Anglican communion. Significantly, however, a poll of the laity in her diocese revealed that fewer than 15 percent opposed her consecration. And in September 1989 the House of Bishops unanimously approved the legitimacy of priests' and bishops' authority regardless of gender.

Any such authority, Her Excellency insists, must be used with compassion. It is a proposition worth consideration by her critics.

Sandra Day O'Connor
First Woman Supreme Court Justice
(1930–)

In the summer of 1952 Stanford University granted law degrees to 102 students. Ranked No. 1 in the class was a William H. Rehnquist. No. 3 was Sandra Day O'Connor. But then he was 27, and she was only 22.

She was born in March 1930 in El Paso, not very far from her family's cattle ranch in southeastern Arizona, where a few years later she was herding cattle on horseback, driving trucks and tractors, and repairing this and that and other things as needed. At least that's how she happily spent her summer vacations. (Many years later she would tell Ronald Reagan that "the best place to be is on a good cutting horse working cattle.") During the school year she lived with a grandmother in El Paso and went to a private school for girls, since her parents justifiably felt that the local rural school couldn't do the future justice justice. She did go to a public high school, however, graduating in 1946.

The family traveled about a great deal, through much of Central America and all the western United States, including California, home of Stanford University. That would be the college for her, she decided. There she earned her B.A. in economics and then her LL.B. Her editorial work on the *Stanford Law Review* brought her into contact with a slightly younger fellow student named John Jay O'Connor, whom she married shortly after her graduation.

During the year before *his* graduation she applied for employment with several Los Angeles and San Francisco law firms, but her ranking third in a class of 102 wasn't a strong enough recommendation to overcome her gender. No women need apply. When one of the firms relented just enough to offer her a job as legal secretary, she took a job instead as a deputy county attorney. After John's graduation the couple moved to Frankfurt, West Germany, where they spent the next three years practicing law for the U.S. Army, touring Europe, and learning to ski (skillfully).

After their return and the birth of the first of their three sons in 1957— John having embarked on what would be a highly successfully legal career— she devoted herself chiefly to running their household in Phoenix, Arizona. But only chiefly. She had plenty of energy left over for service on public boards and committees, in the state hospital and the Salvation Army, in a school for minorities. In the time remaining she turned to politics, serving on a precinct committee and as district chair for the GOP from 1960 to 1965. Between 1965 and 1969 she held a full-time job as assistant attorney general for the state and filled her off-hours employing her talents for a state personnel board, a Native American museum, a historical society, and the Arizona State University Law School.

Given such noticeable activity, it was no great surprise when in 1969 the governor appointed her to fill a vacancy in the state senate. She would occupy the seat through two elections over the next five years, during which she earned a reputation for conscientious diligence and scrupulous, astute attention to detail. Her colleagues, impressed, elected her majority leader, making her the first woman to hold such a position in any state senate. Her voting record was rather typically "moderate," conservatively conservative: chary of government spending but willing to fund flood control and to rectify unfair taxation, supportive of penal reforms but also the death penalty. No feminist zealot, she nonetheless worked actively to reduce sex discrimination in employment and property rights, supported abortion rights though not public funding of abortion, and voted faithfully in favor of the Equal Rights Amendment. She also helped found the Arizona Women Lawyers Association and the National Association of Women Judges.

After five years of making law she switched to judging by it. In 1974 she was elected to the Maricopa County Superior Court, bringing to it her characteristic painstaking approach and soon winning respect for severe but fair dealing. As an ever more prominent Republican she took part in national politics but refused to run against the Democrats' Bruce Babbitt in his run for governor of Arizona. It was a consequential refusal. The next year, 1979, Governor Babbitt reciprocated by appointing her to the state's appellate court as "the finest talent available" with "astonishing intellectual ability and judgment." The Arizona Bar Association later released much less enthusiastic evaluations of her performance yet strongly recommended that she be continued on the bench.

Meanwhile Ronald Reagan, noted advocate of relinquishing governmental authority to the states, who in his campaign had promised to appoint a woman to the Supreme Court, had been elected President. In the summer of his first year, 1981, a law-review article by Sandra Day O'Connor argued for greater reliance on state courts even in adjudicating Constitutional questions.

At about the same time Associate Justice Potter Stewart announced his retirement from the Court, and on July 7 Reagan nominated her to replace him. He praised her "unique qualities" without referring to the party dogma that abortion is murder. Despite irate fulminations from the pro-life right, she was endorsed by the right wing's revered standard-bearer Barry Goldwater as well as by the liberals' liberal Ted Kennedy and the National Organization for Women. As for Senate confirmation, she was, of course, a shoo-in. In September she joined the eight male sages, including her former classmate and ardent supporter William Rehnquist, who had been appointed nine years earlier. She also was welcomed by the women on the staff, for whom she sponsored a nonsexist morning exercise regimen.

There could hardly be a better place than the Court for someone who had said that she loved the law "because it's always changing."

Alice Rivlin
Economist (1931–)

At first she had thought of a diplomatic career, but during a summer class at the University of Indiana she opted for economics because "it seemed less fuzzy than history or political science." There's no evidence or reliable testimony that she has ever regretted that statement.

She was born Alice Mitchell in March 1931 in Philadelphia but was brought up in Bloomington, Indiana, where her father taught nuclear physics at the university. After graduating magna cum laude from Bryn Mawr College, she did indeed earn an M.A. and then a Ph.D. from Radcliffe College in nothing less than economics. Between the master's and the doctorate she had married a Washington lawyer named Lewis A. Rivlin, whom she now joined in the Beltway milieu. (The marriage would last through twenty-two years and three children.)

She had already been accepted in 1957 as a research fellow at the Brookings Institution, citadel of liberal cogitation, education, and publication; excepting occasional interruptions for government service, it would be her professional home for at least the next 35 years. Gradually she progressed through its several levels of recognition, from staff member in 1958 through senior staff economist to Senior Fellow in 1969. Meanwhile, of course, she wrote and published most productively on such subject as educational finance, state and local taxation difficulties, unemployment amid prosperity, and population problems.

Her consulting service to the House Committee on Education and Labor and the Department of the Treasury brought her an invitation in 1966 to join

Lyndon Johnson's new Department of Health, Education and Welfare, at first as Deputy Assistant Secretary and then, in 1968, as Assistant Secretary for Planning and Evaluation. As coordinator of the department's economic analyses, she exerted a strong practical influence on its policies, and as manager of its publications output helped fashion its public image.

In 1969, after the change in administrations, she returned to Brookings as Senior Fellow. Over the next five years she wrote and published many provocative articles on a wide variety of subjects in economics, and a book in 1971 significantly entitled *Systematic Thinking for Social Action* and dedicated to promoting greater use of analysis in shaping government policies. In a similar vein she joined in yearly analyses of Nixon budgets, garnished with critical recommendations.

In July 1974 a Democratically controlled Congress, in an effort to wrest some control over government budgets from the Watergate Administration, passed the Congressional Budget and Impoundment Act, creating House and Senate Budget Committees and a formally nonpartisan Congressional Budget Office to do essentially what she had been doing at Brookings for the yearly analyses but to do it officially for members of Congress, giving them some ammunition for their confrontations with the executive's subservient Office of Management and Budget. Not unexpectedly, she was asked if she'd like to be the CBO's first director. Before answering, she consulted her friend John Gardner, head of Common Cause, and asked "if I'd be crazy to take it. He said, 'Crazy? I think you'd be insane!'" And so of course she took it.

Eventually, that is. Because of House-Senate squabbling over the functions of the CBO, it wasn't until November that Senator Edmund Muskie's view of her as a broad-horizons thinker prevailed and she was formally appointed. During the hearings she made a special and evidently successful effort to allay most Republican fears that she would prove an irrepressible liberal in the job. Yet seven months later, after she had staffed and organized the office, her first formal report, although scrupulously nonpartisan from her viewpoint, was depicted in the media as having a strong liberal thrust and thus decisively alienated the Ford Administration and its fellow Republicans in Congress. Nor was the situation helped any by a subsequent report in which, again according to the media coverage, she recommended putting one of the conservatives' sacred cows, the military, on a stricter fiscal diet. So it was hardly surprising that her request late that year for an increase in staff was summarily turned down.

With the passage of time and the advice of Representative Brook Adams, chair of the House Budget Committee, she hired a public relations adviser who helped to word her public announcements to make them less subject to media misinterpretation and thus less controversial. She also reduced the size of the reports and offered them to Congress in bite-size portions shaped to fit individual interest—a customer-sensitive approach that netted her much gratitude.

Before her four-year term was out she could accept with satisfaction the opinion of one of her harshest Congressional critics that she should be congratulated for establishing a "highly professional operation and a tough, lean agency." In 1979 she was rewarded with an increase in staff from 193 to 220 and a budget increase of $12 million.

With the advent of the Carter Administration her name was bandied about concerning candidacies for the top job at HEW, OMB, and the Council of Economic Advisers, but instead she took on the CBO for a second four-year term. Her nonpartisanship became more evident now as her reports begged to differ with Administration optimism and generated criticism in Congress, this time from Democrats. With the arrival of Reagan & Co. and supply-side economics her reports went back to alienating Republicans, so thoroughly that there was a campaign to oust her from office, a campaign with which she proved successfully uncooperative.

When her term ended in 1983, however, despite some optimistic CBO economic forecasts that delighted Republicans, she wasn't asked to stay longer, and she returned quite contentedly to Brookings as its Director of Economic Policy Studies. The appearance of the Clinton Administration on the Washington scene inspired rumors of an offer to head up the OMB, especially after *U.S. News and World Report* for November 30, 1992, showed a picture of President-elect Clinton absorbed in a copy of her latest book, *Reviving the American Dream* (which argues for returning more power and responsibilities to the states).

But it was not to be—immediately. After playing second fiddle to Leon Panetta for about a year and a half at the OMB, when he moved to the White House as Chief of Staff she did indeed become undisputed honcho of that prestigious office.

Barbara Walters
Television Interviewer of Celebrities
(1931–)

In 1984 the mutual admiration society of Barbara Walters and Hugh Downs came full circle when she joined his as cohost of ABC's *20/20*. Ten years earlier she had joined him as co-host of CBS's *Today* show, and ten years before *that* she had been made a regular on the show largely at his insistence. "His generosity," she remembered thirty years later, "was instrumental in my having a career. If Hugh hadn't fought for my opportunity to appear regularly on *Today*, I wouldn't have happened in this business."

This business wasn't what she had in mind in her early years. She was born in Boston in September 1931 to an owner of several nightclubs, although she would have preferred someone in a more conventional line of work, like a doctor or lawyer. Yet she found the show-biz environment stimulating enough to inspire visions of being an actress. The visions lasted through much of her time at Sarah Lawrence College in New York, where she picked up her lisp-embellished accent that she has identified as "Boston with a New York overlay." But after receiving her B.A. in English she switched to visions of being a teacher. These visions evaporated, however, when she was hired by NBC's New York TV station, as assistant to the publicity director, and then by CBS-TV as a writer and producer for public-affairs programs, and, after a brief hiatus, by NBC as a writer for the *Today* show. Although she was generally relegated to writing scripts and background material and to providing the "woman's angle," she found many assignments interesting, as when she accompanied Jackie Kennedy to India and Pakistan. Her reporting on that trip and on Jack Kennedy's assassination later earned her a measure of grudging respect from male pooh-bahs, as well as some occasional on-air time.

While she scribbled away in the background, the show's series of on-camera women, called the "*Today* girls" with inveterate male condescension, were limited largely to contributing decoration and vacuous happy talk. When the last of these, actress Maureen O'Sullivan, suddenly got fed up one day and abruptly quit, someone apparently recognized just how decorative that bright, diligent, shy writer back there was. That was when the redoubtable Downs, as the show's host, picked up the idea and carried it to fruition. The shy writer joined the regular on-camera set and soon was being sent out on interviews. She was even given a program of her own, *Not for Women Only*. The addition of "Not" was her idea.

She had found her niche, of course. Her talent for snagging and interviewing celebrities of all sorts would become a source of wonder for a generation of TV viewers. The names of her prizes began accumulating: Johnson, Nixon, Rusk, Eisenhower, Kennedy, King, Wyeth, Capote, Garland, Bergman, Astaire, Onassis, and Elizabeth, Charles, and Grace. Before long she had come out with a book of advice on ice-breaking ("What was your very first job, Mr. Onassis?") entitled *How to Talk with Practically Anybody about Practically Anything*.

She was no "*Today* girl," generating fluff. As Downs had predicted, she was a solid contributor, "the best thing that's happened to the show since I've been on it." Between interviews she contributed substantial pieces of reporting, on anti–Semitism in Michigan, for instance, and on the problem of loneliness in New York. She ran the gamut from visiting a convent to report on the life celibate to working as a Playboy bunny to report on a life less so. Her reporting and interviewing earned her such an enthusiastic following that ABC in 1976 enticed her away with an offer of a five-year contract with an unprecedented million-dollar yearly salary, which was widely publicized and widely criticized and widely envied, *and* with a spot as co-anchor on the evening news, heretofore strictly male territory on all three networks. ABC's management had considerable trouble with newsman Harry Reasoner concerning his "co-" status: he didn't like it one bit. His behavior toward her, on screen and off, made her life pretty miserable during their fortunately brief association. ("Hell" was her word for it.) They stuck it out for about a year of flat Nielsens while she continued interviewing in separate specials. Some years later, during a book interview with him she treated him respectfully, cordially in a notable class act.

She continued with her freelance kind of interviewing, often asking embarrassing questions that somehow didn't seem to embarrass. She questioned Richard Gere about his sex life, Don Johnson about his lost virginity, and Richard Pryor, rather aggressively, about abstaining from drugs. She asked Nixon if he worried about his image, asked the Carters about their sleeping arrangements, and got Laurence Olivier to confess that he didn't like himself all that much. She interviewed Streisand, Taylor, Castro, Qaddafi, Schwarzkopf, two Hepburns, and the Shah of Iran. For every celebrity an interview, or so it seemed. Her extraordinary success—after all, she was a trailblazer—earned her an extraordinary measure of independence. She was, as some of her more envious male competitors might have put it in a moment of candor, her own man. Baleful stares from the macho contingent might bother but wouldn't deter her. In her day, she once remarked on David Brinkley's *This Week* show, sexual discrimination "was taken for granted." She had to be sure that *she* wasn't taken for granted.

She wasn't. In 1980 she rejoined her good friend Downs on *20/20*, eventually as co-host, giving the show a welcome ratings boost. She had more time now for her beloved daughter Jackie, adopted during the second of her three marriages. She also had more money: in the mid 1980s she signed her third five-year contract for a reported two million a year, and in the early 1990s signed her fourth for perhaps double that. Not bad, except possibly by Oprah Winfrey standards.

Despite increasing competition over the years for interview opportunities—not only from assorted males like Morley Safer and Ed Bradley but also distaff rivals like Leslie Stahl, Jane Pauley, and Diane Sawyer—her quarter-century record remains unmatched. She still treats an interview, a *20/20* producer has remarked, as though it were "a play—she always goes for the emotional revelation."

In her book she describes a number of successful interviews and, at the end, one disaster. Warren Beatty wasn't in a very good mood that day. To all her eager questions he responded with curt and utterly uninformative monosyllables. Even when she asked about his latest movie, he answered with a yawn that the question was a difficult one. Finally, in her exasperation, she gave up. "Mr. Beatty," she said, "you're the most impossible interview I've ever had. Let's forget the whole thing and I'll do a commercial." She did, to stagehand applause.

The lesson for her readers: "You can't win 'em all."

Ruth Bader Ginsburg
Supreme Court Justice (1933–)

An ardent feminist, as a lawyer and especially as a judge, she has shown a remarkable evenhandedness, arguing and ruling for rights for men as well as women. As one of the judges on the U.S. Court of Appeals for the District of Columbia, she voted more often than not with the celebrated (or notorious) conservative Robert Bork, yet voted consistently for freer speech and more accessible justice for all.

She was born Ruth Joan Bader in March 1933 in Brooklyn. Her haberdasher father managed to provide for his bright wife and bright daughter in reasonable comfort despite the onslaught of the Great Depression, even to the extent of sending, or helping to send, the daughter to college. After Cornell University, in 1956 she entered Harvard Law School, where she was one of nine grudgingly accepted women in a class of 500 and where she remembers being taken aback when a dean asked her to explain how she could bring herself to take a spot that could be occupied by a man—and where she nonetheless earned top grades and contributed to the (that's *the*) *Law Review*.

Married in 1954 to tax attorney and, later, superlative cook Martin Ginsburg, she moved with him to New York in 1958, transferring to Columbia University and receiving her LL.B. in 1959.

Although she had graduated first in her class, that wasn't enough to overcome gender discrimination among New York's law firms. Refused a Supreme Court clerkship for the same reason by none other than Justice Felix Frankfurter, she at least found a job clerking for one of the Big Apple's district judges. After a couple of years of this and a couple more as a researcher and project director at Columbia, she was hired in 1963 by Rutgers University as an assistant professor of law. There (after concealing her against-the-rules pregnancy, her second, by wearing oversized and ill-fitting clothes) she would progress to the top of the academic totem pole in conventional fashion until 1972, when Columbia University offered her the exalted rank of Professor of Law. There she stayed (as Columbia's first tenured woman on the faculty) until 1980, when she was appointed by President Jimmy Carter to the D.C. Court of Appeals.

In the 1960s and 1970s she practiced law as well as taught it. Although she spent much or most of her time in court representing women in sex-discrimination cases, especially as counsel to the American Civil Liberties

Union, in 1973 she argued a case before the Supreme Court against a Federal law affording better housing and medical treatment to married males than to married females, and won. In another Supreme Court case she attacked Social Security preferential treatment of widows over widowers, and won again. (She argued six woman's rights cases before the Court, and won five.) In arguing cases like these she obviously was less interested in redressing wrongs of the past than in establishing legal equality for all. She could admire Thurgood Marshall's career, for instance, without emulating it.

Serving on the Court of Appeals with not only Bork but also the spectacularly conservative Antonin Scalia, to some extent she took on the role of consensus-builder, despite her shyness bridging the gap between left and right. In 1993, with Scalia now on the increasingly reactionary Supreme Court, President Bill Clinton, after a few newsworthy false starts, nominated her to fill the vacancy created by the retirement of Justice Byron White, and her nomination was confirmed in August by a vote of 96 to 3, one of the three being provided, not unexpectedly, by the Neanderthaloid Jesse Helms. For all their differences in judicial viewpoints, her good friend Scalia was delighted. One story has it that when he was asked whom he'd prefer to be stranded on a desert island with, Gov. Mario Cuomo or Harvard's law guru Laurence Tribe, he answered Ruth Bader Ginsburg.

Part of the reason for her middle-of-the-road position is that she can make distinctions. She fully agrees with the conclusion of the historic *Roe vs. Wade* decision on abortion, for instance, but not with its resting on a questionably constitutional right of privacy. From her viewpoint the decision would be on much firmer footing if it rested on the Constitution's assertion of equal protection under the law.

When she was practicing law in the early 1970s, a thirtieth of the country's lawyers were women; today every fourth lawyer is a woman. She has obviously been on the cusp of this change. A related change was Harvard's change of heart. In the 1950s its law school regularly granted a diploma to transfer students who had been there for two years—to male students but not to her. With her appointment to the Court of Appeals in 1980, it offered to send her the diploma. She declined it as just a bit too late.

Dianne Feinstein
Liberal Senator (1933–)

Her national career was born in a tragedy that brought her to national attention. In November 1978 George Moscone, mayor of San Francisco, was assassinated. Dianne Feinstein, as president of the city's Board of Supervisors, was chosen automatically to complete his term as mayor.

She was born Dianne Goldman in June 1933 in San Francisco to a Jewish father, a prominent professor and surgeon, and an alcohol-addicted Catholic mother in a child-abusive atmosphere that has left her religiously eclectic. Perhaps the most positive early influence on her career was that of a dyspeptically liberal uncle who regularly took the teenager with him to meetings of what he called the city's "Board of Stupidvisors" and urged her to "get an education and do a better job." After four years at a convent high school, in line with his advice she majored in history and political science at Stanford University and served as vice president of the student body.

After graduating in 1955, she entered into a three-year marriage during which she gave birth to her daughter Katherine and learned about woman's role the hard way. Before the baby's arrival in 1958 she worked on a scholarship for the state board charged with supervising minimum-wage regulations, but thereafter accepted the role of homebody until 1962, when the governor appointed her to a four-year hitch on the state's parole board. That year she came out of retirement also in another sense, marrying a busy, prosperous neurosurgeon twenty years her senior. Bertram Feinstein would prove less demanding in the home than his predecessor and more supportive outside it, and she would keep his name.

After serving on a couple of city crime commissions, she was elected to its Board of Supervisors and served on it between 1970 and 1979, including almost three two-year terms as its president, the third being interrupted by the assassination of Mayor Moscone and a fellow Board member, Harvey Milk. No longer a homebody, she employed a housekeeper to handle the homemaking details, leaving her free "to spend Class A time" with her husband and daughter. Ironically, it was many years later, when her daughter joined her in a political campaign, that they would become close friends.

The opportunity for such important family time was a reason, she would explain later, for her seeking city jobs rather than state or national office. Another was that the country's problems were predominantly city problems, and that's where they would have to be solved. And so, urged by the city's liberal constituency to run for mayor in 1971 (a supporter has maintained that she "identifies with the underprivileged in her gut"), she decided that staying in office might be worth the effort.

It might have been, but in a three-way race she ended up a disappointing third, with only 25 percent of the vote, perhaps largely because of her stand for restraints on development and her condemnation of prodigal pornography and sleazy strip joints, the latter earning her the unwelcome political moniker of "Mrs. Clean." She tried again in 1975 with about the same result when Moscone was elected mayor. After the assassinations of Moscone and Milk, the words chosen by the *San Francisco Chronicle* to describe her conduct that tragic day were *poised, eloquent, restrained, reassuring* and *strong*.

She clearly wasn't the choice of the city's celebrated gay community. For that very reason she made a point of appointing a homosexual man to succeed the gay Harvey Milk on the Board, although she chose a moderate gay activist rather than the more zealous lesbian preferred by the gays. It was, she felt, obviously a time for reconciliation and for moderation.

Bertram Feinstein had died in the spring of 1978, and two years later, after she recovered, she married a very affluent investment banker, Richard Blum, who proved even more supportive than husband No. 2, with sound political advice enriched with that mother's milk of politics, money. The inevitable charges of corruption could never be made to stick.

She would be the mayor for almost ten years, the elected mayor, until 1988. Her 58 department heads and staff people would find her charismatic, diligent, conscientious, and generally hard to work for—indeed, as the "ulcer-giver" she claimed to be. Her effort to reduce the city's crime rate, increasing the police force by 350 patrol officers, and supporting tough handgun controls, kept her police chief nervously on his toes. On one occasion when she complained that she had been hearing radio news reports about too many robberies and asked him what could be done, he urged her to turn off her radio. But when her anti-gun stance resulted in a 1983 machismo recall election, she won with more than 80 percent of the vote.

Although in 1969 she had promoted legislation banning discrimination against homosexuals, as mayor she alienated the city's gays by closing down its bathhouses. She also alienated many women and other workers by vetoing a comparable-worth bill designed to raise women's pay to a level comparable with men's. (Too complicated, she maintained, and too expensive, especially in view of the state's notorious Proposition 13, that curtailer of property taxes.) Yet she won two terms as mayor, her legal limit, her second ending in 1988.

As she looked forward to 1990, it seemed that California, after eight glacial years of a veto-addictive, tax-fearing Republican governor, might be ready for a live-wire Democrat eager for government to *do* something, and she might be that Democrat. She was telegenic in a television age, had for starters a great deal of personal financial resources in a state where it could cost a million dollars just to win an assembly seat, and probably could expect no substantial organized opposition amid the state's political chaos. The people wanted change, and she would be their candidate.

But first she would have to win in the Democratic primary against a state's attorney blessed with strong party ties. Those ties put her at a disadvantage, since her independent cast of mind militated against her being known as a team player. Her campaign also was hampered by her lack of broad experience, confined as it was essentially to the rather parochial office of mayor. This latter drawback was transformed into a boost by repeated TV showings of a "grabber ad" picturing her on the steps of the city hall after the assassinations and effectively taking charge: "Forged by Tragedy!" It continued: here she was rapping with black children, there she was discussing problems with cops, and everywhere she was illustrating the ad's theme: "Tough and Caring."

After two weeks of the ad on TV, a poll of the formerly neutral showed half of them now favoring her. It was, as one campaigner happily put it, a sea change. Women, especially those active in organizations, had been strong in support of her male opponent because of his record (and to some extent hers), but now they began to find the stimulating idea of California's first woman governor ever harder to resist. And she was already the favorite of the black community, as well as the clear winner in the charisma sweepstakes.

As the gap between them narrowed, her opponent's ads grew nasty—and so did hers. But only toward the end, and no doubt inconsequentially. In that end she came out comfortably ahead.

In the early stages of her campaign against her Republican opponent, San Diego's ex-mayor and California's Senator Pete Wilson, the *Washington Post* published a photo of each candidate in virtually identical poses with nearly identical expressions, commenting that they were the same age, height, and probably weight. With Wilson reputedly a liberal Republican and Feinstein a conservative Democrat (with him for abortion choice and her for the death penalty), there was indeed a Tweedledee-Tweedledum aspect to the campaign ideologically. But not financially: there it was Mercedes-Volkswagen. To put it simply, he started out with about seven times as much money and a larger, smoother-running organization full of focused money.

The Republicans spent four times as much as the Democrats on voter registration, making some 18 million contacts with potential Wilson voters, mailing out over seven million absentee ballots and associated literature. By election day, Democratic registration had fallen since January by 30,000 and Republican registration had risen by 50,000. Wilson won the day with a margin of 2.6 percent. Feinstein had won the women's vote, but only three-fifths of it, and she had been hurt by some well publicized gaffes, including her suggestion that some new taxes might be necessary. But at least she had discovered that she could raise money. The campaign had ultimately cost nearly $50 million, with her share about two-fifths of that. She may have relied too heavily on expensive TV advertising.

On the other hand, she looked good on TV. In the fall of 1992 she looked especially good to women who had watched the Senate committee's preposterously masculine treatment of Anita Hill in the Clarence Thomas hearings and had come to realize the importance of having women in Congress. And so they, and a sufficient number of sympathetic men, voted for her to fill Pete Wilson's Senate seat for the final two years of his unexpired term. Wilson meanwhile was struggling with the state's painfully intractable fiscal predicament and smarting from a drop to 36 percent in the popularity polls. It could well be that with rue his heart was laden.

Jocelyn Elders
Surgeon General (1933–)

Bill Clinton knew that he was nominating a woman with a strong tendency to speak her mind, indeed a veritable firecracker, and she didn't disappoint him. Although he disagreed, she argued publicly for at least a study of the likely effects of legalizing drugs, especially marijuana. She insisted on the need for more health clinics in schools, especially for pregnant teenagers. Asked if the clinics would provide condoms, she answered that she wouldn't have them "put on lunch trays, but yes." She drew a torrent of flak when she described the Roman Catholic Church as dominated by celibate males, although she was obviously if not laboriously laboring the obvious. She proposed raising taxes on alcohol and tobacco to help pay for the medical consequences. As for Bill Clinton, she has pointed out, she was his health director in Arkansas, and so he knew what he was getting when he nominated her to be Surgeon General—he "didn't pick me to be a rubber stamp for him." Clinton agrees but has said that he sometimes feels like Abraham Lincoln meeting Harriet Beecher Stowe for the first time and saying rather ruefully (as he did), "So this is the little lady who started this great war."

She was born Minnie Jocelyn Jones in August 1933 in Schaal, Arkansas, about a long morning's walk from Clinton's citadel of Hope. She and her seven younger siblings lived with their sharecropper parents in a cabin with three rooms and no conveniences and worked with them in the fields. Yet she and four of those siblings would eventually go to college. As for her, she won a scholarship and, while scrubbing floors in her leisure hours, attended Philander Smith College in Little Rock, where she saw a medical doctor for the first time in her life. Suddenly her life's ambition rose from laboratory technician (she'd seen one of those) to physician. And so she enrolled in the University of Arkansas Medical School.

After earning her bachelor's degree in three years, she joined the army as a first lieutenant. Then, after the army had trained her as a physical therapist, she returned to the Medical School under the G.I. Bill, graduating in 1960 as a physician specializing in pediatric endocrinology—and as the only woman in her class. Following an internship at the University of Minnesota, and her marriage to basketball coach Oliver Elders (which would produce two sons), she returned for her residency to the university's Medical Center in Little Rock, where she became a research fellow in pediatrics in 1964, receiving a master's in biochemistry from the Medical School in 1967. A few months after receiving the M.S. she was hired by the School as assistant professor of pediatrics and began ascending the academic ladder, attaining the rank of full professor in 1976 and, in 1978, being certified formally by the medical board as a pediatric endocrinologist.

Soon thereafter she met Bill Clinton. In 1979 her brother was murdered by a deranged man in a tragedy reported in the press, and the governor paid a visit to her parents' home to express his sympathy. Whether she impressed him at the time is not recorded, but his act of kindness certainly impressed *her*. Over the next few years something about her must have impressed him— perhaps her work on the state's commission for economic development—for in 1987 he appointed her the state's chief director of public health, heading up a department of some 1500 people, to whom she eventually would add another thousand. During the next five years, with her professional bent as a pediatrician, she instituted programs to vastly expand the screening of youngsters for childhood diseases and immunizing the vulnerable, to provide pregnant girls and women with more prenatal care, to offer mammograms to the poor, to improve home care for the aged and the chronically ill, and to improve testing and counseling facilities for HIV patients. It was during those years that she developed her public reputation for outspokenness, starting with that remark about condoms and lunch trays.

And so it was that in 1992 President Clinton asked her to come to Washington and "do for the whole country what you've done for Arkansas." She warned him that, given his experience with her, he ought to "know exactly what you're getting if you name me Surgeon General." He did, and he did. Her confirmation hearings involved some petty questions on personal ethics, readily answered, and an intriguing proposal from the graybeards of the American Medical Association, who, apparently assuming that no black woman could possibly be more highly trained than a practical nurse, recommended that only a qualified physician should be appointed Surgeon General. There was also, of course, considerable turmoil in what she has called "the religious non–Christian right" over her promotion, in Arkansas, of sex education and birth control, her preference for abortion over irresponsible procreation, and her being crowned "condom queen" by the Traditional Values Coalition. After some delay occasioned by Republican opposition, she was finally confirmed in September 1993, with the rank, incidentally, of Vice Admiral.

She has received her share of awards and honors, among other things being named as one of the Outstanding Women in Arkansas, Personalities of the South, and Distinguished Women of America, in addition to her several honorary degrees. In the White House, however, concern was growing over the effects of her impolitic suggestions that legalizing drugs is worth serious study and that antiabortionists should "get over their love affair with the fetus." And then, In December 1994, she was asked during a UN public meeting about promoting masturbation as a way to discourage riskier if more companionable sexual activity among children. Masturbation, she replied, is "a part of human sexuality and a part of something that perhaps should be taught."

The rest is history—political history.

Ann Richards
Texas Governor (1933–)

As for men, when you can't lick 'em, join 'em. Well, maybe not join 'em, but at least kid 'em along.

Ann Richards, nee Dorothy Ann Willis, was born in September 1933 in Lakeview, a rustic, lakeless little Texas town near Waco. Her father Cecil Willis was a truck driver, a man of spunk and principle whose membership on the local school board was notable chiefly for his spirited and successful defense of a teacher whose serviceman husband was overseas and who was threatened with dismissal on account of her pregnancy. Determination will get you just about anything, he told his daughter. Also, don't tolerate injustice.

The family was hardly affluent, but she was given lessons in piano and, more to the point, in elocution. When it came time for high school they moved to the relatively big city of Waco so that she could take advantage of its much better high school. And take advantage she did, excelling in her English and speech classes and being chosen to represent Texas at a student-government convention in Washington, D.C. She was simply Ann Willis now, having dropped her first name in deference to big-city ambiance. (Three names betokened country.) By graduation time she was considering offers of debating scholarships from a number of colleges. At her parents' urging she opted for Waco's Baylor University, majoring in speech and government. She joined a sorority but quit it within a year after discovering that the selection of pledges was too elitist for her democratic tastes.

In the summer of 1953, between her junior and senior years, she married David Richards, a high-school sweetheart. On their honeymoon he cut his feet on some coral, the cuts became infected, and "it was fourteen days after we got home before he could get out of bed. There were lots of remarks by my friends that I would take David off on a honeymoon and he couldn't get out of bed for two weeks."

After her graduation the following year she joined him at the University of Texas at Austin. While he worked toward his law degree she took education courses, earning a teacher's certificate, and, between 1955 and 1957, taught history and government in a local junior high school. Toughest job she ever had, she would recall some thirty years later. After a couple of years of it she quit to present her husband with the first of their four children. By this time he had received his law degree, so they decided to move to the greener legal pastures of Dallas. There one of her activities was to work for the NAACP, a pursuit not exactly traditional for a white woman in Texas.

She went further than that. In 1969 she moved to Austin with the children and her husband, who had taken a job with a law firm there. In 1972 she accepted an offer from Sarah Weddington, the pro-choice attorney in the celebrated *Roe v. Wade* Supreme Court abortion case, to manage her campaign for the state legislature. (No male politico could be found to take it on.) The campaign was successful, and she became Weddington's administrative assistant until 1975. It was in this administrative job that she first became steeped in Male Condescension as she has described it: "Me Tarzan, you Jane." It partly inspired her to promote the campaign of a woman, Wilhelmina Delco, who would become the first Afro-American in the Texas assembly.

In 1979 the Democrats needed someone to run for county commissioner and asked David Richards if he'd be interested. He wasn't. But Ann might be. They asked her. She hesitated, being worried about the effect on her duties as wife and mother, but with David's urging finally agreed to give it a shot. As a result she was elected the county's first woman county commissioner. Family duties gave way before the demands of the public executive. Her responsibility for maintaining the county's roads required her to supervise a number of adamantly macho road crews, generally irate at having to work for a woman. But when she was told that they had named their mangy old pet dog Ann Richards and she *laughed,* they had a change of heart. They soon come to recognize her as a conscientious, diligent, and fair overseer with a disarming sense of humor. They didn't give her any trouble.

She also was responsible for the operation of about forty social agencies, many of which she instituted—a center for raped and/or battered women, for instance, and a training program for parents of children with Down's syndrome. In 1979 she joined President Jimmy Carter's Advisory Committee on Women, engaging in an ultimately futile effort to get the Equal Rights Amendment into the Constitution. Two years later the state's Women's Political Caucus nominated her Woman of the Year.

The strain of all this activity, with its private-public conflicts, was too much. Her marriage began disintegrating, and she drifted into consolatory drinking, heavily enough to worry her friends and finally to justify treatment at a rehabilitation center in Minneapolis. That stopped the drinking, but in 1984 her marriage ended in a disheartening divorce. Yet the drinking hadn't kept her from running arduously for and winning the job of state treasurer, making her the first woman to hold a statewide office in fifty years. As treasurer she saved the state hundreds of millions by automating outmoded, labor-intensive procedures ridiculously vulnerable to human error. She also managed to hire more minority employees while, almost conversely in Texas, raising the department's morale. Her contribution during her two terms in the office did her reputation no harm at all, and in 1985 she was elected to the Texas Women's Hall of Fame.

Her reputation also won her the honor of seconding the nomination of Walter Mondale at the 1984 Democratic National Convention and, after the electoral debacle, an appointment to the steering committee of the Democratic Policy Commission. This in turn led to her first fifteen minutes or so of national celebrity when she made the keynote speech at the 1988 convention, the speech with memorable lines. "Twelve years ago," she announced, "Barbara Jordan, another Texas woman, made the keynote address to this convention. Two women in 160 years is about par for the course. But if you give us a chance, we can perform. After all, Ginger Rogers did everything that Fred Astaire did. She just did it backwards and in high heels." On a more political adversarial level, she ridiculed George Bush's belated discovery of issues like child care and education and his being "born with a silver foot in his mouth." (She later received a foot-shaped silver pin from Bush.)

In 1990 she ran for governor. First there was the three-way race in the Democratic primary, during which her male opponents tried to brand her as a dependable alcohol and drug abuser but an undependable officeholder. She won a plurality nevertheless, and in the runoff was elected candidate. Her Republican opponent was s filthy rich Texas rancher and businessman, a good ol' boy who managed to alienate many women and doubtless not a few men with his strenuous opposition to abortion choice and gun control, as well as with a celebrated comparison between unpleasant weather and rape: "If it's inevitable, just relax and enjoy it." Guffaws from the hee-haw constituency but not from voters generally.

Even a woman could win in Texas against uncouth idiocy, although narrowly, and that's what she did. As governor she introduced the bureaucracy to some unprecedented efficiencies, took on the insurance companies and the lobbyists, and reduced the hazards of waste disposal among other things. She accomplished this with the cooperation, of course, of a predominantly male legislature, whose goodwill she assiduously cultivated as groups of the ol' boys broke bread with her in an atmosphere of friendly badinage. Laughter, she maintains, is "the great equalizer."

Carla Hills
U.S. Trade Representative (1934–)

Carla Hills earned the sobriquet of "velvet crowbar" as a result of her amiably tenacious negotiating style during her four years as her country's trade representative. And indeed she did manage to pry an agreement from the adamantine Japanese to accept more American high-tech products through the formidable wall of their trade barriers, and to prod a reluctant European Community into tolerating U.S. farm products.

Carla Helen Anderson was born in Los Angeles in January 1934 into a prototypical family (father, mother, boy, girl) prosperous enough to have a home in Beverly Hills and a ranch in Burbank. Growing up, she was physically active, athletic, even tomboyish (earning an earlier sobriquet, "Butch"). She rode, sailed, played tennis and, in her private all-girls high school, indulged vigorously in volleyball and basketball. In her bookworm mode she studied hard and read a great deal. On the verge of her teens she became entranced by a biography of Alexander Hamilton and thereafter could hardly wait to become a lawyer.

After high-school graduation and a tour of Europe in 1951, she entered Stanford University, majoring in economics and history and winning prizes as captain of the school's tennis team. A fellow law student was Roderick Hills, whom she would marry and by whom she would have four children. (In today's milieu, a cautionary "thereafter" probably should be added here.) In 1955, after spending the preceding summer at Oxford University, she received her B.A., cum laude, and set her sights on Yale Law School.

Her father objected. He wanted her in the family's building-supplies business and was not disposed to contribute to her hankering after a life of litigation. Luckily, she had spent earlier summers working as a bookkeeper and bank teller and had enough money saved up to get her through her first year. Impressed with her resolve as well as her grades, he then agreed to underwrite the rest of her stay at Yale. In June 1958 she received her LL.B., in September married Roderick Hills, in 1959 was admitted to the California bar, and by the mid–1970s was a busy mother of four.

Practicing law and responsible motherhood created some obstacles in her life but nothing insurmountable. She resolved severe conflicts usually by explaining to the judge that she would have to be absent from court because of "a conflicting appointment," knowing from experience that she wouldn't have to explain further that the conflicting appointment was a school visit or a birthday party.

The law she practiced at first was in the public sector. Despite her credentials from Yale, she simply couldn't get a job in a private law firm—a result, she was convinced, of sex discrimination. And so she became an assistant U.S. Attorney in the Justice Department's civil division in L.A. In 1962, together with her husband and three other attorneys she founded a private law firm—ironically if inevitably receiving a lower salary than the men until she insisted on equality. Dealing chiefly with lawsuits in federal courts, she became the firm's strategist in antitrust litigation. She also did some teaching and served on a variety of legal committees and councils.

And so it went until 1973, when U.S. Attorney General Elliot Richardson offered to put her in charge of the department's entire civil rights division as an Assistant A.G. The offer was put on hold after he was summarily fired by the embattled Richard Nixon for adamantly refusing to fire Watergate investigator Archibald Cox. Although the department did revive the offer, it wasn't until April 1974 that she was sworn in. It would turn out to be a challenging job, this, supervising a motley crew of some 250 Washington lawyers and 94 U.S. attorneys throughout the land.

The challenge proved ephemeral: she barely got her feet wet. In March 1975 she became the third woman in U.S. history to be appointed by a President to his cabinet. In this case it was Gerald Ford, who invited her to head up the Department of Housing and Urban Development. With characteristic sagacity he conceded that she didn't know much about housing or urban development, but her questions about her duties "were bright and to the point." Despite her inexperience, she made a good witness before the Senate's Banking, Housing and Urban Affairs Committee, impressively enough for confirmation.

Six years later she had accumulated enough expertise and Republican "less-government know-how" to be appointed vice-chair of Ronald Reagan's Presidential Commission on Housing, as well as having her name bandied about as possibly the first woman on the Supreme Court. (Another possibility was named O'Connor.) Meanwhile, however, with Ford replaced by Carter, she had returned to private practice. establishing a D.C. office of the L.A. firm, representing a variety of American companies. For more theoretical distractions she chaired the Urban Institute, one of the capital's think-tanks, between 1983 and 1988. A key to her judicial and political thinking may have been revealed most poignantly in her September 1987 testimony before the Senate Judiciary Committee in support of Judge Robert Bork's nomination to the Supreme Court.

The next year George Bush, en route to the White House, named her to his cabinet as U.S. Trade Representative. Again, her appointment was criticized because of her lack of experience, and again she won confirmation with an impressive performance, this time before the Senate Finance Committee. She would work against trade barriers, she promised, "with a handshake wherever possible" but "with a crowbar where necessary"—hence the "velvet crowbar." Indeed, in her dealings with her Japanese and European counterparts she offered carrots but always kept her several sticks well within view, unhesitatingly threatening retaliation, imposing sanctions, at times vowing to pick up her marbles and git. She was generally quite effective earning a more flattering sobriquet from the European Community's mission chief in Washington, who described her negotiating as "a class act."

An ardent promoter of the North American Free Trade Agreement, she enjoyed a golden moment in October 1992 near the Alamo in San Antonio when, in the beaming presence of presidents Bush and Salinas and Prime Minister Mulroney, she and the Canadian and Mexican trade representatives signed the treaty documents which, if and when approved, would create the largest trade zone in the world, inhabited by 263 million people and boasting a gross domestic product of seven trillion dollars.

Ahead of treaty ratification lay considerable controversy over its effects on American workers and on the environment. In the news photo of the signing ceremony, however, her grin was dazzling.

Edith Cresson
First French Woman Prime Minister
(1934–)

The status of women in France can be readily surmised from the fact that they weren't granted their right to vote until after World War II. So it was quite a shock to Gallic manhood when President François Mitterand appointed a woman Prime Minister less than half a century later, in May 1991. The ensuing controversy took on an especially French color when the opposition charged that there just *had* to be something more than political in the relationship between the President and his new appointee—who could only shrug and explain ruefully that no French woman had ever been appointed to an office "without the explanation that she slept with so-and-so. Unfortunately, we're still at that stage."

Edith Campion Cresson was born in January 1934 in an affluent Paris suburb and an affluent family of Campions. Her tax-inspector father provided her, and her mother and younger brother, with a comfortable living in their suburban and vacation homes. She was supplied with a nanny, an English-woman from whom she learned another, less musical language, and was enrolled in a prestigious business college, where she earned a bachelor's degree in business and a doctorate in demography. Not long thereafter, in the early 1960s, she married a Peugeot auto executive and began working for conservative causes.

In the mid-sixties, however, she met Socialist Mitterand, veered left sharply enough to support him actively in his unsuccessful race for the Presidency against Charles de Gaulle, and thereafter served him as a trusted aide. Ten years later, as the new first secretary of the Socialist Party, he supported her formal acceptance into the Party and her appointment as head of its youth department. In October 1975 she ran for a National Assembly seat and, although defeated, conducted her campaign with a vigor and or virility that earned her a reputation as a tough political fighter. A couple of years later she won the mayoralty of a small town, and in 1979 a seat in the European Parliament, which appointed her to its Agricultural Commission.

Her experience in serving on this commission prepared her for another appointment, in 1981, as the newly elected Socialist President Mitterand's Minister of Agriculture, the first woman in that office. French farmers, already seething over depressed farm prices, rose up in male conservative umbrage at this insult to their traditional *virilité*. Tens of thousands of them erupted in demonstrations, brandishing signs protesting against "La Parisienne," and, when feasible, tossing some of their homegrown tomatoes at her. On one occasion their demonstrative masculinity became so ominous that she had to be rescued by helicopter. She was philosophical about the situation, conceding that appointing "a woman as minister, and a Socialist to boot, amounted to a provocation." Nonetheless, during her two years in the office she promoted agricultural exports while farmers' income rose by significant, and mutually gratifying, amounts.

In 1983, after winning the mayoralty of another, much larger town of atlas-map importance (Châtellerault), she was appointed Minister of what shortly became the Department of Industrial Redeployment and Foreign Trade. Promptly she invited controversy by enforcing the government's budget-actuated restrictions on travel abroad, insisting that the French ought to be proud to tour their own "magnificent country." More popular were her efforts to promote French business abroad, stressing French quality and organizing trade junkets throughout Europe and in America and the Far East. No doctrinaire socialist, she undertook the revival of the nation's steel industry, cut out a great deal of anti-business red tape, and urged tax reductions to promote capital investment She even encouraged many businesses to issue capital stock, in the form of what she called "certificates of investment." The alternative was to provide government funding with taxpayers' money, and she couldn't see any point to *that*.

Such capitalist behavior, however, gave her less trouble as a socialist than her gender. At a party congress in 1985 she and a few other women, demanding time at the speakers' platform to argue for equal treatment, were greeted with catcalls advising them to get back to their kitchens and their brooms. Her only advantage to being a woman in politics, she felt, was that men individually often were "much nicer to you" (although even then she usually felt that they were being condescending).

In 1986 she campaigned for a seat in the National Assembly, and this time she won, but in 1988 she rejoined the executive as Minister for European Affairs. She would resign angrily in October 1990 over French failures to meet foreign, especially Japanese, competition. She devoted the next six months to favoring private business with her flair for international networking.

Meanwhile Mitterand had decided that he could use her flair for business networking, especially in preparing for the dropping of trade barriers in

Europe expected in 1993. And so in May 1991 he asked her to become France's first woman Prime Minister, with the acidulous consequences described above. Unfortunately, her attempts to stimulate French industry into meeting foreign competition were so thwarted by its lack of initiative that in her frustration she became a Japan-basher, warning rather stridently that the Japanese "strategy of conquest" could do to the French auto industry what it had done to the similarly lackadaisical American industry.

During the summer of 1991, what with such fulminations and a satirically suggestive TV comedy series intimating a Mitterand-Cresson close relationship, her popularity in the polls fell from two-thirds approval to less than half within a single month. Mitterand, anxious over her effect on French-Japanese trade, as well as needing someone to take the fall for his country's disconcertingly high unemployment rate, in April 1992 asked for her resignation, opting for a less colorful male replacement.

Descriptions of her political career as resembling Margaret Thatcher's pleased her enormously.

Jane Goodall
Primatologist (1934–)

When one considers recent events in Bosnia and Somalia as well as Vietnam, Korea, and two world wars, Jane Goodall can hardly be blamed for preferring to spend virtually all of her adult life with chimpanzees in a remote area of Tanzania, especially since her work has contributed so much to our understanding, our often reluctant understanding, of human as well as humanoid behavior.

She was born in London in April 1934. Her father was an engineer and businessman, her mother a novelist. Maybe because her mother gave her a stuffed chimp doll in her second year, she later wrote in the *National Geographic* that she couldn't "remember a time when I did not want to go to Africa to study animals." That study attracted her irresistibly as a child: on one occasion she went to sleep with a collection of earth-worms under her pillow only to have her experiment interrupted by fastidious adults, and on another she spent five hours waiting for a hen to lay an egg, out of curiosity over the manner of emission.

After finishing high school she didn't bother with college but did get a job as a secretary at Oxford University because she felt that such secretarial experience would make her mobile, employable even in Africa. She also worked as a documentary film editor and as a waitress, principally to save enough money to take advantage of a former schoolmate's invitation to visit the family farm in Kenya. In 1957 she traveled to Africa, paid the visit, and then took off for Nairobi, where the paleontologist Louis S.B. Leakey and his wife Mary were conducting their famous searches for ever more prehistoric human remains. After working with her for a while and noting her fascination with animals, the maverick Leakeys decided that she could make a real contribution to the study of prehistoric humans by studying the behavior of some chimpanzees located near Lake Tanganyika in Tanzania. Would she be interested?

Would she ever!

First she returned to England for some intensive library research on chimpanzees. Then, since a woman wouldn't be allowed to live in the bush country alone, she and her stouthearted, generously cooperative mother sailed for Africa in July 1960 and set up their tent camp by the lake shore in what is now the Gombe National Park. She climbed a hill, "met a troop of barking baboons and knew then that my dream had come true." Chimpanzees, however, proved much more elusive than baboons. It wasn't until she found a clearing on a hill high above the lake and settled on it as a continual observation point that the animals favored her with more than a fleeting glimpse.

Her appearance there early every morning with binoculars and notebook, and her quiet, inoffensive presence invited the chimps to satisfy their curiosity and eventually to accept her as an unthreatening addition to their territory. About a year passed before a chimp finally approached her and, receiving a bit of fruit, gently held her hand for an exhilarating moment. More than ever before, she felt a sense of communion with another species.

Over the years she discovered that chimpanzees, heretofore considered quite bestial, are intelligent enough to devise and use simple tools (e.g., to fashion a twig into a smooth, thin stick and employ it for digging tasty termites out of their mounds, and to make a comfortable bed each evening out of sticks and leaves) and to communicate nonverbally, with sounds and gestures. Like their human cousins, they can demonstrate aggressive hostility but also affection. She observed them holding hands and hugging and kissing, and on one occasion even she was surprised to see a male gallantly kiss a female's hand. Their behavior can be so human at times, she has said, that "it seems like a caricature." Indeed, her observations and reports soon radically changed zoological opinion about the "higher" apes. The ability to fabricate and use tools, for example, could no longer be considered the defining human characteristic. Opinion retreated to the notion that maybe it was the ability to speak. In sentences.

Gradually she became almost one of the family. The animals' initial timidity was replaced for a while by efforts at intimidation (fierce staring, jumping about, brandishing sticks). When these displays proved fruitless (she ignored them, pretending to be absorbed in nibbling on the surrounding foliage), they gave up and let her follow them through the forest and watch them at their foraging, their relaxing, their continual cooperative grooming. After she got the idea of leaving bananas on the ground near her tent, they even began paying her visits, letting her get to know them as distinct individuals, as well as giving her first husband Hugo Van Lawick opportunities to take some celebrated pictures for the *National Geographic's* magazine and TV specials.

It was in the 1970s that she discovered just how human the chimps could be, to her considerable chagrin. For some reason the Gombe community of chimps (who could be quite fierce in killing prey for food) began dividing into two groups, northern and southern, and then became hostile, then violently so, and finally engaged in a four-year-long, all-out war that virtually eliminated the southern group. She had found, she wrote later, the "dark side of their nature," the disturbingly human side. Before the decade was out she even was told of an instance of infanticide, the killing of an infant chimp by an apparently jealous female.

Her research methods, at first bitterly criticized by her overwhelmingly male fellow primatologists as unorthodox, gradually gained acceptance and praise. In 1965 she was granted a doctorate by Cambridge University despite her lack of an undergraduate degree, a rare honor, though only one of many in more recent years. (In 1975, after her divorce, she married Derek Bryceson, the Tanzanian parliament's only white legislator.) Lately she has taken up the cause of protecting the chimpanzee, which she insists should be classified as "endangered" instead of merely "threatened."

"Dedicated" seems too tame a word for her. "I expect," she wrote in a foreword to her 1989 book, *Chimps*, "to continue observing the Gombe chimpanzees for the rest of my life and hope that the study will continue after I am gone."

Geraldine Ferraro
Vice Presidential Candidate (1935–)

There were some men in her life who helped her in her career. And there were others, and especially another woman, who didn't.

Geraldine Ferraro was born in August 1935 in Newburgh, on the Hudson River some seventy miles north of New York City, into a large and fairly prosperous Italian-American family. Large initially, that is, but by the time of her arrival only one of her siblings, her brother Carl, had survived. As the only daughter she was her parents' darling, especially her father's. He affectionately filled her first eight years with games and toys and movie matinees before he died. His death in 1943 was so traumatic for her that her health was affected, causing her to miss a year of school.

No longer affluent, her mother moved with her two children into an unpretentious flat in the Bronx and then in Queens. Working at home as a seamstress and mercilessly pinching pennies, she contrived to enroll her conspicuously intelligent daughter in a tony Catholic girls' school. There the daughter's record earned her a scholarship to Marymount College. In 1956, armed with her B.A., she took a job teaching in the Queens grade schools and spending most of her evenings in law-school classes at Fordham University. But not all her evenings: in 1960 she received not only her law degree but also a marriage proposal from John Zaccaro, a prospering real-estate developer.

They were married that year. She kept her maiden name for professional reasons (she would be admitted to the New York bar in 1961 and to the U.S. Supreme Court bar in 1978), but she was bound, quite willingly, to a prenuptial agreement that she would devote herself to the role of wife and mother during the early years of the marriage. Their three children kept her fully occupied over the next fourteen years but not so fully as to close the door completely on her vast storehouse of energy. She acted as her husband's attorney as her home duties permitted and predicaments required, and gradually her legal work drew her, again quite willingly, into local political activities. When her cousin Nicholas Ferraro needed her help in his campaign for a New York senate seat, she helped most energetically. His victory involved her further in other campaigns, earning her a reputation and associations that would prove useful later.

In the traditional political spirit of durable reciprocity, he helped her into a full-time job in 1974, after he had returned to Queens and been elected district attorney. As assistant D.A. in the Special Victims Bureau, and after 1976 as its chief, she handled rape and child-abuse cases The crimes were often ghastly and she suffered from sleepless nights, but she built a reputation as a trustworthy plea-bargainer and effective prosecutor. Also, in discovering the importance of destitution and social neglect as causes of crime, she found her political instincts switching irreversibly from conservative to liberal. In 1978, emotionally exhausted, tired of dealing with crime rather than its causes, and irritated at being paid less than her male counterparts, she quit. Perhaps politics would prove more meaningful and less bigoted.

In a congressional seat, perhaps. And so she ran for the U.S. Congress from a blue-collar Queens district in which a bleeding heart liberal was thought to have about as much chance as a prohibitionist. But with her cousin's political help and her family's financial help, and with her own ringing endorsements of law, order, and neighborhood improvement, she not only won the Democratic primary handily but even defeated her Republican opponent in a campaign notable for his contribution of oratorical mud. She would be the district's congresswoman for the next six years and would at least enjoy equal pay.

Her first committee assignments were hardly breathtaking, but she worked hard enough and proved liberal enough to attract the attention of

Speaker Tip O'Neill, who became mightily impressed with her industry and her spirit of Democratic cooperation. Her occasional departures from the liberal party line occurred on issues important to her blue-collar constituency, quite in line with its political philosophy. She was somewhat stronger, for example, in support of military spending and law-and-order measures than were most of her fellow liberals, but she could be counted on for support of social programs, including government funding for abortions. (She valued women's much-neglected rights and wasn't about to impose her Roman Catholicism on a pro-choice society, however explosive the hierarchy's denunciations.) She supported legislation designed to make up for the defeat of the Equal Rights Amendment and generally acted in concert with her feminist colleagues without being abrasive about it. Congress was overwhelmingly male, and she believed in being practical.

Tip O'Neill appreciated this respect of hers for the business of the House. She began getting some choice assignments, including one to the prestigious and highly educational Budget Committee. She also was appointed to a commission establishing the rules for choosing delegates to the 1984 party convention, and this led to her becoming the first woman to chair the Democratic platform committee. She used the position quite successfully to keep controversial specifics out of the platform and, incidentally, to brighten her own political luster. There were rumors, after all, that some party bigwigs thought it was time to nominate a woman as the party's vice-presidential candidate. Among these, apparently, was Walter Mondale, who, after his nomination, named her as his running mate.

The selection was not universally popular. She was praised for the sureness of her political instincts and denounced for the same reason. The choice was condemned as a triumph of ambition over experience and as a political ploy in place of sound statesmanship. During the campaign, questions arose about her husband's separate tax returns. She answered with a release of some of the returns and, unfortunately, an admission that she herself had just the other day sent the IRS a little over $53,000 in back taxes because of an accounting mistake. There were also uncomfortable questions about her family's substantial and allegedly illegal (and quickly repaid) contributions to her 1978 campaign for Congress. The revelation of the Zaccaro-Ferraro assets of nearly four million dollars shrouded her campaign in fat-cat ambiance. The press conference on her finances was an ordeal, but she handled it well enough to win plaudits from *Time* and some congratulatory roses from the acidly conservative George Will. He later told her that she had done "a superb job," but his card with the roses had been irresistibly condescending: "Has anyone told you you are cute when you're mad?" She had to promise him on the phone that, if elected, she would not be a cute Vice President.

In all likelihood the financial dustup made little or no difference, for Mondale already had begun digging his political grave with a promise, in his acceptance speech no less, to raise taxes. Against Ronald Reagan's genial promise of eternal no-tax prosperity, with no mention of debt, the Mondale promise was actually a threat. With the American voters embarked on a "no new taxes" economic binge, the Mondale-Ferraro ticket sank into a 49-state defeat and political oblivion.

Well, not quite oblivion. She had widespread name recognition now, which she used to support other candidates in New York and elsewhere as part of the political reciprocity game. By 1992 she felt that she could take on New York's incumbent Senator, Republican Alphonse D'Amato. Indeed, some polls were giving her a 47–39 edge. Yet it would be State Attorney Robert Abrams who would run against D'Amato, and lose. Another woman, New York City's Comptroller Elizabeth Holtzman, running against her and Abrams for the Democratic nomination in a notoriously vicious campaign, made it a mutually suicidal three-way race. As a result neither woman would be among the 54 women—the 10 percent—in the 103rd Congress.

But in Ferraro's career there were plenty of memorable moments to treasure—like reading a letter in the fall of 1984 from a mother celebrating not only her 20th wedding anniversary but something else as well: "My recent graduation from college is due to your inspiration."

Sylvia Earle
Marine Scientist (1935–)

She calls the sea "the deep frontier." As the person who made a perilous, record-breaking 1250-foot dive off Oahu in 1979, she has every right to do so. Her fascination with the sea, the underwater sea, may be more understandable to landlubbers after they've read her description of exploring the sea bottom a hundred feet under the surface in the pellucid waters of the Indian Ocean: looking straight up, she and her fellow divers could "see Venus and some of the stars. We could use the moon for orientation. It was like walking through the woods by starlight!" And by lantern light, provided by luminous fish in a plastic bag.

Sylvia Alice Earle was born in August 1935, in Gibbstown, New Jersey. Her father was an electrician and her mother was a former nurse who imparted her love of animals to her daughter and two sons. That included deep-sea animals, which she visited many years later in her first oceanic dive at the age of 18. Given such genes, it's hardly surprising that the daughter would make her first open-sea dive in her teens and would go on to spend some 6000 hours of her life under water.

As a child in New Jersey she grew quite fond of, and curious about, the residents of a pond in the family's backyard, filling jars "with fish and frogs and tadpoles" and describing their behavior in notebooks just for her own satisfaction. After the family moved to Florida in her early teens, she was thrilled to find the pond replaced by the Gulf of Mexico. She waited impatiently until she was seventeen to take a summer course in scuba diving. Her first dive was a "glorious" experience. She "practically had to be pried out of the water!"

She had already embarked on a formal-education agenda, which—although interrupted by the first of her three marriages and the birth of a daughter and son—led eventually to a botany doctorate from Duke University in 1966. Four years later she spent two weeks fifty feet under the sea off the Virgin Islands in an underwater "habitat" with four other marine scientists—all women, for these were somewhat prissier times. (This experiment was part of NASA's effort to predict the effects of long-term isolation in space, although the women spent many hours every day exploring their submarine environment.) After emerging from their watery sojourn, they were hailed by the press condescendingly as "aquababes" and subjected to personal Presidential congratulations and a ticker-tape parade in Chicago. Deep-sea programs, however, would never receive any respectable fraction of the government money allotted to space.

She made her most famous, and surely most hazardous, dive in September 1979, taking her 1250 feet down to the ocean floor off Oahu. To withstand the crushing water pressure of more than 600 pounds per square inch, she had to be encased in a monstrous diving suit that makes astronauts' spacewalking suits look like casual wear. There were no stars overhead on this trip, rather an enveloping darkness relieved in spots by a light from the accompanying submarine. She would see well enough, however, to see "an 18-inch-long shark with glowing green eyes swimming gracefully past only a few feet away," to watch a "lantern fish gliding by with lights on its sides, looking much like a miniature passenger liner," and to spend 150 fascinating minutes taking copious notes, collecting copious specimens, and planting a U.S. flag for the edification of passersby.

In 1982 she joined with Graham Hawkes, British designer of the monster diving suit (and her husband from 1986 to 1990), in starting up a business, Deep Ocean Engineering, to design and fabricate cheap (*relatively* cheap) and user-friendly submersibles for dives about a mile deep or less, which they hoped would treat even more people to the wonders of the ocean deep. Later they would design a more costly submersible able to carry the more intrepid about seven miles down. Another of their products is an undersea robot for use in exploring for oil and gas deposits.

With her photographer Al Giddings she published a book on the Oahu dive, *Exploring the Deep Frontier*, and made a documentary film on the lifestyle of humpback whales, shown on PBS as *Gentle Giants of the Pacific*. A board member for several environmental groups, in 1989 she participated prominently in studies of the effects of the notorious *Exxon Valdes* oil spill in Prince William Sound.

A year later she became the first woman to be appointed chief scientist of the National Oceanic and Atmospheric Administration, although she resigned less than 18 months later, in January 1992, reportedly because of some discomfort with George Bush's rather casual environmental policies. The resignation left her free to pursue a variety of academic projects in collaboration with natural history museums and marine laboratories, meanwhile gathering a number of prestigious awards and having a marine plant and a sea urchin named after her.

Her profession has made her very fond of fish, which she admits to eating occasionally—"but not anybody I know personally." Surely not *Diadema sylvie*, that sea urchin.

Barbara Jordan
Legislator and Orator (1936–1996)

Churchillian oratory was and is her speciality. Although she has never had as much opportunity to exhibit it as the old war dog, she put it to memorable use on at least three notable occasions, during the Watergate hearings and at a couple of Democratic National Conventions. On these occasions, despite the circumstance, she said something worth listening to. Eloquently.

Barbara Charline Jordan was born in February 1936, in Houston, Texas, into genteel poverty—never hungry, never homeless, but certainly never affluent or extravagantly comfortable. She was the darling of a solicitous grandfather of contagiously independent mind. Her father, despite his degree from the Tuskegee Institute, worked in a warehouse until 1949, when he became the pastor of a missionary Baptist church. In this role he was greatly helped by her mother, whose notable eloquence was a captivating feature of the church services. Her two older sisters, apparently more deeply captivated by the hymns, eventually became teachers of music. That left the eloquence to Barbara.

She did well in her public school classes, well enough to whet her ambition to be somehow extraordinary. She thought of taking up pharmacy but decided against it because "who ever heard of an outstanding pharmacist?" Then a speech on careers by a black woman lawyer gave her ambition more focus, especially since she was beginning to develop something of a golden tongue. In 1952, her high-school graduation year, she won first place in a national oratory contest despite her topic, "Is the Necessity for Higher Education More in Demand Today than a Decade Ago?"

Although depressed by the racial bigotry all around (or above) her, she was sufficiently encouraged by her family's confidence in her abilities to enroll at Texas Southern University (for blacks only, separate and unequal), to major in history and political science, and to head up the prize-winning debating team. Her B.A., magna cum laude, and her family's selfless generosity got her into Boston University Law School, where she met with discrimination not so much because she was black as because she was a *woman*. Women students (1 percent of the student population) were rarely asked for class input except on occasional "Ladies' Days."

After receiving her feverishly earned but genderless LL.B. in 1959 and passing the Massachusetts bar, she heard a call of duty and returned to Houston to practice law. She enjoyed the relative freedom that Boston offered but felt that she had "to be relevant." Her clientele wasn't the most lucrative in town: for some time she did business on the family dining-room table, before graduating to a downtown office. Until 1966 she did double duty for sustenance, working in the office of a county judge. But in 1960 she had time to help out mightily—oratorically—in getting out the black vote for John F. Kennedy. Suddenly politics seemed to offer a way to scratch the itch of ambition. She *had* heard of outstanding politicians.

And so in 1962 and 1964 she ran for a seat in the state's house of representatives, running well, although not well enough. But then that Yankee Supreme Court ordered redistricting to provide for equitable representation of blacks, et al., and in 1966 she ran from a redrawn district for the state senate. She won, becoming the first black member of that senate in 83 years. Much spinning could be heard in Texas cemeteries.

She was also the only woman among the 31 senators. She tried to make it clear that she was no African American female zealot bent on tossing about monkey wrenches but preferred rather to work for justice within the establishment. Working genially with her fellow committee members, she successfully promoted legislation setting up a state Fair Employment Practices Commission to curb racial discrimination in hiring, promoting, and firing; imposing an unprecedented minimum wage; improving workmen's compensation; and establishing a government department to focus on the problems of the state's ever more crowded cities. A color-sensitive bill designed to restrict voter registration also received her very close, and in this case very negative, attention; it was defeated.

By the end of her six years there she had earned a solid reputation as a highly effective legislator, elected by her appreciative colleagues in 1972 as the legislature's first black president pro teem. Meanwhile the 1970 census had resulted in some refashioning of U.S. Congressional districts. The Eighteenth, 85 percent minorities, offered an irresistible invitation in 1972, and by the following January she was ensconced in the U.S. House of Representatives (along with the other virtually unprecedented black Representative from the South, Andrew Young.) Fate and Lyndon Johnson's still considerable influence got her a seat on the Judiciary Committee.

She would be in the House for three terms, through 1978, supporting liberal legislation—for aid to education, busing, expanded Social Security, and protection of the environment; and against racial discrimination, Vietnam entanglement, and carte blanche for Presidential war powers. But 1974 would be her memorable year, the year in which the Judiciary Committee pondered the articles of impeachment brought against Richard Nixon. She was, asserted Bruce Morton of CBS, "the best mind on the committee." Certainly she had the best voice, its deep, resonant quality nicely suited to the measured cadence of her oratory. As a black, she asserted, she had been left out of the original U.S. Constitution, but subsequent amendments had changed all that. Now it was in some jeopardy, and she meant to defend it. "My faith in the Constitution is whole. It is complete. It is total. I am not going to sit here and be an idle spectator to the diminution, the subversion, the destruction of the Constitution.... Has the President committed offenses and planned and directed and acquiesced in a course of conduct which the Constitution will not tolerate? That is the question. We know that. We know the question. We should now forthwith proceed to answer the question."

Her eloquence brought her to the attention of party pooh-bahs, and in 1976 she was asked to give one of the two keynote speeches at the Democratic National Convention. After Senator John Glenn had virtually put the delegates to sleep, she reawakened them with a stirring call for a national consensus, a common dedication to social equality. It was a thoroughly partisan speech in a thoroughly partisan setting. Much cheering and applause.

After the election Jimmy Carter invited her to discuss a Cabinet appointment with him but proved unwilling to appoint her to the one post that interested her, that of Attorney General. She doubtless would have been a good AG, except that her health was deteriorating. In December 1977 she opted for a less public, less all-consuming role. Her third term would be her last. She returned to Texas and in 1979 took up a new career, teaching policy development and political values at the University of Texas at Austin. Despite her reputation as a hard taskmaster, her classes have never had enough room for all the students eager to join them.

She continued with ad hoc political activities, culminating in her seconding speech at the 1988 Democratic National Convention for soon-to-be Vice Presidential nominee Lloyd Bentsen, although by this time a neuromuscular affliction had her using a walker and a wheelchair. Soon thereafter she almost drowned in her swimming pool while exercising, but she recovered quickly enough to join in the game but futile Dukakis-Bentsen campaign. She was still durable enough to accept an appointment in 1991 as Texas Governor Ann Richards' special counsel on ethics. In the state, government ethics needed considerable refurbishing.

"I am," she told *Time*'s Bonnie Angelo at the time, "the ethics guru," interviewing prospective appointees on ethical matters, helping to "raise their sensitivity quotient." Asked about (for example) George Bush's chief of staff John Sununu, whose penchant for self-indulgent official travel had resulted in terminal leave, she offered some practical advice: "If you're going to be ethically insensitive, at least be insensitive in moderation." As for politics in general, she didn't hesitate to single out the central problem, the funding of political campaigns: "It's the money that has become an obscenity, has been so corrupting."

The following year she was well enough to accept an invitation to be one of three keynote speakers at the 1992 Democratic National Convention. Once again her oratory awakened the delegates, calling for a change and for a return to the American dream after twelve exhilarating years of neglect:

"We can change the direction of America's economic engine and become proud and competitive again. The American dream is not dead. True, it is gasping for breath, but it is not dead. However, there is no time to waste because the American dream is slipping away from too many. It is slipping away from too many black and brown mothers and their children, from the homeless of every color and sex, from the immigrants living in communities without water and sewer systems. The American dream is slipping away from workers whose jobs are no longer there because we are better at building war equipment than we are at building decent housing."

After all, she had a reputation to uphold. Seven years earlier she had been named by the International Platform Association as Best Living Orator and had been inducted into its Orators Hall of Fame. And two years earlier she had been received into the National Women's Hall of Fame. A golden tongue can be a powerful open sesame.

She died January 17, 1996, in Austin, Texas.

Barbara Mikulski
Politician (1936–)

The U.S. Congress's first woman to serve in the House *and* the Senate, she may also be the most energetically aggressive member on Capitol Hill. "Nobody would ever use the term 'mellow' to describe me," she once remarked to a reporter. "I'm not caffeine-free, that's for sure."

Barbara Ann Mikulski was born in July 1936 in Baltimore to parents whose grocery store provided enough wherewithal to give their three daughters a parochial grammar and high school education. In 1958 she received her B.A. from Mount St. Agnes College, and during the next seven years, while working for Catholic Charities and then the Baltimore Social Services Department, earned her master's degree in social work from the University of Maryland. She had thought at times of becoming a nun but wisely concluded that the disciplined life was not for her, thereby doubtless sparing some convent considerable turmoil.

As a granddaughter of Polish immigrants, she developed great sympathy for "ethnic America," for the working-class families she dealt with in her social-service jobs, people who were building their new country into a powerful nation yet who, as she put it in a *New York Times* article in 1970, "were discriminated against by banks, institutions of higher learning and other organizations controlled by the Yankee Patricians." They were her special concern (especially the very young and very old) during her tenure on the Baltimore City Council between 1971 and 1976, when she became known as "Queen of the Ethnics."

It was during that tenure on the council that she became involved in national politics. Appointed as cochair of the Democratic Party's Commission on Delegate Selection and Party Structure, she engineered changes in rules and procedures that promoted party unity, resulting in a much more harmonious convention in 1976 and, probably, the election of a Democratic President, Jimmy Carter.

In 1974 her vigorous campaigning for the U.S. Senate against an entrenched, respected, liberal Republican, Charles Mathias, was pitifully underfunded. Her herculean effort, including 10,000 miles of electioneering as a camper, nonetheless earned her the admiration of party bigwigs, who began thinking of her as worthy of considerable support.

Early in 1976 Democrat Paul Sarbanes, who represented Baltimore in the House of Representatives, announced his intention of running for the Senate, and she seized the opportunity to take his place in the House. Her work on the Council and in the Senate campaign had brought her more than enough political support, and early 1977 saw her ensconced in the House (and Sarbanes in the Senate). There, as a neophyte with political savvy, she supported the powerful if less liberal Jim Wright of Texas for majority leader and became the first distaff member of the important Energy & Commerce Committee as well as a member of the Merchant Marine & Fisheries Committee so important to Baltimore as a port city. During her eight years in the House she voted Democratic 88 percent of the time, earning high marks from labor and liberal organizations. She promoted legislation against child abuse and for insurance reform, worked strenuously for the ill-fated Equal Rights Amendment, and helped to organize the Congressional Women's Caucus. With the arrival of Reagan & Co., needless to say, she became stridently adversarial.

Early in 1986 she heard opportunity knocking again when Senator Mathias finally announced his retirement. This time her Republican opponent was another woman, and a formidable one: silken, well-spoken, intelligent Linda Chavez, whose fashionable attire and slender appearance introduced a note of silk purse vs. sow's ear into the campaign. To meet the silky competition,

Barbara got herself a professional pollster to encourage inhibition. She also hired a professional makeup consultant, changed her spectacles from horn-rimmed to rimless, lost a few dozen pounds, radically improved her wardrobe, and learned to cultivate that electable look on TV. For her efforts she was elected, and on her arrival in the Senate was genially assigned, at least for the time being, to the seat occupied by her long admired Harry Truman. More important, her appointment to the Senate Appropriations Committee, dispenser of the people's money, was a prize assignment for a newcomer.

Since then she has served on several major committees (labor, environment, public works, small business) and a dozen subcommittees, industriously looking after Maryland's interests and those of the underdog. At the Democratic National Convention in the summer of '92 she was asked to deliver a passionately political speech and did so with characteristic vigor. That November she was elected to another six-year term.

Elizabeth Dole
Cabinet Member (1936–)

During her six years as a member of the Federal Trade Commission she proved herself, according to its chairman, "a pillar of competence"—high praise, in a man's world. Further, the American consumer owed her "a deep debt of gratitude for a job well done."

She was born Elizabeth Hanford in July 1936 in "the wonderful little Southern town" of Salisbury, North Carolina. She and her much older, much beloved brother John enjoyed a pleasant childhood, especially since she was enchanted by school and its opportunities for organizing social activities like her Girl Scout troop and a book club. Her adolescence was pretty conventional; on hayrides, for instance, some of the girls' mothers would follow in a car immediately behind the wagon, headlights ablaze. Her enchantment with school continued at Duke University (its "Women's College"), where she was president of the student body ("excellent practice for the real world"), May Queen, and "Leader of the Year." She also earned her political science degree with honors and a Phi Beta Kappa key.

After Duke came Harvard, the hard way: a job as secretary to the librarian at the Law School—a foot in the door, she has said. She spent the summer of '59 doing postgraduate work at Oxford University, touring England as time permitted, and even briefly visiting Moscow and Leningrad, where she had a taste of police-state living, conversing with a friend in a room with the radio turned up to neutralize any listening device. She then returned to Harvard for an M.A. in education (a female's insurance policy against unemployment) and finally, in the spring of '62, to the Law School. Although she was one of only a couple of dozen hardy women in her class of 550, she eventually was elected president of the international law club—she whom a male classmate had harassed because the women were taking the place of men students "who could *use* their education!" She has never identified the cad but has never forgotten him either.

In 1965, armed with her J.D. and eager to test the Washington waters, she applied for a White House fellowship but was nosed out in the final selection. Undaunted, she took off on a drive across the country and a Far Eastern tour. On her return she gained admittance to the D.C. bar and found a job suited, surprisingly, to the particular mix of educational qualifications in her resume. As staff assistant to the assistant secretary for education in the Department of Health, Education and Welfare, she was responsible for education of the handicapped. Leaving the job in 1967, she practiced law for about a year, particularly in defense of impoverished clients like the man charged with annoying animals at the zoo (by petting them). She won that case, her first, by pointing out that in the absence of reliable animal testimony, the charge of annoyance could hardly be proved beyond a reasonable doubt. Still on the lookout for government service, in 1968 she joined the Committee on Consumer Interests as associate director of legislative affairs, advocating laws against commercial sharp practices at first for the Johnson, then for the Nixon, administrations. In 1971 she was appointed deputy director of the new White House Office of Consumer Affairs, moving from advocating to administering the laws and often causing acute discomfort in the chicanery department of commercial enterprise. Under the Southern velvet there lurked some unexpected steel. (The steel wasn't tough enough to get her into one meeting, to which she'd been invited and for which she had assiduously prepared, because it was held at the Metropolitan Club. No Women Allowed.)

Among her responsibilities was the promotion of a consumer-interest plank in the GOP's 1972 platform. (She was no longer a registered Democrat.) This meant appealing to the chairman of the Republican National Committee, Bob Dole of Kansas, in his Senate office and at the convention. He found her extraordinarily persuasive. She found him "awfully attractive" and, of all things, "bashful."

Her burgeoning reputation in consumer protection persuaded Nixon to appoint her in 1973 to one of the five seats on the Federal Trade Commission, an ostensibly nonpartisan agency dedicated to commerce without chicanery. Her job, she maintained, was to try to give the consumer an even break: the pressures exerted on government by business surpassed, she insisted, "by a long shot, anything I have ever seen on the consumer side." Her opinions in that role were, said one builder, "about as welcome as a belch in a choir loft," but her performance earned her a place in *Time*'s 1974 list of 200 "young leaders of America."

In December 1975 she married the very Republican Senator Dole and soon thereafter took a leave of absence to join her new husband's campaign on the Republican ticket with Gerald Ford against Jimmy Carter. Although White House lawyers had assured her that no conflict of interest was involved, in 1979 she resigned from the FTC to join her tirelessly ambitious husband's abortive campaign for the Party's presidential nomination and then, after his withdrawal, to chair the Voters for Reagan-Bush Committee and to promote absolute truth as a member of the GOP "truth squad" charged with countering Democratic inaccuracies and accuracies. During the transition she headed the team's "human studies" unit, and in December 1980 Reagan appointed her "assistant to the President for public liaison." As such she would "provide a means for developing a consensus for administration policies and programs," such as they might be. (The administration mantra, of course, would be The Less Government the Better.) Over the next six months, for example, in more than 300 speeches and meetings she spread The Message with the vigorous enthusiasm of the convert.

The 1982 Congressional elections revealed a disturbing lack of such enthusiasm among women voters generally. Although the phrase "Republican woman" seemed increasingly oxymoronic, and although she was no great favorite of feminist organizations, the Reagan staff felt nonetheless that admitting her to the male inner sanctum (at least ostensibly) might counteract some of the feminine disenchantment. And so in January 1983 she became Reagan's nominee for Secretary of Transportation. In this job she wouldn't have to be quite so vigorously enthusiastic about The Message in contrast to Senator Bob, who, with at least one eye focused on the 1984 Presidential race, was proving much less so. ("Now that Elizabeth has given you the administration line," the Senator would counter, "let me tell you what's really happening.") Her appointment was praised generally in the press—she was skillful, accomplished, competent—and was confirmed by a 97–0 vote in the Senate. "I regret," asserted her quotable husband, "that I have but one wife to give to my country's infrastructure."

It was a pretty responsible job. The department's current budget was $27 billion. Her background in consumer protection served her well. She became the secretary for passenger safety, especially in autos. To her efforts we owe the emphasis on automatic seat belts, air bags, and mandatory brake lights in rear windows, as well as random drug testing of crucial personnel in truck and airline operations. And to her efforts the department's female employees owe a 20 percent increase in women employees, a doubling of women in management jobs, a women's exercise room and a child day-care center. Yet she did this gently enough, it seems, that even among the men, according to a 1983 issue of *Life*, she made "astonishingly few enemies."

In August 1988, to her considerable chagrin, she felt she had to resign to concentrate on the Republican primary battle between Bob Dole and George

Bush. The couple's mutual effort, although downright heroic, wasn't enough to counter the Bush campaign tactics. "I wish," said the senator to a TV reporter in a futile complaint, "that he'd stop lying about my record." After the Bush victory many advisers recommended Elizabeth as an experienced, popular, charismatic running mate, but who could resist Dan Quayle?

She campaigned actively for the ticket, of course, and in December President-elect Bush asked whether she'd like to become Secretary of Labor. When she replied that first she'd like to know more about the department, his office worked a fax machine almost to the breaking point with reams of background material. She accepted. After all, it was another cabinet job, and it wasn't as if she didn't know the ropes.

In that job she had to go along with the Administration's reluctance to raise the minimum wage, but she did what she could to improve job training and to inveigh against the notorious glass ceiling against which competent, ambitious businesswomen continually bump their heads. The job entailed a measure of frustration. Almost by definition the department was, after all, something of an anomaly in a Republican administration.

Meanwhile the American Red Cross search committee, after interviewing some 200 candidates for the organization's recently vacated presidency, repeated an earlier offer: would she take the job? Here was an opportunity to help people in urgent, conspicuous need, as well as to continue in a challenging executive role. The offer seemed irresistible after some contemplation. In October 1990 she resigned as Secretary of Labor. The Administration, commented the *Boston Globe*, had "lost one of its classiest members."

In February 1991 she became the ARC president. During that first year she would forego her pay of about $200,000 a year to stress the importance of volunteers—her fellow volunteers during that year—to the organization's work. Senator Bob didn't think much of *that* idea, but news of it helped her in her role of recruiter and money raiser. And her talent and experience in networking soon helped in ensuring the safety of blood donations in spite of the AIDS crisis and in improving the organization's response in emergencies. The latter proved to have been worth the effort when, in the summer of 1993, the great flood, perhaps the greatest in its history, would devastate the Missouri-Mississippi river basin.

The loss of that year's salary didn't doom the Doles to hardscrabble penury, of course. As they approach their golden years they can look forward to a retirement rendered comfortable, according to the National Taxpayers Union, by some four million simoleons.

This, and her departure from politics, should make their happy marriage more serene, less susceptible to outbreaks of any ideological disharmony. Not that such discord was ever a serious problem against the background of their mutual, and mutually appreciated, senses of humor. If he could say that she would help him make the bed only when a news camcorder was present and that her pie-crust recipe belonged with the Federal Highway Commission, she could, and did, claim that she was an authority on air bags because she'd been riding around with one for years.

Score one for the distaff side.

Hazel O'Leary
Head of the Department of Energy
(1937–)

There are the two worlds of government bureaucracy and private business, and rarely the twain shall meet, especially on the question of government regulation of industry. But they did meet in Hazel O'Leary, who, before heading up Bill Clinton's Department of Energy, had been both regulator and regulatee: "In the public sector, I've regulated industry broadly. In the private sector, I've been forced to live with those regulations, and, perhaps more importantly, I've seen how those regulations, if not carefully crafted and balanced, can impact jobs and lives and economies of people who expected and hoped for better from their government." As someone (David Garrick?) has said, a kindred feeling makes us wondrous kind.

She was born Hazel Reid in May 1937 in Newport News, Virginia. Her parents, a doctor and a teacher, were educated, cultivated blacks who had all they could do to shield their two girls from Southern racism, enrolling them for instance at a grammar school for black children in a precautionary concession to that racism. Their father cautiously drove them about town as necessary, and when it came time for summer camp he chose one in Massachusetts, where skin color was less provocative. After graduation Hazel took up the study of music at a school for gifted children in Newark, New Jersey, where she had been sent to live with an aunt under less primitive conditions.

In 1955 she was old enough to return to the South on her own initiative, and in 1959 she graduated from Fisk University, cum laude and Phi Beta Kappa, with a B.A. in history. Determined to became a lawyer, or at least to know the law, she refused to be sidetracked by a rather brief marriage and the birth of a son and, although she was delayed somewhat, received her J.D. degree from Rutgers in 1966. After working a while as a county and state prosecutor in New Jersey, she moved to Washington and was taken on as a partner by a large accounting firm.

Her experience there working with public utilities and other energy producers prepared her for her appointment by Gerald Ford as Director of the Office of Consumer Affairs in the Federal Energy Administration and, in 1977, her appointment by Jimmy Carter to Deputy Director and then Director of the Economic Regulatory Administration in the new Department of Energy. In this job she had to cope with the unnerving effects of the startling rise in prices of Arabian oil, which kept the organization's staff of 2000 professionals busy with the effort to impose price controls on the country's oil and gas companies and electric utilities. It was a kind of regulatory baptism by fire. One of her fellow battlers was Deputy Secretary of Energy John F. O'Leary, whom she married in 1980 and by whom she would have a son before his death seven years later.

With the arrival of Reagan & Co. the couple went into private business, founding O'Leary and Associates to advise firms in the energy business and to lobby state and Federal bureaucracies in their interest. As the partnership's vice president and general counsel, she spent much of her time restoring the standing of the General Public Utilities Company after the widely publicized catastrophe at its Three Mile Island nuclear power installation.

Dissolving the firm after her husband's death, and following a period of mourning, in 1989 she joined the Northern States Power Company, a giant Midwest producer of gas and electric energy and operator of three nuclear power plants, with headquarters in Minneapolis. As executive vice president for corporate affairs she promoted practical conservation measures, for example introducing a method of predicting future markets more accurately and thereby saving the company and the environment a great deal of superfluous energy production. She also promoted more efficient use of energy among the firm's customers. More controversially, she supported its storage of exhausted nuclear rods on a Mississippi River island against the protests of environmentalists and a resident tribe of Native Americans. (She also took up golf "to be part of the prevailing corporate culture.")

Her performance during this controversy earned her a promotion to the presidency of the firm's recently formed natural gas division, but before she could occupy her new office she took a phone call from President-elect Clinton asking her to take over the Department of Energy. Her selection was generally applauded by managers of the country's energy industry. Environmentalists were less enthusiastic but were willing to wait and see. She faced, after all, the staggering problem of cleaning up the leavings of the nation's nuclear weapons network. This in addition to the daily management of a department with a $20-billion budget, installations at 95 locations, and 20,000 employees supervising contracts with firms employing some 150,000 people. One of her first moves, in April 1993, was to reorganize the department for greater efficiency and for great emphasis on nonnuclear sources of energy. She also made its decisions subject to review by the Occupational Safety and Health Administration, an unprecedented concession to a rival bureaucracy.

An advocate of governmental openness, she has established procedures for better communication with citizens affected by the department's actions. This preference for openness showed up quite clearly toward the end of her first year in office. For years various Defense Department agencies had been subjecting people to various kinds of testing, including radiation. In the mid-1980s Congress had published a revealing study, *American Nuclear Guinea Pigs*, to which the DOE at the time gave scant attention. The Energy Secretary of 1993, however, appalled by the records, promised to get them declassified and made public and to thoroughly investigate the situation. The government, nervous over an outbreak of litigation, proved less committed but nonetheless susceptible to public pressure created by the publicity. The guinea pigs, she insisted, should be compensated.

As an energy-conscious conservationist in a public office, she has been handed a large plateful of major problems. But meanwhile, as a private motorist, at least she drives a car that can run on natural gas.

Eleanor Holmes Norton
Civil Rights Attorney (1937–)

When some Ku Klux Klansmen were prosecuted for some maliciously unlawful buffoonery, she defended them in court. When Alabama's racist governor and Presidential candidate George Wallace was refused permission by New York City in 1968 to put on a rally at Shea Stadium, she volunteered to represent him in a lawsuit against the city (and won it, although he backed down on appeal). Remarkable behavior, this, from a liberal black woman. But not so remarkable for an attorney, a professional fully aware of the importance of civil rights, even for uncivil rightists.

She was born Eleanor Holmes in June 1937 in Washington, D.C., the first of the three daughters of her civil-servant father and schoolteacher mother, and grew up amid child-puzzling segregation. Her college-educated parents having stressed the importance of good schooling and personal responsibility, she kept her nose to the educational grindstone through high school, Antioch College, and Yale University, earning a J.D. from Yale in 1964. The next year, while working as a clerk for a Federal judge in Philadelphia, she met and married fellow lawyer Edward Norton, who thoroughly approved of her having her own career. That winter, after their move to New York City, she was hired by the American Civil Liberties Union as assistant legal director.

It was in this job that she represented the Ku Kluxers and George Wallace as well as accused felons, antiwar demonstrators, antisexism protesters, even Julian Bond when Georgia tried to refuse the young black politician his legitimate seat in its legislature. As for representing the Ku Kluxers and Wallace, she responded to criticism by laboring what should have been the obvious, that freedom of speech is a freedom for all and that the right to legal counsel shouldn't depend on the nature of the accusation. Indeed, in that fall of '68 she also represented the racist National States Rights Party before the Supreme Court in another rally-refusal case. Such leisure time as she had was devoted largely to teaching courses in black history at the Pratt Institute in Brooklyn.

In 1970, newly appointed by the mayor as chair of New York's potent Human Right Commission, she promised to devote herself to the proposition that neither any man nor any woman should be "judged by the irrational criteria of race, religion, or national origin." Women were especially vulnerable, she noted, to the subtleties of contemporary discrimination ("Do you expect a pregnancy?"), even more than blacks, who are so used to discrimination of every kind. She offered the Commission, for instance, as a court of first appeal for women's complaints, inducing various companies to improve their maternity benefits, and various restaurants and cabarets to observe equality of service. With the help of women's organizations she initiated changes in laws permitting discrimination in real-estate transactions and against women workers in their pay and benefits and in the neglect of day-care facilities. She also initiated modifications in laws restricting access to abortion.

In 1973 she joined in founding the National Black Feminist Organization to promote more opportunities not only *for* but also *in* employment. At about that time she took on the city's Board of Education, citing statistics showing that, although minorities constituted more than half of the student body, they made up less than a tenth of the teaching staff and less than a twentieth of the principals. She also was appointed to a committee investigating welfare abuses and agreed with its conclusion that long-term welfare mothers, mostly black, should be taken off the rolls if they refused to accept work after their benefits ran out.

During the Carter Administration, as chair of the Equal Employment Opportunity Commission, she enhanced her reputation for articulate disputation. In 1988 that reputation brought her an invitation from Jesse Jackson to preside over panel discussions in an effort to move his campaign closer to conventional Democratic principles and viewpoints, a challenging assignment indeed. The next year she collaborated with about a hundred other authorities in a study of blacks' disadvantages in American society, disadvantages that had been greatly if inadequately ameliorated, she herself had already concluded, by the introduction of affirmative action.

By now she was a tenured professor in the Georgetown University Law Center as well as a member of the board of directors for several companies and charitable institutions. She surrendered all such positions, however, with her election in 1990 as the District of Columbia's representative in Congress. Reelected in 1992, she is a nonvoting delegate, yet she at least has had some opportunity to have her eloquent say.

That eloquent say, among other things, has earned her, among other things, some fifty honorary degrees.

Lynn Margulis
Molecular Biologist (1938–)

Two billion years ago one variety of the primeval ooze was an assortment of vast mats of microbes spread over the earth's surface. She wasn't there, except perhaps inchoately, but she has spent much of her current life amassing evidence that cells having nuclei (like human cells) have their origin in symbiotic arrangements among the bacteria of that time living in the sea or in that primeval ooze. When she first tentatively suggested this idea professionally in the 1960s, it was summarily dismissed by the scientific establishment. By the 1990s, however, it had become a perfectly respectable and widely tolerated, even widely accepted, theory of the evolution of the cell.

She was born Lynn Alexander in March 1938 in Chicago to a successful attorney and his travel-agent wife. From his three marriages she garnered a collection of seven siblings, and doubtless as a result she had to start earning her own pin money at part-time jobs early on. This "up-&-at 'em" spirit was accompanied by a love of reading and writing, including the writing of plays, which she also directed and in which her sisters served as compliant directees. When this activity palled in her middle teens she enrolled at the University of Chicago, where she became interested in the natural sciences and in a bright young fellow named Carl Sagan, the future star astronomer, who eagerly encouraged her interest in science and whom she married in June 1957 after her graduation with a liberal arts degree.

The newlyweds moved to Madison, Wisconsin, where she earned a master's in genetics and zoology in 1960. The next move was to Berkeley, California, where she worked for her doctorate, although by the time she received it in 1965 she had already been divorced and had moved with her two sons to Massachusetts, where she joined the faculty of Brandeis University. In 1966 she moved again, to Boston, where she stayed and taught at Boston University for the next 22 years, rising from the lowly rank of instructor through professor to the giddy heights of "university professor" in 1988. Since then she has been teaching botany at the University of Massachusetts at Amherst with the even giddier title of "distinguished university professor."

Meanwhile, of course, from her graduate-student days in Wisconsin, she had been pursuing her curiosity over the location of genes in the cell, especially in the cytoplasm, outside the nucleus, despite much professorial disapproval. In the process she came across some turn-of-the-century articles positing extranuclear genes, also amid much negative reaction from the establishment. With her late-twentieth-century instruments and techniques, she extrapolated and bolstered their suggestions into what eventually became known as her serial endosymbiotic theory for the evolutionary development of the nucleated cell.

By the mid–1960s she felt confident enough to publish, but she had to submit her paper to fifteen hidebound editors before getting it accepted and published by the sixteenth, in the *Journal of Theoretical Biology* in 1966. Inspired by the negative reactions to it, she set about preparing and writing a much more detailed explanation of the theory, published in 1970 as *Origin of Eukaryotic Cells* (i.e., cells with nuclei), and then, in 1981, a further explanation titled *Symbiosis in Cell Evolution*. After the first book was published her requests for grants to support further research were turned down by the National Science Foundation, among others, on the grounds that her theory was "totally unacceptable" to "Important Molecular Biologists" (caps added). By the time her second book appeared, however, the theory had gained wide acceptance. (The theory of continental plate tectonics, incidentally, had a very similar rejection-acceptance history.)

As a result of her microbial studies she devised a new system of classification for living things to replace the traditional kingdoms of plants and animals (as opposed to the nonliving minerals). She proposed five kingdoms: cells without nuclei, cells with nuclei, funguses, plants, and animals. Although still controversial, this system too has been gaining ever wider acceptance. She has cannily chosen to explain it in a 1992 book for youngsters, *Diversity of Life*, engaging the attention of the coming generation.

Her next assault on traditional thinking actually had its beginnings in 1972, when she became interested in the Gaia hypothesis proposed by the British chemist James Lovelock. (Gaia was the Greek earth goddess.) Lovelock's hypothesis fit in nicely with her research, suggesting as it did that living things have always participated in their evolution, going beyond mere passive reactions to environmental change and, through the addition of their own chemical liquids and gases, have actively contributed to the process. The hypothesis has been airily dismissed as merely fanciful and imbecilic—so here we go again.

In addition to her teaching, lecturing, committee work (some for NASA), and tireless publishing (including three books co-authored with her son Dorion Sagan), she has for the past couple of decades made a point of at least yearly visits to Baja, California, to muck around in an extensive bed of microscopic life resembling the primeval ooze and containing millions of microorganisms in every cubic inch—"literally knee-deep in her research," as son Dorion has put it.

She would have liked to spend her life eliminating human destitution and ignorance through moderation of the population explosion and education, she has said. But since these are impossible goals, "I spend my time deducing the early evolutionary history of life on earth." Amen.

Janet Reno
First Woman U.S. Attorney General
(1938–)

Florida's Dade County is splendidly or notoriously Republican, depending on one's viewpoint. In 1988, for instance, it gave Bush 69 percent of its vote and Dukakis all the rest, and in 1992 it gave the Bush-Perot axis 63 percent and Clinton all the rest. Under these circumstances it's quite a tribute to lifelong Democrat Janet Reno's competence as chief prosecutor for the Greater Miami Area that she was elected and consistently reelected to that job from 1978 until 1992, when she was called to Washington as her country's first woman Attorney General.

She was born in July 1938 in Miami to unconventional parents, both journalists, her father a police reporter and her mother an investigative reporter and, local tradition maintains, an alligator-wrestling poet. Her vigorously colorful personality inspired her two daughters and two sons into a spirit of similarly energetic self-confidence. When the family left Miami in the mid–1940s to live some twenty miles closer to the Everglades, the move meant building a house to last them for the rest of her life and many years beyond. (It survived Hurricane Andrew.) She dug the foundation, laid the bricks, installed the plumbing, and worked with her father in the evenings on the heavier construction. Janet liked the televisionless country environment—camping and canoeing, and visiting the nearby Miccosukee Indians. (But it was her mother who was made an honorary princess of the tribe.) The Everglades gave her thoughts of becoming a marine biologist, but she discarded that idea for becoming a doctor, then a baseball player, and finally a lawyer—a career that seemed to offer the greatest degree of independence.

Her choice confirmed by some spectacular success at debating in high school, she took aim at Harvard Law School, which she entered in 1960 after earning a B.S. in chemistry at Cornell. At Harvard she and her fifteen distaff fellow hopefuls (including Colorado's Pat Schroeder) constituted just 3 percent of their class. Three years later, armed with her LL.B., she was rejected by a large law firm in Miami on grounds of unacceptable gender but was accepted by a smaller, less barnacle-encumbered firm.

In 1971, as staff director for the state assembly's Judiciary Committee, she helped to reorganize the court system through a revision of the state constitution. The next year she ran for the assembly and lost, nursing her wound with the memory of Lincoln's loss in *his* first race and with absorption in a new job as counsel for the senate's Criminal Justice Committee. In that office she attracted the attention of the state attorney for Dade County, who persuaded her to join his staff but thereafter left her to an underling for assignment. Casually assigned to set up a juvenile division, she surprised everyone by promptly doing so.

Although she left that office to join a private firm in 1976, she also left behind a reputation that earned her, in 1978, a recommendation to the governor to appoint her as replacement for the county's retiring state's attorney. She thus became Florida's first woman chief county prosecutor. That November she was elected as such by 74 percent of the voters despite her Democratic imperfections. The job, no sinecure, meant supervising more than 200 attorneys and about 700 other employees with a caseload of 120,000 a year amid pressing problems of illegal immigration, drug peddling, and racial hostilities.

In May 1980, although she was and is a member of the NAACP, she incurred the wrath of blacks and liberals when her office failed to persuade an all-white jury to convict four white cops accused of beating a black suspect to death. (The verdict brought on a riot that caused 18 deaths and a $200-million property loss.) It took her several years of hiring blacks and Hispanics (she speaks fluent Spanish) and of minority community involvement, as well as referring such cases to less impressionable and better heeled Federal prosecutors, before she earned minority respect and trust.

She earned it also with her vigorous prosecution of fathers neglecting their child-support responsibilities, eliciting baritone as well as soprano praise, since such delinquency hurts faithful supporters as well as impoverished victims. Steering a course between toughness and compassion, she vigorously prosecuted child abuse but introduced an unconventional court process that continues today to direct initial and nonviolent drug abusers into counseling rather than into prison. (More than half of the counseled have stayed free of drugs.) Apparently quite aware that our country's penal system focuses less on justice than on vengeance, she has pleaded more recently for more preventive treatment to go along with the largely ineffective practice of incarceration. This attitude hasn't endeared her to the vengeful, such as the ex-police chief who decried her poor record of not "putting bad guys in jail" and "leaving too many damn criminals out on the street," and who doubtless suffered a stroke after hearing her assertions that her "highest priority is to protect the rights of the guilty, not to convict the guilty" and that we simply "can't build enough prisons."

After Bill Clinton's election she (among others) was asked if she'd be interested in being Attorney General, but her beloved mother's terminal illness made it impossible at that time. Several months later, in February 1993, after a couple of newsworthy attempts to fill the post, she was available, and Clinton nominated her chiefly because, he said, of her reputation for "unquestioned integrity." (She regularly returned unspent campaign contributions!) It didn't hurt to have had Hugh Rodham, Hillary's brother, as a cofounder of, and public defender in, her state's special drug court. Although her distaste for the death penalty, with its endless delays, seemed to raise questions among some vengeance-seekers on the Senate Judiciary Committee, she was nonetheless unanimously confirmed.

The job, with its responsibility for 90,000 employees and a budget of $10 billion a year, hasn't been easy. She stirred up political turmoil almost immediately with her request for the resignations of the 77 politically appointed U.S. attorneys, a traditional procedure for a new administration but one that incurred charges that she was trying to hobble the investigation of Ways and Means Chairman Dan Rostenkowski. The uproar died down when she insisted that the investigation would continue unabated. When accused of failing to be a "loyal soldier" she retorted that Clinton had hired her not to be "a loyal soldier" but to be "a lawyer for the people." A more serious and heart-wrenching matter was the death of 86 members of the Branch Davidian cult, including 17 children, after she ordered an attack on their compound specifically because she feared that the children were being abused. The first bitter criticism of her was turned to public sympathy by her conspicuous remorse and her honesty in discussing her decision, as well as by the flaky character of the cult. More recently she lost a deputy AG after a serious dispute over the Administration's crime bill. But they parted amicably.

Her forthrightness and her obvious concern for the plight of ghetto children with their teenage pregnancies and drive-by shootings have made her one of Clinton's most popular choices. Although her serious concern is manifest in her public demeanor, she has a sense of humor. On her property near the Everglades, for example, she has over the years accumulated a total of 35 pet peacocks. And they're all named Horace, regardless of sex. Indiscriminately.

Maxine Waters
Congresswoman (1938–)

There is no question about whose side she's on—the disadvantaged, the dispossessed, the disenfranchised, the discriminated-against, the dispirited. That, after all, is essentially her constituency.

Maxine Carr Waters was born in August 1938 in St. Louis, Missouri, and in precarious poverty. Of the thirteen children in the family she was number 5, which meant that at the age of 13, after her parents had separated, she had to get a job to help her mother, dependent on welfare and on successive husbands' niggardly patronage, in feeding those hungry mouths. A high school diploma and marriage to Edward Waters five years later, followed by the birth of two children in the early sixties, did nothing to improve the financial outlook. Nor did a move to Los Angeles, land of promise, turn out very promising: minimum wages, maximum discouragement.

But in 1966 Lyndon Johnson's War on Poverty brought the Head Start program to Los Angeles, and she was hired as an assistant teacher. Later advanced to supervisor of volunteers, she found great satisfaction in helping people in conspicuous need of help. Politics, she decided—at least Lyndon Johnson's brand of domestic politics—offered a way to do just that.

She got involved. After a great deal of volunteer campaigning at the tenderfoot level (which interfered with her marriage enough to end it in divorce), in 1973 she managed the campaign of a liberal candidate for a spot on the L.A. City Council. After his victory he appointed her his chief deputy, giving her hard-earned experience in extravagantly practical politics, as well as time to earn a B.A. in sociology from California State University—an educational gloss for any political hardball.

In 1976 the electoral shenanigans of her district's incumbent state assemblyman so incensed her (and many if not most of the district's voters) that she ran against his protégé in the Democratic primary. After winning the nomination, she won the election, handily. Her reputation as a pretty tough pol with a mind of her own preceded her to Sacramento, where she found herself "absolutely resented" and harassed with assorted obstacles as "this black woman coming from Los Angeles who needed to be taught a lesson."

She was a fast learner of lessons. Within a couple of years she had shepherded a bill through the assembly that ensured pregnant women as much as four months of maternity leave and a comparable job on their return. It eased many a pregnancy over the next six years, although at the end of that time a Federal judge voided it because it discriminated against men—pregnant men, presumably. Her 1984 bill banning the strip-searching of women and children arrested for misdemeanors met with considerable law-and-order opposition, including a veto by a hard-shell Republican governor, but eventually was enacted and stayed on the books, in slightly modified form, without judicial interference. Similarly, her bill against California investments in South African businesses ran into so much opposition that she had to add it to the calendar six times over eight years, but it finally became the law. She also was involved in setting up an unprecedented Child Abuse Prevention Training Program and in providing financial support for businesses in poor neighborhoods. No bleeding-heart liberal, she actively and successfully pushed for a bill specifying longer prison terms for armed drug dealers.

Shy, retiring, obsequious she wasn't. Indeed, she could be abrasively spunky at times, enough to turn people off but also to turn people on. As her regularly reinstated incumbency moved her into the 1980s, enough of her colleagues were turned on to elect her as the first female majority whip in the assembly's history. She also became the first woman on the powerful Rules Committee and the first nonlawyer on the Judiciary Committee.

By this time she had her eagle eye on the Congressional seat for the Twenty-ninth District, which was substantially the same as her own state electoral district. Early in 1989, when the Twenty-ninth's Democratic Congressman Augustus Hawkins, in his eighties, decided to call it quits after almost thirty years in Congress, the eagle eye developed an ambitiously focused glint. She won the primary election with nearly nine-tenths of the vote and the general election in an exhilarating breeze.

In the House of Representatives, appointed to the Veterans' Affairs Committee, she exhilarated her fellow members by vigorously opposing its chairman, a Mississippi Democrat who, as a Republican in transparent disguise, urged the committee simply to defeat anything requiring new expenditures. She also argued consistently for greater consideration of minorities, particularly, for instance, in arranging for veterans' job rights during and after the Gulf War. Her relentless pressure further resulted in the addition of two African Americans to the committee's preposterously white staff.

Home was still Los Angeles, where her second husband Sidney Williams and her two children and grandchildren lived, and she commuted regularly. But in April 1992 she had a special reason for commuting, since that was when the riots (the rebellion, she called them) broke out following the spectacular, camcorded beating of Rodney King by the arm of the law. Her squeaky-wheel pressure tactics helped to restore electric power to the community. ("We couldn't even watch the riots on TV!") The riots (in which her district office was destroyed by fire) were a special reason for her increased emphasis on government help to the contemptuously and contemptibly neglected inner-city ghettos. When George Bush, persevering in that neglect, called a meeting of legislators to discuss the L.A. troubles, he neglected to invite her. But she heard of the meeting, heatedly demanded to be included, and was, forthwith.

With the election of a Democratic President (whom she ardently supported, of course, during the campaign), to the glint in her eye was added a glimmer of hope.

Marian Wright Edelman
Senator (1939–)

Crediting her with "real power in Congress," Senator Ted Kennedy once described this lawyer as "the 101st Senator on children's issues." Amid all the talk of greedy, self-promoting lobbyists, here's one promoting the interests of neglected children and thus the future of the country.

She was born Marian Wright in June 1939 in Bennettsville, South Carolina, where she and her two older sisters and three older brothers attended separate but unequal grammar and high schools. The shortcomings of that education (which did include voice training and piano lessons, the latter a great source of comfort during a hectically busy life) she made up for with voracious reading because, she later testified, reading was the only excuse that her father would accept for neglect of household chores. It also lessened her contacts with the town's prevailing Caucasian contumely, readily apparent in the restricted swimming pools, neglected black victims in traffic accidents, and continual casual incivilities.

Her father, a Baptist minister, died when she was fourteen but not without urging her on his deathbed not to "let anything get between you and your education." Taking his advice to heart, she enrolled at eighteen in the liberal arts program at Atlanta's Spelman College, a school for black women. In her junior year she went to Europe on a scholarship, studying at the Sorbonne and the University of Geneva and, that summer, visited Moscow on a fellowship. For someone her age she had become a very experienced traveler, a traveler now with a strong itch to enter her country's foreign service.

During her senior year at Spelman, however, her growing awareness of the emerging civil rights movement changed her mind. After joining a sit-in demonstration at city hall and spending a night in jail, she decided that maybe blacks needed more lawyers to defend them from the legal injustices of segregation. And so, after receiving her B.A. in 1960, she applied to Yale Law School and was accepted. When she was granted her LL.B. in 1963 she was already in training with the NAACP's Legal Defense and Educational Fund and would eventually become its state director.

After her year of training in New York, she headed for Mississippi, where there was one black lawyer for every 300,000 black residents. Ironically, her first work there, in Jackson, in the summer of '64 was focused on northern white college students who had come south to help with black voter registration and who needed lawyers to get them out of jail (when the lawyers weren't there themselves).

During her four years as the state's first black female lawyer, she came to the realization that there wasn't much point to winning desegregation cases in court if blacks were too poor, for example, to take advantage of the desegregated facilities—especially youngsters and, most especially, children. As lawyer for the state's Child Development Group she went to Washington and managed, despite roadblocks righteously provided by the state's Neanderthal delegation in Congress, to persuade the legislators to restore the state's just share of Federal funds for Head Start.

Toward the end of her stay in Mississippi, in 1967, Senator Robert Kennedy paid the state an eye-opening visit during which she treated him to a tour of a few of the many areas of appalling destitution, a tour during which, for instance, Kennedy could elicit no response from a starving infant and after which the elimination of such poverty became a top priority in his political agenda.

Kennedy was accompanied on the trip by a young white aide named Peter Edelman, with whom she developed an affectionate rapport that would ultimately result in three sons.

They were married in July 1968 and moved to Washington, where of course he worked and where she now thought it might be wise for her to work, especially toward promoting Head Start nationally. When the Poor People's Campaign visited the city, she offered her services as legal counsel, and that year she founded the public-interest Washington Research Project. When Peter moved to Boston in 1971 for the vice presidency of the University of Massachusetts, she moved with him and was appointed director of Harvard's Center for Law and Education. She was also included in *Time's* list of the country's 200 foremost young leading lights.

Still deeply concerned with the plight of children in families living in poverty, she established in 1973 the Children's Defense Fund, as an offshoot of the Washington Research Project, particularly to work with Congress and various Federal agencies on behalf of otherwise unrepresented children. Funded privately, the CDF conducted a study of poor children's most pressing problems and then spent three years pressing Congress for child care legislation until that body finally passed a bill in 1990, its first such bill in almost twenty years.

Meanwhile the Fund was growing as an organization, with about a hundred people in its Washington headquarters and an annual budget of over $10 million, while she kept up a steady drumbeat of speeches and articles. In 1987, her book *Families in Peril* decried the neglect of ill and starving children in a world spending a trillion dollars a year on armaments. (One reviewer described it as "a small, readable book with a large, urgent message.") In 1992 her slim volume *The Measure of Our Success*, similar in theme but more personal (addressed to her young adult sons), hit the best-seller charts.

During the 1992 political year the Fund's promotional efforts on television and other persuasive devices were nonpolitical reminders of the reductions in Federal spending for poor children that had taken place during the preceding twelve years. Although she has many friends on both sides of the aisle in Congress, some of the mossbacks tend to cut and run when they see her coming.

For all her executive ability and lobbying talent, she is frustrated by the slow pace of progress in the public nourishment and encouragement of children. No amount of frustration, of course, will defeat her, for she has come to realize "what I was sent here to do."

Wangari Maathai
Kenyan Political Activist (1940–)

Her environment is rugged not so much in the Western sense—air pollution, urban blight, traffic gridlock, frantic activity—as in the African, particularly the Kenyan, sense—tribal hostilities, ingrown sexism, brutal despotism. It's particularly rugged for anyone highly intelligent, well educated, principled, determined, and of independent mind—especially a woman.

Wangari Maathai was born in April 1940 in Nyeri, Kenya, a comparatively small town about a hundred miles north of the capital, Nairobi. She and her parents and five younger siblings worked a hardscrabble farm, where she'd probably be today if her extraordinary parents hadn't found a way to get her to school and if her teachers at the Loreto Limuru Girls High School hadn't encouraged her to apply for one of the many scholarships then being offered by the Kennedy Administration. That scholarship got her all the way to Atchison, Kansas, in the early 1960s, where she enrolled at Mount St. Scholastica College.

The blandishments of American living standards didn't weaken her resolve to return to Kenya and use her education to help her people. On the way back, however, she stopped off at the University of Pittsburgh with her bachelor's degree in biology, and there she earned a master's in the same discipline. When she did get back to Kenya in 1966 she found that her education would indeed prove valuable, although the fact that she was the only woman with an advanced degree for hundreds of miles around made her highly suspect in a milieu of primitive roosterism. In this respect she only made things worse when, while working in the veterinary medicine department at the University of Nairobi, she used her spare time to become the first woman to earn a doctorate at that university and, later, the first woman to teach there.

The academic life, however, couldn't fully satisfy the activist in her, especially after her participation in her husband's successful campaign for a seat in the country's parliament opened her farm-girl's eyes to the grinding poverty, the pitiful condition of the urban poor. After the election their plight inspired her to action, setting up a job-search organization to provide the destitute with employment, both public and private. Before long, as a biologist concerned about deforestation (wood being *the* fuel used for cooking), she began focusing the organization's employment activities on the planting of trees.

The effort languished, however, until 1977, when she obtained the support of the National Council of Women of Kenya in establishing a Green Belt Movement, a system of nurseries to provide local communities with plants and seedlings. The Movement addressed the needs and caught the imagination of so many people that by the early 1990s a thousand nurseries, operated by 80,000 workers, had supplied Kenya with ten million trees and had introduced the system to several neighboring countries. (She has written a couple of books about it.)

Meanwhile her private life had succumbed to male resentment over her academic and other achievements, credit for which the resident chanticleers felt, she "should have gone to my husband rather than to myself." Her husband sued her for divorce on grounds not of over achievement but adultery and, despite her angrily vigorous defense, won. As a result of her furious charge that the censoriously male court's reliance on hearsay evidence betokened either incompetence or corruption, she was sentenced to six months in jail or until she apologized. After three days in a Nairobi jail, she apologized.

Her dedication as an environmentalist, combined with her spunky determination, brought her into direct confrontation with government despotism in 1989. In one of Nairobi's rare parks the government planned to set up an elaborate commercial complex, complete with skyscraper, theaters, hotels, offices, a TV broadcasting station and, of course, an imposing statue of President Daniel Arap Moi. Loudly objecting to the plan as a concrete-jungle scheme that would cost debt-ridden Kenya about a quarter of a billion dollars, she called for a public debate on the proposal. Her opposition stirred up such a storm of popular protest and flurry of rhetorical abuse from the politicians—including Moi's pronouncement that it was simply "un-African and unimaginable for a woman to challenge and oppose men"—that vital foreign investment evaporated, and the project was abandoned. In retaliation the government evicted her Green Belt Movement from its publicly owned office space, forcing her to move the headquarters into her Nairobi home.

Further government harassment has attended her political activity in support of the growing popular interest in democracy. On one occasion, during a demonstration against the protracted imprisonment without trial of some dissidents, she was beaten senseless with a club. Her struggle against the government's incitement of tribal violence has brought on such reactions as to cause her to adopt disguises to avoid menacing official notice. From outside Kenya notice of her has been much different, including numerous awards and honors from environmentalist and feminist organizations.

Western aid, she has argued, shouldn't go to self-serving governments but to people's efforts to supply their fundamental needs, "adequate food, clean water, shelter, local clinics, information and freedom." This appeal has done nothing to increase affection for her in government circles.

Cynthia Moss
Elephant Scientist (1940–)

The rest of us generally go camping over a weekend or for a week or two. Cynthia Moss went camping for a couple of decades. In the wilds of Africa yet. With elephants. She came to know them as individuals, to admire them, to grow fond of them. And in the process she became a universally recognized authority on these gargantuan pachyderms and an ardent advocate for their survival as a species.

She was born in July 1940 in the nonwilds of Ossining, New York, the younger of two daughters of a newspaper publisher. The nearest thing to elephants in her affluent neighborhood were horses. She took eagerly to riding, especially in the rapidly disappearing woodlands nearby. She deplored the inroads of "developments," becoming in her early twenties, almost incongruously, a city-bred easterner with membership in the Sierra Club. The African wilderness, however, never entered her mind.

Indeed, her degree from Smith College in 1962 was in philosophy, although she found herself more given to scientific analysis than to metaphysical speculation. Yet within a couple of years after graduation (and after the death of her parents) she was exercising her considerable writing talent for the theater and religion sections of *Newsweek*. It was only after receiving some entrancing letters from a college chum on tour in Africa that she became intrigued enough at least to pay the exotic continent a visit. And so she did, in 1967.

That did it. For many visitors Africa weaves a magic spell; she was utterly bewitched. Within a week she felt completely at home, especially after meeting the elephants in the Lake Manyara National Park in northern Tanzania and their devoted observer, the zoologist Iain Douglas-Hamilton. When he asked her to join him in studying the elephants' habits in their environment, she was overjoyed. Kismet. Somehow she knew this was her destiny.

She moved to Africa to stay in January 1968, working with Douglas-Hamilton at first continuously and then intermittently until he finished his project in 1972. To supplement her earnings as his research assistant she had to leave her colossal friends occasionally to do some veterinarian research and to conduct various animal studies in Kenya. She also participated, more eagerly, in a study of elephant ecology for the University of Nairobi in the Tsavo National Park. On the side she contributed to the documentary film *The African Elephant*, wrote freelance for *Time* and *Life*, edited a newsletter for what is now the African Wildlife Foundation, and accumulated research material on East African mammals for her book *Portraits in the Wild*, published in 1975 and replete with intriguing tidbits (e.g., giraffes use their heads as bludgeons, very effectively).

Meanwhile the elephants came back into her life when an opportunity arose in 1972 to conduct a study of the elephants in Kenya's Amboseli National Park with another elephant-watcher, Harvey Croze. With interruptions for her writing and editing, she and Croze built up a file on the park's 500 or so elephants, identifying them by their ear peculiarities (holes, notches, vein patterns) and setting a zoological precedent by giving them names instead of merely numbers. This practice had been discouraged in the past as being too likely to remind a researcher of a person with the name assigned, but she has found that, on the contrary, seeing the human name separately reminds her of the elephant.

The difficulties of part-time researching were dissipated when the African Wildlife Foundation offered to fund full-time research into the lives of the Amboseli elephants. The high praise her book had received from reviewers had brought her considerable esteem as a scientific researcher, and this surely contributed to the AWF's confidence in her study methods. Those methods had already confirmed previous reports that the elephant families of calves and adult females, presided over by elderly and very sage females, are visited by the peripatetic males only sporadically, for mating at their male convenience, as in some human arrangements.

After setting herself up in a permanent camp, primitive but comfortable and affording an exhilarating view of towering, snow-capped Mount Kilimanjaro, she began her long-term study of, eventually, over a thousand elephants. (Croze had left for other projects.) The families, she discovered, are organized into larger, companionable herds, and these into still larger clans. Elephants seem puzzled and saddened by death, covering their dead with soil and foliage rather lugubriously. Youngsters learn to walk soon after birth but thereafter must be taught by their elders what food to eat and water to drink and how to conduct themselves in accord with elephant protocol. Females in heat, she found, can be quite flirtatious with pursuing males—behavior not unknown in more "developed" environments. In this connection she and Joyce Poole, a fellow researcher who has been working with her since shortly after Croze's departure, learned that African male elephants, like their Asian counterparts, often have a condition called must, or musth, which makes them uncharacteristically aggressive, probably because of an elevated testosterone level, and correspondingly lecherous. In 1988 she confided it all to a popular book, *Elephant Memories*, which follows the fortunes, and misfortunes, of an extended elephant family.

Meanwhile Africa's human population explosion and, more especially, the insatiable demand for ivory were decimating the continent's elephant population, from 1,300,000 in 1979 to less than half that in 1989, and unraveling its organization because of poachers' genocidal preference for big males with big, profitable tusks. Though not conservation zealots, she and Poole alerted the AWF to the alarming trend, and the Foundation's subsequent advertising appeals did much to shrink the market for ivory throughout the world. The Moss-Poole team also contributed to the action in 1990 by the Convention on International Trade in Endangered Species which classified the elephant as an endangered species and thus prohibited trading in ivory. Since then such trading has dwindled enough at least to give the elephants a chance at survival.

Such activity has enhanced her reputation, bringing her opportunities to contribute many articles to scientific and wildlife journals, as well as to participate and appear in TV documentaries. In 1985 her alma mater awarded her a medal for alumna achievement, and she has been honored for her conservation efforts by the Friends of the National Zoo and the Audubon Naturalist Society.

What makes her really happy, of course, is studying her elephants and waking up in the morning to the gratifying sight of Mount Kilimanjaro.

Pat Schroeder
Political Gadfly (1940–)

If the House Armed Services Committee is the Pentagon's ointment, Pat Schroeder's the fly in it. And has been for more than twenty years. Among other things.

She was born Patricia Scott in July 1940 in Portland, Oregon. As part of a highly mobile family, she attended grammar and high schools in various cities (and incidentally learned to fly a plane) before transferring her considerable scholastic talents to the University of Minnesota in Minneapolis. After graduating with honors and a Phi Beta Kappa key three years after her arrival, she took those talents to Harvard's Law School, earning a J.D. in 1964. By then she had met and married James White Schroeder, a fellow devotee of the law and politics. After graduation the couple moved to Denver, where she worked as an attorney for the National Labor Relations Board until rudely interrupted by the birth of a son in 1966.

After a couple of years of focused mothering she dipped a tentative toe into Democratic politics as a precinct committeewoman, began teaching law at local colleges, and tried cases until interrupted again, by the birth of a daughter in 1970. Soon she was back at work, this time as a hearing officer for the state's Department of Personnel and as legal adviser to the state branch of the Planned Parenthood Federation of America.

Meanwhile her husband, having narrowly lost a race for a seat in the state assembly and having decided somewhat ruefully to try his hand at campaign managing, was searching desperately in 1972 for someone to run against the Republican incumbent for the district's seat in the U.S. House of Representatives. Said incumbent, as incumbent, was universally considered such a shoo-in that Pat agreed to run because "I was the only person he could talk into it." She was so confident of losing that she kept right on working through the campaign, to hold on to her jobs. Among some American gothic voters there was considerable consternation over the busy candidate's failure to confine herself to mothering. She responded by reporting that the kids were safe at home in the freezer.

But husband James turned out to be a highly competent and imaginative campaign manager. Despite some unpopular positions against the war in Vietnam and against the neglect of education, children's health, and the environment, she won the Democratic primary and, despite the Nixon landslide and lack of support from the Democratic National Committee, overcame the district's Republican bias to win the election, her first victory in a dozen to date.

The same fossilized prejudice against working mothers followed her into Congress. Soon after her arrival she was asked, by a Congress*man* of course, how she could possibly be "the mother of two small children and a member of Congress at the same time." She replied that she had a brain and a uterus, both in working order. (For the first couple of months, until her administrative assistant arrived from Denver, her wonderfully supportive husband worked in her office. Warned by a sobersides that relatives can't legally be on the payroll, she assured him that wasn't the case. "I just let him sleep with me.")

As a member of the tiny distaff minority (14, or 3.2 percent), she doubtless was expected to seek positions on some of the "soft" committees, but instead she managed to get herself on the Armed Services Committee, where she would be a burr under the saddle of successive chairmen for the next two decades (until Lee Aspin). She deplored the committee's cozy relationship with military officialdom, denouncing it as "the Pentagon's lobby on the Hill." There was no need, she insisted, to kill an enemy fifteen times when five would do the job. There were other things to protect the country from besides military attack, and measures against those other things—ignorance, illness, poverty—required some of the money frittered away by the brass hats. The problem, she asserted, was that whatever new weapons *could* be developed *would* be developed. Hers at least was a very vocal minority.

In other respects as well she was and is a zealous liberal, her zealotry rendered tolerable by a sharp wit and an engaging sense of humor. Her support for educational and health programs for young and old has made her a favorite of school, senior-citizen, and consumer organizations. Her promotion of governmental reform earned her a 100 percent rating from the League of Women Voters. By the time the 1974 election came around, she was so popular with her constituency that her Republican opponent had to focus his diatribes on her support for the pregnant woman's right to choose and the minority child's right to be bused. She won with almost three-fifths of the vote and has been winning ever since.

Her put-downs in Congress and elsewhere she accepts philosophically. That's life. Competent women, she has said, "have dealt with this issue all their life." Not that put-downs are acceptable—that's why she agreed to chair the National Task Force on Equal Rights for Women. She does fervently wish that

Congress, in this respect and others, could be brought into the twentieth century.

And then there was her brief presidential candidacy, for which she stubbornly refused to go into debt. So it died from lack of nourishment. The first sentence in her quasibiography gives a very brief account of it: "What began on June 5, 1987, as an exciting quest for the presidency of the United States ended three months later on September 28, as a search for Kleenex."

Ted Sorenson once introduced her as a politician able to "draft a bill, stir a crowd, fly a plane, bake a cake, coin a phrase—and run for President." She corrected him: "I know a bakery that delivers." (She is now retired.)

Donna Shalala
Secretary of Health and Human Services
(1941–)

Her first year as an assistant secretary of Housing and Urban Development in Jimmy Carter's administration at least gave her some basic training in Beltway battling for her use later as Secretary of Health and Human Services in Bill Clinton's administration. That first year was, she has said, the roughest year of her life. "I thought of myself as aggressive until I went to Washington, but I didn't know what aggressive was." She almost failed to survive "in part because I'm basically a kind of nice human being." That's not just her opinion.

Donna Shalala and a twin sister (also nice) were born in February 1941 in Cleveland. Her father was in real estate, gregariously and prominently active in the city's Syrian and Lebanese communities, but it was her mother whom she took after, a lady who had given up championship tennis to study and then practice law, all without neglecting her family. (She was still practicing law and playing tennis in the 1990s.) At the age of nine Donna gave a clue to her character during a tornado when, instead of seeking refuge in the house, she disappeared and was found later at a nearby street corner, directing traffic.

She was athletic despite her five-foot stature, playing shortstop and left field for a championship girls' baseball team (coached by a young college man named George Steinbrenner, of later renown) and in her teens winning awards for her tennis. She was also a good student, on the honors list at the Western College for Women, from which she received a B.A. in, most appropriately, urban studies.

After her graduation in 1962, she spent two years with the Peace Corps in Iran as college teacher and dean of women, and then another two years in Syria and Lebanon teaching English teachers for the U.S. Information Agency.

In 1968, after her return, she joined the urban community-development program at Syracuse University, which granted her a Ph.D. in social science in 1970. After being imperiously turned down for a reporter's job with the *New York Times* (no gritty reportorial experience), she was hired as assistant professor of political science at Baruch College in New York, where she made something of a name for herself with a report, for a public-interest organization, rather impertinently declaring the idea of statehood for New York City to be passé. (The controversial state-city relationship had been the subject of her doctoral dissertation.)

In 1972 she left Baruch for an associate professorship of politics and education at Columbia University, supplemented with some teaching at Yale Law School. In 1975 she was asked to join the effort to rescue New York City from impending bankruptcy, becoming a director and treasurer of the rescuing Municipal Assistance Corporation, and as such issuing $6 billion in bonds while tugging at lapels in Albany. Despite some gender-engendered resistance, she proved herself financially and politically effective enough to be called to Washington for appointment in January 1977 as assistant secretary for policy development and research at HUD.

Depressed but not intimidated by the Beltway battling, she started a review of the impact of government housing on women—particularly the discrimination against mothers and their children, against older women, and against minorities—and then, despite Washington precedents, followed the review with corrective programs. She managed to put up with the Beltway brouhaha for three years but in December 1979 proved susceptible to a new offer, from New York City's Hunter College. As its youngest president ever, she inherited a school in the financial doldrums, declining enrollment, budget, facilities and campus upkeep.

Enlisting the help of the anxious faculty, she turned the enrollment decline around by offering bright high school students incentives like scholarships and financial assistance. She also fattened the budget by raising millions for research, for books and library additions, as well as completing construction of two 17-story buildings for the campus. She even arranged for a new subway station. She also did some teaching—political science, urban education—"to maintain my sanity." Urban education was a sore point with her: with more than half of the new students at Hunter requiring remedial work, her favorite word for the performance of New York's schools was "rotten."

In May 1987 another irresistible opportunity arose when she was hired as professor of political science and educational policy studies *and* as chancellor of the University of Wisconsin, the nation's fourth largest university with 43,000 students in 26 colleges (half of them four-year) and an enviable reputation in research. Hailed as something of a celebrity, she had an ice-cream flavor named for her by a Madison dairy. With the university then embroiled in racial controversy, she immediately introduced a program of interracial communication as well as increasing minority and distaff representation in both the student body and the faculty. It wasn't the moral argument that moved her to do this, she explained, but rather the educational argument. The school could not "be first-rate unless we have a representative student body, faculty and staff."

Concerned about racial invective, she made the mistake of agreeing to a campus speech code that was later voided on First Amendment grounds. Concerned also about alcoholism as perhaps the chief problem with college students, she often went with police on raids of local bars to warn students of the perils of alcohol addiction. In an effort to boost undergraduate morale (suffering somewhat from graduate student elitism) she vastly improved the Badgers' football program and also mixed most sociably, even helping newly arrived students to unpack. As part of her money-raising activity she urged that emphasis be shifted from graduate research to elementary education, especially for "at-risk children [who] will shape colleges' futures far more than anyone now enrolled."

At Hillary Rodham Clinton's urging and with Bill Clinton's enthusiastic concurrence, she became in early 1993 the Secretary of Health and Human Services, head of a department with more than a half-trillion-dollar budget. Long something of a sinecure, the job now took on particular significance in view of the Clintons' intense interest in reforming health care. What with all the Beltway battling ahead, she would have plenty of opportunities to be nicely aggressive or aggressively nice.

Elizabeth Holtzman
Politician (1941–)

She supported George McGovern in the 1972 Democratic primaries as well as in the election. In the 93rd and later Congresses she voted consistently for legislation promoting women's rights, low-cost housing, food stamps, wage and price controls, press freedoms, health care, mass transit, and environmental conservation—and restricting Richard Nixon's homicidal airborne shenanigans in Cambodia. She has proven rock-ribbed quite often but conservative hardly ever.

Elizabeth Holtzman and her twin brother Robert were born in August 1941 in Brooklyn to Russian immigrant parents. Her father, who became a lawyer; her mother, who became head of Hunter College's Russian department; and her brother, who became a neurosurgeon, all provided her with a competitive environment that surely couldn't brook a lackadaisical nonentity. Indeed, in high school, when her brother ran for president of the student government, she ran with him as vice-president, and won.

From Radcliffe College she took a degree in American history and literature, magna cum laude, in 1962 and then joined fourteen other young women in constituting 3 percent of their class at Harvard Law School. No reclusive scholar, she used her spare time gaining practical experience in litigation with a civil rights attorney in Georgia. In 1965, armed with her new law degree, she was taken on as a practicing lawyer by a small law firm in Manhattan.

In 1967 politics enticed her away from law when New York's Mayor John Lindsay, acquainted with her law-school record, invited her to become an aide in his office with special responsibility for the Department of Parks, Recreation and Cultural Affairs. After spending the next three years fighting the bureaucracy on behalf of the city's libraries, parks, and playgrounds, she decided that she might be more effective in the Democratic State Committee. She ran for it in 1970, won, resumed her law practice, and, while representing her Flatbush district, began casting an opportunistic eye at the Congressional seat of Representative Emanuel Celler.

During his half-century in the House, Celler had contracted some hardening of the political arteries. Although a stalwart Democrat, he had a miserable attendance record, and he seemed to have lost interest in issues of vital concern to her—the Equal Rights Amendment, Social Security increases, peace, the environment, school support. Furthermore, he seemed to have lost interest in his constituents, as shown in his failure to maintain an office in his Brooklyn district. Fifty years earlier he had won his first election with the slogan, "It's Time for a Change," and now she opened her primary campaign against him in 1972 with the same slogan. In his 25 Congressional primaries he had been opposed only once before. Expecting to win handily, he ran a rather relaxed campaign while she wore herself out with bell-ringing and buttonholing. Her efforts brought her a narrow victory, 50.5 percent to 49.5 percent, but in the election that November she won over her Republican opponent by a margin of 3 to 1—after which she opened an office in her Brooklyn district and promised to be available there every weekend.

In the House she immediately began working for the causes mentioned above as well as decrying the Nixon Administration's foot-dragging and obstructionism in matters of social concern. Impatient with Congressional tolerance of the war in Southeast Asia, she filed suit in April 1973 to bring the bombing to an abrupt halt. (She was joined later by three bomber crewmen.) Although she won her case at the Federal District level, she lost on appeal, despite Justice Thurgood Marshall's opinion that the bombing probably was unconstitutional. She had voted earlier against the War Powers Bill of 1973, which cut off funds for any bombing after August 15 of that year, arguing that it implied approval of any bombing before that date, but the law's delay kept the slaughter going until the cutoff date finally ended the bloody exercise in futility.

On her arrival in the House she had been appointed to the House Judiciary Committee and was therefore part of the Watergate hearings and impeachment proceedings. Considering her liberal antagonism, she conducted herself quite conservatively, with perhaps heroic restraint.

In 1980, completing her fourth term in the House, she decided to run for the Senate. Although she won the Democratic primary, she lost the election to the very Republican Alphonse D'Amato. In 1981, rather than return to private practice, she campaigned for the office of Brooklyn district attorney and served as such until November 1989.

On one occasion during her term as district attorney, a judge in a rape case approved a defense counsel's request to have the alleged victim get down on her hands and knees in court and reenact the attack. And so the D.A. protested to the Commission on Judicial Conduct and repeated her complaint in a publicly released letter. For the latter action (an alternative to a quiet disappearance of the complaint in the Commission's files), she was disciplined by a judicial committee governing lawyers' conduct. She appealed its ruling, but the judicial establishment closed ranks all the way to the Supreme Court, and she lost.

So perhaps it's not surprising that in the November 1989 elections she ran for the office of Comptroller of the City of New York. As such she is relatively removed from judicial incompetence and inner cohesiveness.

Lesley Stahl
Television News Reporter (1941–)

As every couch potato still conscious knows, CBS's TV newsmagazine *60 Minutes* has been a Neilsen phenomenon, maintaining its exalted ratings for more than a quarter century, as well as a very respectable reputation. And so CBS veteran Lesley Stahl was delighted to receive an invitation in 1991 to join the crew of dazzling old-timers like Wallace, Bradley and Safer, and, of course, all this and Andy Rooney.

Nor was she daunted by the prospect of some pretty unusual assignments. Her first, for instance, was an incognito visit to Romania, where she hid her crown of gold under a dark wig to do an unflattering story on baby selling (to Americans who might otherwise have recognized her). And then there was her visit to Turkey for a story on the precarious predicament of the refugee Kurds. Ironically, her most perilous visit probably was to Miami, U.S.A., for a story on police brutality, where she and an associate producer were twice attacked by would-be carjackers. Her companion, when the thief hopped into the back seat and threatened them, pluckily scared him off by running the car into a wall, although he got away with her (the companion's) briefcase and handbag. The second attacker, fortunately, was foiled by the doors being locked.

Lesley Stahl was born in Lynn, Massachusetts, a suburb north of Boston, in December 1941 and was raised in the smaller, nearby coastside town of Swampscott in (despite the name) comfortable circumstances. Perhaps the most effective of her mother's influences on her was her insistence that a woman could have a family *and* a career. An so she chose a career—medicine. After taking with honors a temporarily irrelevant degree in history from Wheaton College in 1963, she entered Columbia University's premed program. She found herself repelled, however, by the seamier side of such subjects as anatomy and zoology. In her second year, after dropping out precipitously, she opted for marrying a doctor instead. The motivation may have been somewhat misdirected, for the marriage lasted only a couple of years.

In 1967 she had her initial close encounter with reporters as speech-writer for New York's PR-sensitive John Lindsay. Suddenly *that* was the career she wanted. ("How come no one ever told me about journalism?") Eagerly she applied for work at the three networks, and within a year she was working for NBC as a researcher and writer, then as a field producer for the Huntley-Brinkley news program. What she really wanted, however, was to be a reporter, and at NBC that didn't seem to be in the cards. So she applied for a reporter's job at some newspapers, including the *Boston Globe*. When the editors there asked her what she "wanted to be in the end" and she answered "a television reporter," he retorted that he wasn't "in the business of training you media types" and urged her to go across the street to the TV station. She did, and there the media types, impressed with her NBC resume, hired her. The sta tion was a CBS affiliate, and two years later she was assigned by the network (like the others, under pressure from the Federal Communications Commission to hire more women and minorities) to Washington, D.C.

Almost immediately she got her Big Break assignment: the Watergate break-in story. She was new, after all, and only a woman, and could handle a story which, although considered inconsequential, was worth some brief local coverage. With senior correspondents otherwise occupied, she covered it for somewhat more than the next two years. Her model was the beaver: hard-working, dogged, assiduous, meticulous, unfazed by obstacles. Although at times the story seemed to peter out, to be getting nowhere, she got to know the *Washington Post*'s Bob Woodward and his avid pursuit of it, and at his urging she stuck with it, earning her journalistic spurs and outlasting Richard Nixon.

She also enhanced her reputation and celebrity networking by giving popular dinner parties (invariably catered, since cuisine was not her speciality). In 1977, confirming her mother's hypothesis, she married fellow journalist Aaron Latham, who covered Watergate for *New York Magazine*, and about a year later she gave birth to her daughter Taylor.

For eight years, between 1983 and 1991, she moderated Sunday morning's *Face the Nation*, bringing those beaver qualities to her often relentless questioning of evasive guests. Behind a friendly, lovely smile of course. In 1979 she also became the chief White House correspondent and was kept there stubbornly by CBS despite hostility from the Carter press people after her husband's less than flattering article titled, as she recalls it, something like "There's a Slob in the White House." Again, she stuck with it, and before long stories began coming her way—on Carter, then Reagan, and then Bush.

Her performance on *Face the Nation*—for example, her resolute eliciting from Secretary of State George Shultz the startling admission, during the Iran-Contra imbroglio, that he really wasn't "running the show"—and her yeoman service on the floor of political conventions as well as at the White House earned her the admiration of many professionals, including that of Don Hewitt, creator and executive producer of *60 Minutes*. In 1991 he invited her aboard. Since then she's "never been so happy," she told an interviewer. "I can't stop smiling. It's the best job in TV."

Mother was right.

Molly Ivins
Political Commentator (1942–)

Her political inkwell holds an inexhaustible supply of acid—rib-tickling acid, that is—especially when she writes about Texas politics, which offers inexhaustible materials. Once, for example, a maverick in the Texas legislature introduced a bill honoring the Boston Strangler of homicidal note, just to see whether anyone would be interested enough to notice, and it was passed. When the Citizens' Conference of State Legislatures ranked the Texas body 38th out of the 50, she questioned the possibility that "there are twelve worse than *this*?" Similar comments stud her books—for instance, 1991's best selling *Molly Ivins Can't Say That, Can She?* (She can, and she does.)

Molly Ivins was born around 1942 (date classified) in River Oaks, Texas, just west of Forth Worth, to a rigidly conservative attorney father and a proper, matronly Southern belle. So much for home influence. Political sophistication came with omnivorous reading and, later, at Smith College, at the Institute of Political Science in Paris, and at Columbia University's School of Journalism. With her master's degree in journalism she took a newspaper job in Minnesota in the hope that she could get away from endless Texas talk about the weather and football, but when she found that Minnesota talk was pretty much the same she returned to Texas and took over the editorship of the *Texas Observer*, which reported on the Texas legislature from a disgracefully liberal viewpoint.

The job paid destitution wages, yet she remembers that for those six years it provided "more fun than the law allows"—not Texas-type fun necessarily, but fun.

Texas-type fun of the male variety she encountered in 1971 on her first day at the legislature when she noticed "one ol' boy dig another in the ribs" and, with a wink, chortle, "Yew should see whut Ah found maself las' night! An' she don't talk, neither!" As for the legislatin', to others it might be shocking, but to her it was priceless grist for her satirical mill.

The job involved some networking, of course, and she made many friends, among them Ann Richards, the state's future Democratic governor. She collected people, one observer noted, as other people collect china. Indeed, she even made friends among the legislators, who might often get temporarily riled by her literary digs but who in general seemed flattered by the attention. ("Baby, yew put mah name in yore paper!") Eventually she concluded that maybe they *were* gentlemen after all, even conceding that "Texas politicians are unusually civilized people." (Oh, surely she didn't say *that*—unless she meant "very unusually.")

In 1976, offered five times her poverty-level salary, she accepted an offer from the *New York Times*. It's a great newspaper (that she knew), but now she found that "it is also No Fun." Since the Big Apple had nothing to compare with the Texas legislature, newsworthywise, she asked to be sent somewhere else. In 1977 the somewhere else turned out to be Denver, where she spent the next three years as chief of the Rocky Mountain bureau.

Still, it continued to be the good, grey *Times* that she was writing for, and the writing was subjected to much circumspect editing: her "beer gut," for instance, became the paper's "protuberant abdomen." The last straw was her description of a chicken-killing event as "a gang pluck." The *Times* said goodbye, and soon thereafter the *Dallas Times-Herald* said hello. Indeed, it "made me an offer I couldn't refuse": write about whatever you want in whatever way you want to. In Austin, where she set up camp to be near her beloved legislature, she found that the paper would keep its promise throughout the succeeding years—even after she wrote a particularly less than flattering piece about a Texas representative in Washington, including the comment, "If his IQ slips any lower, we'll have to water him twice a day." For quite a while her jibes and quips brought the paper a formidable number of ad- and subscription-cancellations, but before long the threats of the cancellations supporting her views began to outnumber those against her and have continued to do so.

As her reputation expanded, so did her horizons. The arrival of the Reagan-Bush deficit addicts lengthened her firing range to reach Washington. "Calling George Bush shallow is like calling a dwarf short." Her articles began appearing in national publications, ranging in variety from *TV Guide* and *The Reader's Digest* to *Playboy* and *The Progressive*, and *she* began appearing on television shows like PBS's *MacNeil/Lehrer News Hour*. In 1990 she took time off to write a serious book about Texas only to find that she just' couldn't bring herself to do it. And so she wrote another, not so serious, 1993's *Nothin' but Good Times Ahead*. A best-seller, of course.

People have told her that she's a very funny writer, but she protests modestly that "it's all in the material."

Anita Roddick
Successful Businesswoman (1942–)

The beauty business, she has declared, is hateful, "a monster industry selling unattainable dreams. It lies. It cheats. It exploits women." And so for the past twenty years her Body Shops have leveled with their customers, promising merely to "cleanse, polish, and protect the skin and hair" rather than suggesting that their cosmetics will transform drab despair into glamorous celebrity and ungovernable ecstasy. Anita Roddick's honesty has proved the best and highly profitable policy, what with more than 700 stores in more than 40 countries, including about 90 in the United States, racking up yearly sales in the hundreds of millions and profits in the tens of millions and making her one of Britain's half-dozen wealthiest women.

She was born in 1942 during World War II in the relatively peaceful town of Littlehampton, Sussex, by the ocean. Her family, including two older sisters and a younger brother, owned and operated a restaurant catering to fishermen, an enterprise that became especially demanding after the death of her mother's second husband (and her father). She focused her spare time on her high school homework, graduated most honorably, and enrolled at a drama school in the hope of a career in acting. But when her mother urged her to set her sights on the more respectable career of teaching, she decided that it too would entail some dramatics and so spent the next three years at a college of education.

A scholarship in 1962 dispatched her to Israel to study the condition of children in the kibbutzim. Her project was cut short when, as a prank, she laid a layer of stones immediately under the surface in a lake and persuaded a fellow student to walk miraculously, spectacularly on water. She devoted the rest of her visit to peripatetic and highly educational hitchhiking. After returning to Britain and doing some library work and some mutually invigorating teaching, she yielded to the itch of wanderlust and spent her next few years in thoroughly peripatetic fashion, ranging through Europe, the South Seas, and southern Africa.

Expelled from South Africa for the unforgivable sin of going to a Johannesburg jazz club on a blacks-only night, she returned home and established a cozy relationship with a soulmate, an equally itinerant poet named Gordon

Roddick, by whom she had a couple of daughters and whom she married in 1971. Their joint running of a hotel for several years proved too laborious and time-consuming, and they were thinking of seeking other ways of surviving when he decided that now was the time for him to spend the next two years doing something he'd always wanted to do, as the second person in history to ride horseback from Buenos Aires to New York.

Surviving thereupon became an especially urgent problem for her and the children. Drawing on her experience with the natural herbs and lotions of primitive peoples, and hocking her hotel for a loan of $6500, she hired a promising herbalist and in early 1976 opened her first Body Shop in affluent, tony Brighton. Her gift for substituting free publicity for expensive advertising showed up immediately in her handling of a complaint from the owners of the funeral parlor next door, who felt a degree of incongruity in proximity. After leaking their complaint to the press, she was engulfed in curiosity seekers, many if not most of whom turned into customers. The Body Shop was on its way, and she would never have to resort to advertising, unless her aboveboard listing of ingredients on her labels (not required in England) can be considered such.

That fall she opened her second Body Shop. By the time husband Gordon returned from his aborted horseback ride in the spring of 1977, customer demand had become so overwhelming that they decided to grant franchises to shop owners, mostly women, eager to join the bandwagon. Body Shops began appearing in Sweden, Belgium, Greece, all over the map. In 1984, when the company went public, its shares on the second day were selling for half again as much as on the first, and in eight years were worth almost a hundred times as much, with comparable growth anticipated for several years ahead.

Her business success has provided her with the time and the means to support environmental and other causes dear to her heart such as the ending or at least retarding of sea pollution, acid rain, ozone depletion, homelessness, child neglect. Her company employs many Third World workers but pays them First World wages. A recipient of many honors and awards, she expects to continue on course. "We will compromise on almost anything," she promised in her autobiography *Body and Soul* (written, one reviewer commented, "in the key of Me"), "but not on our values, or our aesthetics, or our idealism, or our sense of curiosity."

Accountable, responsible business people, she insists, can change the world.

Charlayne Hunter-Gault
Journalist (1942–)

She began aiming for it at the age of twelve and stayed on target. She was determined to be a journalist. Be practical, she was urged. What hope can a black woman have for a career in journalism? Go into teaching like a good girl. But no—she was going to be a journalist.

She was born Charlayne Hunter in February 1942 in the aptly named little town of Due West near the northwestern corner of South Carolina. She spent most of her young life in Covington, Georgia, and Atlanta. Although her father, a Methodist army chaplain, was often away from home, her devotedly literate mother was conscientious and resolute enough to make up for much of his absence in their daughter's life. In this she was helped greatly by a similarly constituted grandmother who had supplemented her own third-grade education with such omnivorous reading as to be a treasurehouse of varied information and intellectual stimulation—just the ticket for a young, aspiring journalist manqué. So were the frequent visits with that grandmother to New York, so different from Georgia and inhabited by people speaking an almost different language. Also educational were family moves with her peripatetic father to Florida, land of preposterous sunshine, and Alaska, land of preposterous snow.

At the age of sixteen, despite a family tradition of Protestant Christianity that even included more than a touch of strenuous evangelism, she became a Roman Catholic. (Catholics were "the only white people, by the way, ever to show any interest in us [blacks] at all.") Family astonishment in no way diminished family affection, which was fortified by her honors-level work in high school and her (much more interesting) editing of the school paper.

After her graduation in 1959 she wanted to enroll in the University of Georgia's journalism school. The university, however, jealously guarding intellectual values based in pigment, was off-limits to blacks. So she had a close friend, Hamilton Holmes, supported by family and friends and dedicated integrationists, ask a Federal court to issue an order for integration. During the ensuing delay she attended Ohio's Wayne State University, where segregation was limited to the dorms, but where Detroit permitted her, regardless of pigment, to visit its museums! In January 1961, backed by a Federal integration order and despite the governor's conniptions, she and Holmes enrolled at the University of Georgia, its first black students since its founding in 1785.

It was a national TV news event, what with the two of them being federally escorted about campus amid throngs of frustrated collegians stonily observing the proceedings with simian stares and occasional catcall commentary. The sophistication of the poetry created at the university was illustrated, for instance, by the cerebral chant, "Two, four, six, eight, we don' wanna integrate! Eight, six, four, two, we don' wan' no jigaboo!" Its ambiance of touching Christian charity found articulation in "Nigger, go home!" The frustration even reached a rock-throwing stage, although only briefly, and she was endangered, also briefly, by similar attention from an armed lunatic. For her it was an educational experience, she explained later: she had an opportunity to observe the techniques of experienced reporters covering the story. Her more formal line of study earned her a degree in journalism in 1963. On the side she worked for a student newspaper focusing on civil rights and, as a full-fledged celebrity, went on occasional speaking tours.

After graduation, armed with some summertime interning experience with the *Times* in Louisville and the *Inquirer* in Atlanta, she took a job as secretary for the *New Yorker*; she could type but was promised writing assignments. The promise was kept; in 1967, however, she was awarded a fellowship in social science at Washington University in St. Louis. In her spare time there she worked as an editor for the magazine *Trans-Action*, which sent her to cover the Poor People's Campaign in Washington. There, fatefully, she gained some television experience as an investigative reporter and anchor for the news division of the local TV station.

Her next job would prove more durable. In 1968 she moved back to New York and joined the *Times* for local coverage, especially of the black community. During her nine years with the paper (besides marrying her second husband, financier Ronald Gault, in 1971), she won several awards for her thorough, perceptive reporting on crime, politics, civil rights. These brought her to the attention of the producers of the Public Broadcasting System's *Mac-Neil/Lehrer Report* (later expanded to the *NewsHour*), which was and is designed to complement the commercial TV newscasts with some reporting in depth for its several million viewers. The program needed a third correspondent and fill-in anchor in 1978; she auditioned and was hired. She had come to stay.

Although the move put her in some pretty heady company, she has held her own ever since. Robert MacNeil has praised her ability to say "simple, relevant things at the right moment." Her interviews with politician nabobs and other celebrities, her adroit reporting of the Pope's 1979 visit to America, her coverage of New York crime, her newscasts from Grenada after The Great Invasion and from Saudi Arabia during The Great Persian Gulf War, her reports on racial tensions in South Africa, her pieces on health problems among the poor, especially infant mortality—such work has brought her much flattering recognition and many awards, among them the American Society of University Women's Woman of Achievement Award.

Meanwhile black enrollment at the University of Georgia has risen giddily to six percent.

Marcelite Jordan Harris
Brigadier General (1943–)

She did so want to be an actress. Touring with the USO as a college student in the 1960s, majoring in speech and drama, she contracted a thespian urge that has never left her entirely. Even today, after more than a quarter century as an Air Force officer, she concedes that she'd "die to be in a movie." Yet the career she chose involved quite a different kind of command performances.

She was born Marcelite Jordan in January 1943 in Houston. She and her sister and brother capped a long line of achievers, including a great-great-grandfather who was a mayor and state senator in Louisiana and a great-grandfather who was a prominent educator in Texas, founder of Fort Worth's first school for black students. Her father, a postal supervisor, and her mother, a librarian, provided a respect for learning and an urge for achievement.

After her graduation from high school in 1960 she attended Spelman College in Atlanta, where she earned her B.A. in speech and drama in 1964, followed in later years by a B.A. in business management from the University of Maryland. In the fall of '65 after a cold, hard look at the show-biz rat race, she opted for the Air Force. Women would eventually constitute about a ninth of Air Force personnel, about a quarter of them officers. Given her education and natural ability, an Air Force career looked pretty promising.

By early 1967 she was in West Germany, administrative officer for a missile squadron at Bitsburg, and a couple of years later was transferred to a tactical fighter wing as maintenance analysis officer, also at Bitsburg. Back home in 1971, after an intensive course in aircraft maintenance, she was shipped to Thailand as supervisor of maintenance for a fighter squadron. Back home again two years later, after a hitch as a job control officer, she was assigned to Travis Air Force Base in California to supervise field maintenance for an air refueling unit. Two years after that, in 1975, she was called to Washington to serve as a personnel staff officer at Air Force Headquarters, which showed its confidence in her savoir faire by lending her to the White House, where she acted for a while as a social aide to the First Family.

In the spring of '78 she was sent to Colorado Springs, where she was given her first formal command on something of a trial basis, perhaps, since the unit was a cadet squadron at the Air Force Academy. In July 1980 it was back to maintenance, at a base in Kansas, but after that she began getting commands of maintenance squadrons. After a hitch with a logistics support center in Japan and another command job in Mississippi, in 1988 she was made the first woman wing commander in Air Training Command. Two years later, as a new brigadier general (and the Air Force's first black female general officer), she joined the Oklahoma City Air Logistics Center at Tinker Air Force Base as vice commander.

The job obviously was, and is, a responsible one, assisting the base commander in discharging the Center's mission of properly maintaining all aircraft—including the latest fighters and bombers and their weapons and other associated hardware—and thus giving any potential attacker encouragement for sober second thought. Thus the job involved motivating and supervising the more than twenty thousand military personnel and civilian workers at the

Center, as well as filling in for the commander in his absence. With her "kind of contagious energy and enthusiasm" and her "wealth of experience," he has remarked, he has had no qualms about her ability to handle the job when he's away. "She's an excellent role model," he has said (without any gender distinctions), "for people in and out of uniform."

She and her husband Marice Anthony Harris, a retired Air Force officer, have a son in college and a daughter entering her teens. Out of uniform, with her shapely form encased in an attractive blue dress and her face wreathed with an infectious grin, she's still a much-decorated brigadier general. But one would never guess it.

Faith Popcorn
Market Forecaster (1943–)

Okay, that's not the name she was born with, which is or was, Plotkin. A tongue-tied boss who couldn't pronounce the name eventually settled whimsically on Popcorn, and she came to like *that* name enough to make it legal in 1969. It certainly individualized her, and if a name like Holly Golightly could be such an asset...

She was born Faith Beryl Plotkin in May 1943 in Manhattan. She and her younger sister, daughters of two very busy lawyers, were raised mainly by her mother's parents, who lived nearby and whose ownership and maintenance of some tenement housing, and whose promoting of their clothing store gave their observant elder granddaughter her first lessons in marketing and personnel management. She absorbed them unconsciously, however, preferring the stage to the marketplace. To get there she studied theater in high school and at New York University, yet upon graduation in 1966 she took a job in advertising, fortunately a field in which her Thespian experience would do her no harm at all.

She spent the next eight years with the advertising company that hired her, acquiring the title of creative director as well as a new and arresting surname. She enjoyed the work, but in 1974 she and an office associate decided to strike out on their own. They did, but they didn't strike out. Their first impulse was to promote truth in advertising, but on sober second thought they concluded that the avidly consuming public wasn't quite ready for anything that radical. And so they organized a company, BrainReserve, peopled by imaginative commercial types who could advise businesses on plans and procedures for meeting consumer demand. Plans required some forecasting of future consumer needs and wants, which the imaginative ones (90 percent women, including her sister) provided from an analysis of nothing less than what she has called "a confluence of psycho-socio-demographic-economic factors." Their calls were accurate enough to build a reputation, and by 1984 BrainReserve was clearly a great success, permitting her to buy out her male partner amicably and to take the helm, as well as earning her the moniker, bestowed by *Fortune* magazine, of "The Nostradamus of Marketing."

For the 1990s BrainReserve predicted accurately, for example, the popularity of salt-free foods, a demand for sporty yet dependable automobiles, fewer divorces and more attention to family, increasing desertions from the rat race, less emphasis on carefree youth, and a trend from evenings out to evenings in (TV, VCRs, etc.). Her estimate of the "New Coke" advertising effort as the marketing disaster it was garnered her plenty of favorable publicity and encouraged her to claim that 95 percent of the firm's predictions were right on the money, although her expectation of a Dukakis victory in 1988 suggested that political marketing might not be her forte. In this connection she also predicted a "Decency Decade" for the 1990s, characterized by a concerted drive by young people to force more national attention to "the three critical E's: environment, education, and ethics," a drive as yet inconspicuous if not inchoate.

Despite criticism that some of its forecasting amounted to laboring the obvious, the firm continued to prosper, counseling an ever-lengthening list of blue-chip satisfied customers. Among these was Bacardi Imports, which took her advice and introduced the Bacardi Breezer, a fruit juice spiked lightly with rum. Within twelve exhilarating months the drink was selling enough to make it the country's third most popular alcoholic beverage. As other firms jumped on the lucrative bandwagon, she was accused once again of setting a trend rather than predicting it, as though in business the difference was important.

For its forecasting BrainReserve relies chiefly on the contents of several hundred newspapers as well as on popular books, movies, music, and video shows. For clairvoyant explication it resorts to its accumulated computer bank of some two thousand assorted experts. Its clients receive "Trendpacks," six of them each year, offering a collection of items symbolic of a major current matter of interest, from physical exercise to the Gulf War. And in 1991 her book, largely a product of her inveterate networking and diffidently titled *The Popcorn Report: Faith Popcorn on the Future of Your Company, Your World, Your Life*, warned businesses that, with a "socioquake" impending, they'd better take her trend-forecasting seriously or be left out in the unmarketable cold. And so they, mostly, take it very seriously indeed.

She doesn't claim to be infallible. But she does keep in mind the cautionary shibboleth, reputedly coined by Casey Stengel, that the future ain't what it used to be.

Billie Jean King
Tennis Champion (1943–)

Billie Jean Moffit was a tomboy. She was the only girl in her neighborhood who played football, and she could, and regularly would, tackle hard enough for the boys to be glad when her mother called her home. She played softball so expertly that the local firemen invited her to play shortstop and third base on their team. But because her tomboy reputation bothered her a bit, she told her parents that she'd like to find a game which would be challenging but in which she'd be considered a lady. Her father suggested tennis. "What's tennis?" she asked.

He told her, and she spent most of her leisure time thereafter on the public tennis courts of Long Beach, California, where she'd been born in November 1943. It was fun, and after she started taking lessons from the park coach it was even more fun—especially at the net. The coach ultimately persuaded her that she'd have to learn to play at the back of the court too, and she did (obviously), but that line close to the net would always be her favorite place. Even though her 20/400 vision meant wearing those unprecedented glasses on the court all her life, she was hooked on tennis.

She trained and trained, serving to hit a particular spot across the net, returning her own serves against a backboard, walking some seven miles to and from school each day to strengthen her legs. After six months of this she entered a tournament for the first time, at age eleven. It was a tournament for girls, and she was told that she wouldn't be allowed to play in a T-shirt and shorts: girls have to wear tennis dresses. Resentfully, she changed to a dress and signed up.

She didn't do very well. Her style was too vigorous, causing her to play sucker to the other girls' sly restraint. She kept up her assiduous training and learning, and four years later she tasted victory in her first national tournament for young girls in Ohio. State funding for such trips was available only for boys, but her performance inspired some Long Beach fans to provide the travel money, and so off she went to Ohio. This time her game was better, though not good enough to take her into the semifinals.

The next year, however, she entered the national tournament for older girls (16–18) and made it to the finals, losing only to 17-year-old Karen Hantze. If you can't beat 'em, join 'em: the next year, 1961, she and Hantze traveled to England and won the women's doubles at Wimbledon, the youngest pair ever to do so. In 1962 they did it again, and in the singles competition she fell just short of the semifinals.

Back home, at college in Los Angeles, she began seeing quite a bit of a law student named Larry King. He proved to be a serious distraction but not enough to keep her from playing at Wimbledon again in 1963. This time she made it to the finals but lost to Margaret Smith of Australia, who analyzed her game and gave her some daunting advice: practice even harder. That left her in a quandary because Larry had asked her to marry him, and she was ready to settle into a homemaking routine. The quandary evaporated, however, when he told her that she had great talent and a promising career. She ought to pursue it. It didn't have to interfere with their marriage; he could act as her manager. They were married in September 1965.

But first she spent three rigorous months in Australia in training with a highly reputable coach, a hard taskmaster who enormously improved her stamina, her breathing, and her return strokes (less swinging, greater control). Nevertheless, in 1965 at Wimbledon she lost again in the finale to Margaret Smith, although afterward she felt that she had come *that close*. Sure enough, in 1966 she beat Smith in the semifinals and Maria Bueno of Brazil in the finals to become that year's Wimbledon champion at the age of 22. And the following year she won three titles: singles, doubles, and mixed doubles. The trophies were almost too much to handle. But she managed, quite cheerfully.

Later that year she made the same triple play at Forest Hills, earning the status of the world's top-ranked female amateur tennis player. This seemed a good time to turn professional, but there was a catch. Although professional playing could be very lucrative, pros were barred from the world's principal tournaments. Her timing, however, proved extraordinary, for in 1968 the bar was officially lifted. She turned pro and not only won again at Wimbledon but also won the championship of Australia in a kind of ultimate triumph.

She was gradually becoming aware that the sport harbored a good deal of sex discrimination. Not only were the men's cash prizes much larger, but male facilities were much better—for a massage, for instance, she had to go to the men's locker room, eyes averted in maidenly consternation. In May 1970, after winning a Roman tournament, she watched the winning male accept his $7500 prize before receiving her own prize of $600. That tore it. She complained to Larry, who recommended that she join in the current move to organize women's pro tournaments for respectable cash prizes. In 1971 she joined a tour sponsored by Virginia Slims cigarettes (oops!) and won prizes totaling more than $100,000, more than any woman and few men had ever won.

In 1973 her reputation brought her a challenge from a man, Bobby Riggs, a noted Wimbledon champion who, at 55, was still a smart, energetic, formidable tennis player. Here's your chance, he insisted, to prove your contention that women players are as good as men. Actually, what she had said was that women could draw as good crowds, and so she declined. He then challenged Margaret Smith. She accepted, and on Mother's Day he won so handily that the match became known among the hairy chested as the Mother's Day Massacre.

Again he challenged Billie Jean. Women were vulnerable, he maintained, because "they always choke" in a pinch. This time she found his attitude, and the prize of $100,000, irresistible. It was a night game, under the lights of the Houston Astrodome, watched by 30,000 spectators and some 50 million TV viewers, the largest audience ever for a game of tennis. The promoters played it for spectacle, with her entering on a feather-bedecked throne carried aloft by four sinewy Adonises, followed by him in a rickshaw pulled by five nubile Aphrodites, after which he handed her a huge lollipop and she gave him a small male (chauvinist) pig. Then they took their places on the court, and she creamed him in straight sets.

Not long thereafter she won again at Wimbledon and was elected president of the Women's Tennis Association, which she had helped to organize for dealing with tournament pooh-bahs and television moguls. Before her legs gave out in the early 1980s she would win a record twenty championships at Wimbledon. By then, rather than submit to blackmail, she had gone public concerning her bisexuality—announcing, as she put it in her autobiography, that "yes, I had an affair while I was married, and it was with a woman."

She was afraid of what the revelation would do to her reputation and to women's tennis, but, as she also put it in her autobiography, rather ironically, she decided to "take it like a man." The revelation did do her and her loyal husband some damage financially, but she found the judgmental coterie quite limited. It was especially heartening for her when, as she came out on court for an exhibition match in San Diego, a conservative stronghold, she was greeted with a standing ovation.

Cokie Roberts
Political Commentator (1943–)

From the women who write to her, Cokie Roberts has observed, "I get the feeling that the country is full of women who've never gotten a word in edgewise when the men talk politics."

That wasn't much of a problem for the women in her family, into which she was born in New Orleans in December 1943. Her father was Hale Boggs, Louisiana's very Democratic majority leader in the U.S. House of Representatives; after his disappearance in the skies over Alaska in 1972 her mother Lindy, his campaign manager, replaced him in the House and stayed there until she retired in 1990. ("One or the other of my parents sat in Congress for fifty years.") Her sister Barbara served for seven years as mayor of Princeton, New Jersey, until her tragic death from cancer in 1990, and her brother Thomas is a very active and controversial Washington lobbyist. At the dinner table, or anywhere else in the house, the talk was politics, and tender age was no barrier to participation. Corinne—her name was mangled into "Cokie" by her little brother—joined enthusiastically in the general hubbub, and she's been talking politics ever since.

One reason is that in 1962, on her way to a B.A. in 1964 from Wellesley College, she met Steven Roberts, editor of the *Harvard Crimson*, at a student conference. She found him smart, funny, cute, and easily political enough to be lovable, and so she fell in love. So did he, surely for much the same reasons. Their attachment, despite some consternation in his Jewish and her Catholic family, culminated in 1966 in a wedding embellished by the attendance of President Lyndon Johnson and an overflow delegation from Congress.

After graduation she had spent two years as a local TV producer and news anchor, but during the later sixties and early seventies she played willingly dutiful wife and mother of two, accompanying her husband (with children) on his assignments overseas as a correspondent for the *New York Times*. Generally she stuck to her role as traveling homemaker, although when a political coup occurred in Greece in 1974 she couldn't resist filing a report—which wound up featured prominently on CBS's *Evening News*. However, when the *Times* assigned him to a less peripatetic post (not *Post!*) in Washington, virtually her hometown and hotbed of her favorite subject, she signed up with National Public Radio and started making an enviable reputation for herself with her incisive reporting from the Capital, at first for *Morning Edition* and then also for *The MacNeil/Lehrer News Hour*. Before long she was a regular on another PBS political-news show, *The Lawmakers*, and her fee for lecturing on her favorite subject was approaching $20,000. What more could a talented political junkie ask?

One thing she could ask was to be invited by ABC to appear on David Brinkley's *This Week* with the genially bumptious Sam Donaldson and the amiably acerbic George Will. She didn't ask, but she was invited anyway, and countless women have enjoyed watching her hold her own in competitively assertive conversations. Eventually, that is: at first they had to write in complaining that the "token girl" (her term) was being persistently interrupted. That gave her incentive to give as good as she got, and thereafter, whenever she failed to appear on the show letters arrived asking, "Where's Cokie?" Obviously, to quote the show's executive producer, "she added a spark." (She's become known for her risible chuckle.) One Sunday morning, for example, when the discussion centered on the need for a certain government official to be "taken to the woodshed," the ever-curious Brinkley asked if anyone knew the real meaning of the expression. After Donaldson announced that he knew its meaning because of his many visits there as a child with his mother, Cokie suggested with a grin that there clearly hadn't been enough such visits. One gets the impression that if he'd been *her* child...

With her boy and girl now in their twenties and her husband comfortably ensconced as a senior writer for *U.S. News & World Report* and regular panel member on PBS's durable *Washington Week in Review*, she has found time to fill in quite often for Ted Koppel on ABC's *Nightline*. Oh, yes, and for appearances on frothier offerings like *Entertainment Tonight* and Dave Letterman's relief hour for insomniacs. Be she serious or frivolous, male fans, she says, seem to like her commonsense approach to politics. Women fans seem to like her commonsense approach to men. After all, that's merely what they are. Just men.

Sharon Pratt Kelly
Mayor, District of Columbia (1944–)

"Government, by nature," she has observed a bit ruefully, "moves slowly. I am, by nature, impatient, so nothing is moving as rapidly as I would like." Crime, corruption, Congress and corrosive poverty have made, are making, the city of Washington what it is. A mayor determined to improve things—including this first black woman to be mayor of a principal U.S. city—has to work through a city council and the U.S. Congress, who furnish the molasses.

She was born Sharon Pratt in January 1944 in that city, the older of two daughters of a partner in the law firm of Pratt and Queen. After her mother's death in 1948 she and her sister lived with their grandmother and an aunt, but the matronly ambiance didn't keep her from daily baseball practice in emulation of her hero Satchel Paige. As for formal education, her elementary mediocrity was transformed into high school preeminence (straight As and the senior-class presidency), leading to a BA and then, in 1968, a JD from Howard University. As an undergraduate she majored, significantly if somewhat prematurely, in political science.

In 1967 she married a fellow student, Arrington L. Dixon, and, after receiving the JD, settled down into a role of helpmate, homemaker, and mother of two daughters. He had some political ambitions, leading to membership in and then the presidency of the Washington city council, attained with considerable wifely support. In 1971 she joined her father's law firm and spent five years in part-time private practice, teaching law on the side at a local college. In 1976 she took a job with a local utility, starting off as associate general counsel. Within three years she was director of consumer affairs and, within six, a vice president, the first black woman to hold that exalted position in the firm.

As vice president of consumer affairs, she was inevitably involved in government regulation and in lobbying, a highly political activity. This wasn't entirely unfamiliar territory. She had already been elected, in 1976, to the District's Democratic State Committee and, a year later, to the Democratic National Committee. A few years after that she became the Party's treasurer, the first woman and the first black to fill that treasured position. As is so often the case, her political activity was hard on her marriage, which ended in divorce in 1982.

That was the year also of her entry into District electoral politics, in support of Patricia Roberts Harris's campaign to thwart the reelection of Marion S. Barry, Jr., by running against him. Although the campaign proved an exercise in futility, it obviously was an acute educational experience that could become valuable if opportunity happened to knock some day.

Meanwhile she, along with many others, was becoming increasingly concerned over reports of the city's alarming deterioration: a rising financial deficit, a frightening increase in crime, a ballooning municipal bureaucracy, and rumors of rampant corruption in city hall, even involving drug dealing. In April 1989, having decided that somebody should do something, almost anything, about the situation, she volunteered by quitting her job to run for mayor, although the mayoral salary of $90,705 was less than two-thirds of her utility salary. Besides Barry, three experienced members of the city council were also running, and even after Barry's resignation during his trial for possession of cocaine, she remained at the bottom of the electoral totem pole. Underfunded, unknown to most potential voters, and even opposed by some overzealously black activists because of her light skin color, she was running conspicuously behind by a discouraging number of furlongs. Even an endorsement by the Coalition of Concerned Citizens for a Better D.C. seemed to make no difference.

Taking advantage of her lack of name recognition, she began presenting herself as a new broom—indeed, as a new shovel—who for starters would clean out all that bureaucratic deadwood. The tactic—embroidered with her invigorating oratory and her petite charisma (at 5'2", "I'd be a perfect size 6 if it weren't for these hips!")—seemed to work. In the November 1990 election she won spectacularly (86 percent of a record turnout), evidently profiting from voter discontent with things *in situ*. Her inaugural address in January 1991 was full of pledges to loosen up traffic congestion and the gridlock in housing availability, to control air pollution, to get a handle on gun possession and drug dealing, to confront a niggardly Congress. Yet to her dismay, on her first day in her office she discovered that "nothing worked"—not the elevators, not the phones, not the ventilation system, nothing.

Within her first three months she used that situation to extract a hundred million dollars in emergency funds from a cautiously closefisted yet admiring Congress. Her success at extraction, however, alienated some of the city council, ever jealous of its administrative prerogatives and thus wary of strings attached to any Congressional largesse. Nor did her honeymoon with the Congress prove very durable: in the fall of 1992 that fickle assembly not only cut her proposed budget by $42 million but also began throwing its weight around, denying unmarried city workers health insurance for their live-in partners, demanding a referendum on that instrument of vengeance, the death penalty (in which the voters vetoed the death penalty). By that time her marriage to businessman James Kelly III, in late 1991, was providing gratifying moral support.

Not one to be intimidated by controversy, she proposed in the summer of 1992 a million-dollar-plus plan for the distribution, by specially trained medics, of condoms in Washington's high schools (junior and senior) and in its jails, and of clean hypodermic needles to drug abusers scheduled for therapy. With 70 percent of the city's tenth-graders sexually active or overactive and with long waiting lists for drug-abuse treatment, adversarial appeals for abstinence in either situation seemed somehow irrelevant.

The city deficit, the crime rate, the problems of poverty and homelessness, in a city starved of adequate funds, remained undented. Yet she remained undaunted.

In the fall of 1994, however, being undaunted wasn't enough. Washington's voters replaced her with a popular former three-term mayor and passionately admired ex-convict named Anwar Amal, né Marion Barry.

Nina Totenberg
Outstanding Broadcast Journalist (1944–)

PBS, the public radio-television network, employs, particularly for its national radio broadcasts, one of Washington's most effective networkers, whose news sources provide her with the kind of leaks that make the national government, as she has described it, "a sieve." At the Supreme Court, her principal beat, her news gathering has been no great source of comfort to some of its august membership.

Nina Totenberg was born in January 1944 in New York City and raised with her younger sisters by mother Melanie and father Roman, a concert violinist. After a conventional elementary and high school education, she attended Boston University but, succumbing to the irresistible lure of journalism, dropped out early to take a newspaper job in Boston (making up for it in the 1980s with honorary degrees from Gonzaga and Northeastern universities). In 1968, offered a job by the late *National Observer*, she moved to Washington, where among other things her profile of the FBI's J. Edgar Hoover enraged that formidable autocrat, who wrote the paper an intemperate letter demanding her dismissal. She'd done her homework, however, and her editors backed her up by simply publishing the rather repellent letter. The backup, unfortunately, apparently was accompanied by some sexual harassment, followed by her departure. At the (also late) *New Times*, where she worked between 1972 and 1975, she continued dipping her pen in acid, her most celebrated article carrying the title, "The Ten Dumbest Members of Congress." (She had to stop somewhere, and the number ten kept the article from interminability.)

In 1975 she moved to PBS and has been with that network ever since as its legal correspondent, joining other journalists willing to forego superfluously high incomes for influence and prestige. Focusing her largely unwelcome scrutiny on the decisions and indecisions of the Supreme Court, she nonetheless didn't neglect Congress, especially the Senate, and most especially the Senate Judiciary Committee, with its advise-and-consent power in considering candidates for the judiciary. She covered the Watergate trials, the imbroglio connected with the nomination of G. Harrold Carswell to the Court, the Iran-contra caper, the controversy over Chief Justice William Rehnquist's record, and the Oliver North and Robert Bork hearings, among other things. In 1987, when the committee was considering Ronald Reagan's nomination of Douglas Ginsburg to the Court, she discovered and reported that he had smoked marijuana at Harvard, not as a student but as a professor. He withdrew his name most circumspectly.

But it was of course George Bush's nomination of Clarence Thomas that brought her most forcibly to national attention. The Administration advocates, aware of his shortcomings in the department of legal experience, and of his embarrassing American Bar Association rating (the lowest in the Court's history), were emphasizing his sterling character. And so it was with considerable chagrin that they heard or read about her story of Anita Hill's affidavit charging Thomas with sexual harassment during their office association at the Department of Labor and the Equal Employment Opportunities Commission.

The story, breaking just two days before the committee expected to vote to confirm Thomas, created the turmoil which anyone with a TV set at the time surely must remember. To this day she doesn't know "if it was good or bad to have the story out," but she felt it would have been a dereliction of duty to sit on it, especially since the Hill affidavit seemed to be the object of the committee's studied neglect. Her own experience of sexual harassment, she maintained, was essentially irrelevant: "Mine was physical, hers was not." She also maintained that the story brought her considerable verbal abuse, particularly from Wyoming's competitively acidulous Alan Simpson, to which she replied in kind.

The publicity spotlight brought her other forms of verbal abuse as well, resurrecting stories that she had had an affair with Justice Potter Stewart, among others, allegations evidently arising out of the envy of some male colleagues who refused to accept that her scoops could be the result of mere perspicacity, hard work, and/or good luck. (Justice Lewis Potter had once remarked that "she takes great care to get the facts straight.") She was accused also of plagiarism (one instance) and marijuana-smoking (one puff), but her reputation survived without serious injury. It has, for example, earned her a contract for appearance on ABC's *Nightline*, as well as awards for "outstanding broadcast journalism" and "protecting public access to governmental information."

One person who found the committee's neglect of the Hill affidavit "outrageous" was the 75-year-old, vigorously healthy novelist and former Senator from Colorado, Floyd Haskell, whom she had married in 1979. Her description of him as "very dignified and restrained" may have encouraged Totenberg-watchers to conclude that the marriage had gradually dulcified her, but she insists that advancing maturity has made her not only older but also wiser and therefore nicer. At least until the next judicial or political dustup.

Mary Robinson
Ireland's First Woman President (1944–)

In a society dominated by professionally celibate males intent on regulating other people's sex lives and pietism, Mary Robinson is a phenomenon. Not only is she an opponent of thought control and an outspoken advocate for women and gays, but she's also Ireland's first woman President.

She was born Mary Terese Winifred Bourke in May 1944 in County Mayo. Both her genteel parents were doctors and all of her four vigorous siblings were boys. Being so heavily outnumbered may well have inspired her ambition to become a lawyer, preferably a lawyer like her hero grandfather, with his "passionate commitment to justice." To that end, after sound schooling in both Eire and France, she enrolled at the law school of Dublin's Trinity College, despite parental disapproval and clerical fulminations against that Protestant-riddled institution. Sure enough, not only did she study uncanonized law but she even met a Protestant classmate and, in 1970, married him. Her parents were not at the wedding. But they did become reconciled, especially since the marriage proved very successful.

Before that wedding, however, she had earned her law degree from Trinity in 1967 and then had spent a year at Harvard for her master's, a year of American political turmoil that she found exciting and enlightening. On her return to Ireland she began teaching law at Trinity, the youngest person ever to do so. Almost immediately she became frustrated, not by her teaching load but by the fact that the college's three seats in the Sinead, Ireland's senate, were regularly held by crusty old codgers. Having joined the left-leaning Labour Party, without further ado she submitted her name and, in 1969, became the country's youngest senator as well as the first Catholic member from Trinity. She would continue as a member of the Sinead for the next two decades, partly because she was defeated twice in races for the lower house.

Although much less powerful than the lower house, the senate gave her opportunities to promote her outrageously liberal causes, including equal treatment for women in employment, divorce, day care, birth control. To legalize divorce would require a constitutional amendment, and in 1976 she initiated legislation for that purpose. It was an exercise in futility: ten years later the submissive electorate reapproved the ban on divorce in a national referendum.

She had a life beyond the Sinead, practicing law in not only Irish but also European courts, stoutly arguing against the imprisonment of gays, the perpetuation of laws against divorce and contraception, the tapping of journalists' phones, the ostracizing of the illegitimate. As for abortion, although she found it personally objectionable, she worked for wider dissemination of information about it. As a result of all this public advocacy, her hate mail luxuriated, with occasional pointed enclosures, such as condoms, including used condoms, unsigned.

She was similarly unorthodox in the controversy over the fate of Northern Ireland. When a tentative peace pact was concluded in 1985, she joined none other than the Protestant fire-brand Ian Paisley in vigorously protesting the pact's neglect of Protestant interests. Since the Labour Party had supported it, she left the party.

She had loyal supporters in the party, however, and in April 1990 it unexpectedly entered her in the race for the Presidency of Ireland, a post that had been in the grip of the Republican Party for as long as anyone could remember. The compliment left her unenthralled. Should she devote a lot of her time and effort to run a losing race for a post that is more shadow than substance? But then maybe she could make more of it than that. The decision took some agonizing, but in the end she decided to try.

And try she did, touring the country thriftily by car over the next six months, four times as long as conventionally expected, and characteristically choosing Simon and Garfunkel's "Here's to You, Mrs. Robinson" as her theme song. A slim, pretty woman, she dolled up her appearance and tried appeasing the righteous with family interviews. By October the polls showed a third of the voters on her side. Shortly thereafter her main adversary, Republican Brian Lenihan, cooperated by getting publicly identified as an influence peddler, being summarily fired from the government, and precipitously dropping in the polls. His party, unable to replace him on short notice with someone electable, desperately attacked Robinson as an abortion provocateur and as a woman whose ambition had led to the neglect of her three children. The vicious attack proved effective enough to restore Lenihan's political fortunes, resulting in a victory for him on election day with 44 percent of the vote to her 39 percent.

That, however, was a plurality, not a majority, and it required a runoff, although not in the American sense. Voters were required to make a first and second choice, the latter being peculiarly determining in the absence of a majority winner. After the second-choice votes were tallied she was declared the winner, 53–47. She hailed the result as "a great, great day for the women of Ireland," many of whom, it turned out, including conservative women, had voted for her without even asking for their husbands' permission. Soon afterward the Republican Prime Minister promised to get the punitive antigay legislation repealed and to take another look at that constitutional prohibition of divorce.

Unfortunately, he didn't last long enough in office. But she flourished in office, attaining an 85 percent approval rating before her first year was out. When a 14-year-old rape victim was refused permission to cross over to England for an abortion, she spoke up, and the girl was allowed to go to England. She continues to use her politically powerless office to exert a powerful influence.

"A society that is without the voice and vision of women," she has said, "is not less feminine. It is less human." And it's pretty clear that the women of Ireland have a wild Irish rose in the bully pulpit.

Antonia Novello
Surgeon General (1944–)

Language like this about a major American industry hadn't been heard from anyone in a Republican administration for years, if ever, although Surgeons General had been warning of the perils of nicotine for the past three decade. For this Surgeon General, appointed by none other than George Bush, charged that "the self-serving, death-dealing tobacco industry and their soldiers of fortune, advertising agencies" were slyly seducing children into the tobacco habit with ads featuring appealing cartoon characters like Joe Camel. "This is an industry," she continued in the same vein, "that kills four hundred thousand per year, and they have got to pick up new customers." She hadn't gotten the message from her free-entrepreneurial colleagues that this is the American Way. Spokesmen for the industry genially assured the media that their ads were aimed merely at getting already addicted adults to switch brands. Tobacco moguls *love* little children.

Antonia Coello Novello was born in August 1944 in Puerto Rico. After her father's death eight years later, she and her two siblings were raised by their school-principal mother and electrician stepfather. By that time she was constantly sick, suffering from a congenital colon problem requiring surgery, which was performed belatedly in her nineteenth year and through several operations thereafter. Yet she was lucky in being treated by capable, caring doctors and nurses whose solicitous treatment of her inspired her into wanting to become a physician.

With her mother's enthusiastic encouragement—a profession could provide a young person with an escape hatch from the Puerto Rican doldrums—she earned a B.S. at the University of Puerto Rico in 1965 and her M.D. in 1970. After graduation she married a naval flight surgeon, Joseph Novello, and happily accompanied him to the University of Michigan Medical Center, where she took postgraduate training in pediatrics while he did likewise in psychiatry. In her first year there she earned the department's title of Intern of the Year. The next year, after a severe attack of kidney trouble, she decided to become a specialist in pediatric nephrology. Indeed, she developed something of an addiction to postgraduate training, transferring to the Georgetown University Hospital in Washington, D.C., for further education in nephrology and then to the Johns Hopkins University School of Public Health in Baltimore to take classes in health services administration and eventually to receive, in 1982, a master's in public health. Five years later she completed a course offered to senior managers in government by Harvard's Kennedy School of Government.

By that time she was indeed a senior manager in government. In 1978, after a couple of emotionally draining years in private practice, she had tried to join her husband in the navy but had been rebuffed by a sea dog of a captain who stressed that what the navy needed was "a few good *men*." And so she turned to the U.S. Public Health Service, which hired her as a project officer in the National Institutes of Health. By 1986 her performance had earned her an appointment as deputy director of the National Institute of Child Health and Human Development and eligibility for that Harvard program.

Besides fulfilling her internal responsibilities, for example in pediatric AIDS and women's health programs, the deputy director acted as liaison with Oren Hatch's Senate Committee on Labor and Human Resources, contributing her expertise to the drafting of legislation, including laws requiring warning labels on cigarette packages. This political assignment, in addition to her frequent articles and her many commendations and awards, brought her some flattering name-recognition, and in the fall of 1989 she was appointed to replace the retiring (yet anything but retiring) Surgeon General C. Everett Koop, who shared her, and the Bush Administration's, disapproval of abortion. (Her attitude was influenced by her realization that, because of her congenitally defective colon, *she* might have been aborted.)

Far more experienced in public health administration than Koop at the time of his appointment, she was readily confirmed by the Senate. As not only the first woman but also the first Hispanic and first Puerto Rican to be Surgeon General (with the rank, ironically, of vice admiral), she welcomed her new status as part of the American Dream. "I might say that today *West Side Story* comes to the West Wing." As a woman she was particularly concerned with protecting the health of children, and this is what led to her fulminations against the tobacco industry's tactics to seduce the young, although as a Republican she was, of course, limited to relying on the industry's generous self-restraint. She became similarly exercised over the liquor industry's use of ads featuring "physically appealing, strong, attractive" people engaging in perilous sports and thus "making drinking look like the way to fun and a wonderful and carefree lifestyle." Prevented by her philosophical milieu from recommending any government restraints, she urged self-imposed restraint on the industry, which of course denied that the ads had any influence on young people.

Tobacco and alcohol were not her only concerns. The effects on children of domestic violence, the neglect of vaccinations and prenatal care, the spread of AIDS, serious injury (600,000 children a year, especially on farms), and the poor quality of health care for Hispanics were among her major worries. Yet there was a basic contradiction in her situation, implied in her husband's description of her as "where Mother Teresa meets Margaret Thatcher." It was a contradiction destined to evaporate for her with the departure of the Bush Administration.

Wilma Mankiller
Indian Chief (1945–)

Three hundred years ago the women of the Cherokee people played a prominent role in the tribal government, but with the coming of the white despoilers they were soon put in their place. Only in recent years have they begun to reappear in positions of influence, as exemplified by Wilma Mankiller, who in December 1985 became not only influential but also the first woman chief of an important Native American tribe.

She was born in November 1945 in Tahlequah, Oklahoma, to a Dutch-Irish mother and a pure-blooded Cherokee father with a surname inherited from a warrior tradition. A hundred years earlier that tradition had been overwhelmed by white warriors with better weapons, and the dispossessed Cherokees had been force-marched from southern Appalachia into northeastern Oklahoma, where those still living were magnanimously granted a parcel of land about the size of New Jersey. There she lived as a child on a small family farm in miserable poverty somewhat alleviated by rural serenity until 1957, when a relentless drought and a "mainstreaming" relocation program under the Bureau of Indian Affairs combined to move them west to San Francisco and introduce them to the lonely joys of minority life in a big city. Not surprisingly, many Native Americans objected to this mistreatment and in 1969 occupied Alcatraz Island in a protest demonstration that lasted a year and a half. One of her first functions as a social activist was raising money in their behalf.

By then she had accumulated some formal education in sociology at San Francisco State University and some experience as a social worker, and she had also married and borne two children. The spirit of the Alcatraz protest had deeply affected her, however, and in the mid–1970s she filed for divorce and took her children back to Oklahoma. There she reclaimed the family farm, built a small house, and in 1977 was hired by the Cherokee nation authorities as a coordinator of economic development. Thus encouraged, she earned a degree in social science from the Flaming Rainbow University and in 1979 enrolled in a program of graduate courses in community planning at the University of Arkansas (with time out to recover from an almost fatal but undaunting auto accident).

The Indians' severe economic problems, she had decided, would have to be solved by Indians. To that end she began accelerating the nation's economic development, establishing a Community Development Department of the Cherokee Nation and, in 1981, becoming its director.

As such she honed her skills in writing proposals for Federal grants, one of which permitted development of a community project called The Cherokee Gardens, which became a profitable nursery, and another that provided the central village with a water system and a number of rebuilt homes. Her effectiveness attracted the attention of the chief, who voted Republican but could appreciate a businesslike liberal Democrat when he saw one—so much so that he asked her to join him on the ticket as deputy chief in the 1983 tribal election. She did, and they won, making her the first female deputy chief in Cherokee history. But this was no dead-end job: two years later, when the chief was called to Washington to head up the Bureau of Indian Affairs, she became the first female chief in Cherokee history. Considering women's prominent role in tribal affairs centuries ago, she observed, her election "was a step forward and a step backward at the same time."

She and her predecessor had worked well together, despite their political differences, because both felt that primary emphasis should be placed on tribal economic independence, with less reliance on Federal largess and more on private investment in farming, ranching, manufacturing, and tourist facilities. In addition, they cooperated in a constant effort to soften the inevitable dissension between pure-blooded and mixed-blooded members of their constituency. As chief she continued on that course and, with the help of her second husband, who spoke the Cherokee language fluently, was reelected to a four-year term in July 1987. It was no piddling job: the tribal government of a thousand employees served a nation of 120,000 people and had an annual operating budget of more than fifty million dollars.

The thrust of her administration can be seen in the titles of organizations it established—the Cherokee Nation's Chamber of Commerce, for example, and the Cherokee Literacy Institute. Indian tribal life, she insisted, belonged to the present as well as the past, blending the best of tradition with the best of innovation. Her work in this respect has been recognized with many awards, including induction into the Oklahoma Hall of Fame in 1986 and being named Woman of the Year by *Ms.* Magazine in 1987. In 1995 it ended with her retirement.

As for her surname, despite her feminist leanings she doesn't consider it all that significant.

Diane Sawyer
Investigative Journalist (1945–)

She considered herself the mess of pottage, her older sister Linda the Grecian urn. Linda she has described as "always so lean and elegant and lovely," adjectives that have regularly been used to describe *her.* Her favorite author is Henry James. Early in her career she spiked her TV weather forecasts with unsolicited bits of poetry, and her morning conversations with Charles Kuralt became known as models of laid-back literacy. Yet this woman of elegant femininity has held her own most manfully amid the rough and tumble of Beltway journalism, competing with some of the more intimidating broadcast bears of investigative TV reporting—or "tough old tigers," to use her amiable description.

Diane Sawyer was born in December 1945 in Glasgow, Kentucky, but soon thereafter moved with the family to Louisville. Her grammar school days were filled with a hectic round of extracurricular pursuits, from music and dancing to fencing and horseback riding. In high school she switched to more artistic and literary endeavors, including editing the school paper. Reasonably gregarious, she nevertheless was always happy to go off alone with, say, Emerson or Thoreau. Somewhat diffident, she nevertheless gained immeasurable self-confidence in her senior year, when winning first prize in the national Junior Miss contest gave her terrifying but invaluable public-speaking experience on tour.

At Wellesley College it was more of the same, earning good grades while choiring, acting, politicking (as vice president of the student body). After graduating in 1967, she got herself hired as "weather girl" at Louisville's ABC-TV affiliate, which also used her as an occasional reporter. She proved to be a better reporter than weather girl, partly because her astigmatism made of meteorology an even more inexact science than it is inherently. Soon she was raised from occasional to regular reporter, developing flexibility with a potpourri of local stories and ad hoc interviews, such as her resolute, equipment-laden pursuit of Supreme Court Justice William O. Douglas on one of his debilitating cross-country hikes. For relaxation she studied some law at the University of Louisville.

In 1970, itching for a broader horizon, she moved to Washington, D.C., couldn't find a job in broadcast journalism, and ended up in the White House as an assistant to the deputy press secretary. Her press releases and drafts of Presidential announcements earned her promotions to assistant to press secretary Ron Ziegler and then to Presidential staff assistant. Although ideologically neutral (she would have accepted an offer "from someone like George McGovern"), before long she succumbed to team spirit, and particularly to the enigmatic charisma of Richard Nixon (to whom she was "the smart girl"). During the bit-by-bit unfolding of the Watergate story—an exhausting, time-devouring and "tormenting" experience for her—she spent most of her time fending off reporters' probing and generally discomfiting questions with graceful rigidity. She was, according to Dan Rather, "a total nonsource" of important information but a competent purveyor of innocuous yet indispensable trivia "if you needed a statistic or a spelling at the last minute."

When Nixon left the White House for San Clemente in August 1974, she went with him, sympathetically, at his request. Anticipating a brief stay, she remained there for four years, chiefly as research assistant in preparing his memoirs. In 1978 the lure of the Beltway called her back to Washington, where she was hired by CBS News as a reporter over strenuous objections from some senior correspondents who argued that she had too little experience in broadcast journalism and too much experience in partisan politics. Nonetheless she was kept on roll and worked hard enough and well enough, especially in reporting on the Iranian hostage crisis, to melt the resistance.

Indeed, within about a year, having proved her smooth competence with on-the-spot reporting of the Three Mile Island nuclear accident, she was promoted to correspondent and, in the summer of 1980, was assigned to cover the State Department with veteran newsman Robert Pierpoint, although she spent part of that summer contributing to the journalistic brouhaha at the national political conventions. She also began appearing often on the network's Sunday morning news show and sometimes anchoring *Newsbreak* in the evenings. Occasionally she joined Charles Kuralt on his weekday morning program, where the duo's mature and articulate discussions persuaded Kuralt and his producer to urge CBS brass to include her as coanchor of the expanded 90-minute version of the program then in the planning stage.

And so in May 1981 the new show was introduced as *Morning with Charles Kuralt and Diane Sawyer*. Declining to be restricted to reading the news and to reporting women's-viewpoint stories, she did her share of spot reporting and specials, as well as conducting interviews with national political figures, including Richard Nixon on the tenth anniversary of the Watergate burglary. For him as for others, her interviewing technique could be inquisitorial, but gently so.

The show, despite rising ratings, failed to demolish the competition and therefore had to undergo major changes, including her transfer to the inordinately popular *60 Minutes*. As part of what was now the Wallace-Reasoner-Safer-Bradley-Sawyer team, she specialized in interviews (Haig, Rickover, Bellow, Von Bulow, Thatcher) but also handled other assignments, foreign and domestic: famine in northern Africa, the melee at the 1984 political conventions. For the Reagan-Mondale debates she was one of the three reporters selected to grill the candidates. That year she received a Matrix Award from the New York chapter of Women in Communications.

In her work for CBS and later for ABC, to which she switched quite profitably in 1989, she has tried ever to keep in mind her conviction that TV news should be not only interesting but stimulating, leaving the viewer with "something he's just burning to tell someone about." Perhaps that's why she's done so well on ABC's *Prime-Time Live*, with formidably ursine Sam Donaldson, and why she's become an ever more important influence on the program's combatively investigative journalism. As that influence has grown, a senior staffer has observed that "three years ago we were a disaster. Now we're a hit."

And so in 1994 ABC, against offers from the two competing networks, offered her a special-treatment contract reputedly paying her at a rate of $19,000 a day. She signed up, insisting that "money had nothing to do with it at all." Her husband Mike Nichols, director of stage and screen, testified that she wouldn't let money enter into their discussions about it. His testimony also seemed quite persuasive, if a bit rueful.

Connie Chung
Television Network News Anchor
(1946–)

She has always been, according to Dan Rather, "willing to do anything." She'd be "the first person off the bench" when an assignment came up, grabbing the Washington news bureau chief's lapels and begging, "Send me in, coach!" As a result her career has included some notable failures. Also as a result, it has been spectacularly successful.

Constance Yu-hwa Chung was born in Washington, D.C., in August 1946. At that moment she was the only American citizen in her family. Her father, a diplomat in the Chinese Nationalist government, lost his first five children to a lack of proper medical care during World War II. He had fled the Japanese bombing of Shanghai in 1944, bringing his wife and four remaining daughters to Washington. The postwar Communist revolution and 1949 victory in China thereafter persuaded him to stay put.

Sixteen years later Connie was enrolled at the University of Maryland. Her major was biology. The only interest she had ever shown in active TV work was in her *very* early years, using a vacuum-cleaner tube as a microphone to interview her miniature friends in play. However, during her vacation after junior year she got a stimulating writing job on the staff of a Congressman from New York; in her senior year she switched her major to journalism, now preferring to dissect politicians instead of frogs, and began working part-time for a local TV station. Her disparaging title of "copy girl" was later degenderized to copy clerk. After graduation she was promoted successively to newswriter, editor, and broadcast reporter—and, significantly, working colleague of Maury Povich, later of Fox TV network fame. Her beat was unlimited: disasters, crimes, lots of politics. In Washington, as she has pointed out, local news includes Capitol Hill and the White House.

In 1971 CBS, like other networks under pressure from the Federal Communications Commission to employ more women and minorities as an affirmative action, hired four women: a blond Caucasian, a Jew, a black, and an Asian. Thus, the Asian has observed, "They took care of years of discrimination." Later, when asked how a young Chinese woman managed to get a job as a reporter on CBS-TV, she replied that the news director liked the way she did his shirts. Soon, as Dan Rather noted, she became known for her willingness to do anything and do it thoroughly. When she covered George McGovern in the early part of his 1972 Presidential campaign, Rather also has noted, she "became a one-woman encyclopedia on George McGovern." She was similarly thorough in her coverage of Richard Nixon's campaign trips that year to the Middle East and the Soviet Union, although for his trip to China, despite or because of her fluency in Chinese, she was relegated to presenting background material. In 1973 and '74 Watergate kept her eagerly busy with the pursuit of various political felons in high places. During the Gerald Ford years she was assigned to Vice President Nelson Rockefeller and enjoyed trying to needle him into stepping away from the rigidly conservative party line, and sometimes succeeding.

In 1976 she was offered a lucrative anchor job by the CBS affiliate in Los Angeles. Ever willing to try anything, she took the job. For a while her friend from Washington, Maury Povich, shared the anchor desk with her, though only briefly before moving on to other things. "If you blinked," she said later, "you missed us." Over the next seven years the ratings for the station's news show rose substantially, and her salary increased approximately twentyfold, making it the highest in the country for a local news anchor. Awards multiplied flatteringly.

None of this was enough, however, to keep her from taking a chance to report on the upcoming 1984 Presidential campaign when NBC offered her an anchor job for a sunrise network news show, as well as assignments as political correspondent for the evening news, and as on-the-air reporter for three 90-second prime-time news broadcasts each week. It meant taking on a rough work schedule for a reputed 30 percent cut in pay, as well as moving to New York—where she would rejoin and marry Maury Povich (to her parents' vast relief, for she was their only husbandless daughter). The move, a professional gamble, would at least put her in the journalistic swim again, and she'd try anything.

That anything developed into eighteen hours a day during the week plus busy weekends, a work routine devoted largely to a rather desperate effort to make this and that TV newsmagazine crapshoot pay off. Her documentaries and celebrity interviews received mixed reviews (one critic sniffing at "Connie Funn's popumentaries") and were generally short-lived. A highlight of this period, however, was her 1987 visit to China, full of touching interviews with relatives, and her work as floor correspondent at the 1988 party conventions was conspicuously first-rate.

The following March she was hired by CBS at a gratifying salary of well over a million a year. Besides filling in for Dan Rather during his absences and anchoring the Sunday night news, her major assignment was to act as the on-air honcho of *Saturday Night with Connie Chung.* The show's use of actors to dramatize incidents in the news made it perilously innovative, but then she'd try anything. The innovations brought down the wrath of most critics, one of whom deplored "the bastardization of the newsmagazine format," and it did not otherwise make television history. Nevertheless, her contributions to various ill-fated shows earned her three Emmy awards.

Still the only childless Chung daughter, in mid–1990 she reduced her work schedule drastically in an effort to remedy that embarrassing situation, although within a few months, rather crestfallen but still determined, she was back on the treadmill. Meanwhile the three major network evening news shows continued losing viewers (25 percent since 1970), especially CBS. In an effort to remedy *that* embarrassing situation, the network pooh-bahs decided to give "Gunga Dan" Rather's evening news a gentler, feminine touch by following local news shows' successful formula of bisexual coanchoring. In June 1993, in addition to hosting her own prime-time newsmagazine, she began sharing the anchoring—and definitely making it more decorative.

Maybe she should have married earlier. Maybe she shouldn't have made that move to L.A. But, she has said, she's always been a "big should've, could've, would've person." On balance, she did pretty well for herself.

Judy Woodruff
Chief Washington Correspondent (1946–)

For getting that first job her legs were at least partly responsible. After that she had to rely on other qualities, like talent, industry, intelligence.

Judy Woodruff was born in November 1946 in Tulsa, Oklahoma. She and her younger sister were army brats, moving restlessly from post to post with their parents and seeing a good deal of the world between a tour of duty in West Germany and another in Taiwan. The continual adjustments to new environments taught her, she feels, to cope with the unexpected development, without being intimidated by the unforeseen—which is partly "what being a reporter is all about."

Not that being a reporter was her consuming ambition in high school, during a posting in Georgia. There it was treading the boards that attracted her during basic training with the drama club and a community theater troupe. Her interest was heightened when she entered a junior-miss beauty contest and won first prize.

But it was in North Carolina, at a liberal arts college and then at Duke University, that her interest switched to political science. Besides majoring in that discipline, she spent a couple of engaging summers interning in the Washington office of her district's Congressman. By 1968 she had decided that television news reporting was just what the career doctor ordered. Armed with a strong B.A. from Duke and her Capitol background, she was hired almost immediately by a local TV news director with an outspoken appreciation for her shapely legs. (He proved harmless: This wasn't a case of sexual harassment but was merely an instance of esthetic appreciation, however disconcerting.)

Soon tiring of office-girl assignments, she applied for a reporting job but was told, in the finest traditions of tokenism, that the station already had a woman reporter and needed no more. Eventually she was assigned to an on-camera job, as weather girl on the late Sunday night news. Frustrated by this sideline duty, she applied for reporting jobs to news directors all over the country. Her frustration wasn't lessened by the persistent knee-jerk responses that they needed a reporter but not a woman. However, in early 1970, the token woman reporter for the CBS TV station in Atlanta, who had been relegated to feminine fluff, quit her job to have a baby, at least ostensibly. Judy was hired to replace her and, at her entreaty not to be put on the fluff detail, was assigned to report on Georgia politics.

She couldn't have asked for a much hotter baptism by fire, especially since she soon graduated from the turmoil of assembly politics to the turbulence of Jimmy Carter's campaign for governor, involving her in competition with the region's most experienced political newsmen. Having met the competition successfully, she was promoted to anchoring the noonday news. A jump in the show's ratings inspired management to promote her again, to coanchoring the evening news as well. The magic unaccountably failed this time, however. When the show's ratings did not surge, she was returned after a while to general reporting, while continuing as anchor of the noon news.

General reporting was to be her thing for the next few years, including her first few with NBC's national news organization, which she joined early in 1975. She reported on anything and everything—Cuban and Vietnamese refugees, crime, disasters, and of course politics, allowing her to offer, as she has put it, "a first draft of history." She began receiving awards, including an Emmy in 1975. And she began covering Jimmy Carter's campaign for the Democratic nomination for President in 1976. She covered him against the superior male judgment of the network's New York office, insisting that he was a much more effective campaigner than people imagined. Soon she was show-ing up repeatedly on the evening news, but when Carter began to look like a shoo-in she was shouldered aside and replaced with an older, more experienced correspondent. Male, of course. In response to her inevitable protest she was informed that her ladylike delivery wasn't as authoritative as a forceful male baritone.

After Carter's inauguration, someone in New York suddenly recognized that it was *she* who was experienced, since she had been covering Carter, off and on, for years. And so, in January 1977, she became an NBC White House correspondent, reporting regularly on White House shenanigans for news shows, specials, whatever. She was well acquainted with Carter & Co., but at first, as she has put it in her journalist's autobiography, she "knew even less then about Washington and how it works" than they did. "And while I'd like to think that I caught on a little faster than they did," she continues (writing this in 1982, after Carter's replacement by Reagan), "the only proof that I can offer is that I'm still here." It didn't hurt to be married, as of April 1980, to the *Wall Street Journal's* well-known Washington bureau chief Al Hunt.

Most of her job was dull routine—dogging the footsteps of, lying in wait for newsmakers who just might have something quotable, and extractable, to say. But on March 30, 1981, when President Reagan and his press secretary Jim Brady were shot, she was anything but bored. Soon thereafter she was on the air although three months pregnant, with "the first eyewitness account mil-lions of viewers would hear." The incident gave her a new appreciation of dull routing—anything may happen anywhere, any time, and patience is a virtue. Along with other incidents involving male competition, it also gave her more appreciation of the journalistic truism that "nice reporters tend to finish last." She was developing a measure of ladylike aggressiveness.

She also was developing into a celebrity, stopped on the street with, as she tells it, "Aren't you Leslie Stahl?" To which she would answer simply, "No, I'm Sam Donaldson."

Her name-and-face recognition facilitated a measure of ladylike aggres-siveness, and this was just as well. After nearly six years on the White House beat, in mid–1982 she requested a new assignment and was made the network's chief Washington correspondent. This involved not only many background pieces but also many interviews requiring her ladylike aggressiveness for hard questions delicately, or if necessary not so delicately, put. She spent a year polishing her technique and then, in mid–1983, took it to *The MacNeil/Lehrer*

News Hour on PBS, where she and Charlene Hunter-Gault would enjoy "the wonderful luxury" of being the distaff contributors to the only hour-long news show on national television. The hour was a solid hour, without a quarter of the time being spent on commercials, offering "a chance to go behind the headlines." She would be taking such chances for the *News Hour* over the next ten years until, in 1993, she was enticed away by an offer from CNN.

Linda Bloodworth-Thomason
Television Writer and Producer (1947–)

As a television writer and producer extraordinaire, Linda Bloodworth-Thomason has treated viewers to the extraordinarily popular sitcom *Designing Woman*, besides *Evening Shade* and *Hearts Afire*. As a writer-producer with a political viewpoint, she treated Democratic delegates at the July 1992 national convention to the sentimental stimulus of *The Man from Hope*, the brief, very personal and effective film biography of her good friend Bill Clinton. In both instances she was invading male territory, with alarming success.

She was born Linda Joyce Bloodworth in April 1947 in Poplar Bluff, Missouri, just north of the Arkansas state line. Her family had migrated from Corning, Arkansas, just south of the line, because her father's father, C.T. Bloodworth, a crusading attorney and civil-rights maverick whom she remembers as her hero and inspiration, had prudently decided to make the move after being clumsily but ominously shot by an overwrought Klansman. There he sired five sons, all of whom grew up to be lawyers, generally of the fire-breathing, anti-establishment sort.

Given such a Bloodworth bloodline, it's hardly surprising that she developed a bristly mind of her own, which eventually alienated her from the South's legacy of racial intolerance and sexual prejudice. She was conventional enough in high school, however, to be voted its "most popular" senior and at the University of Missouri to be granted an English-major degree. Although she had meant to join in the family's practice of law, after graduation she accepted a casual invitation from some friends to move with them to Los Angeles. There she spent the early 1970s in advertising and writing jobs for various newspapers until an idealistic impulse inspired her to try teaching English in a public high school. After a couple of years the excess of students and dearth of ordinary supplies made her efforts seem so idiotically futile that she quit in frustration.

With a friend, a TV actress, she began writing and submitting proposed TV scripts. At first this seemed another exercise in futility, but after Larry Gelbert, producer of *M*A*S*H*, happened to see and appreciate one of her efforts, she began freelance writing not only for that show but also for *The Mary Tyler Moore Show*. Her first script for *M*A*S*H*, nominated for an Emmy, inaugurated seven fertile years of successful freelancing until 1982, when one of her many pilots proposed for new shows was accepted by CBS. Her *Filthy Rich*, a kind of parody of the hit soaper *Dallas*, did well at first but lasted only the one season.

Also working for CBS at the time was producer Harry Thomason. They wasted no time, as she has put it, falling "madly in love" and were married in July 1983. Their almost common origins (he was from Missouri) and their almost identical career interests prompted them into forming Mozark Productions and creating a series, *Lime Street*, starring Robert Wagner as an American insurance investigator in London and Samantha Smith as his daughter. The series, plagued by fate—Samantha Smith died in a real airplane crash after making the fifth episode—and by bureaucratic interference, was panned by critics, ignored by viewers, and given an early coup de grace.

Determined to brook no, or at most less, interference, she thereupon focused her talents on a series starring four modern Southern women whose sophistication could belie the TV Southern yokel stereotype. It was undeniably *her* baby—she herself wrote the scripts for the first 35 episodes, an unprecedented achievement. CBS bought the series, *Designing Women*, and craftily scheduled it for Monday nights in the fall of 1986, opposite ABC's *Monday Night Football*, thereby doubtless creating serious dissension in many an American household.

The first reactions to the program consisted of mixed reviews, the negatives complaining chiefly about its reverse sexism. Some male critics may have been discomfited by her presentation of four women expressing strong, intelligent opinions on controversial subjects like sexual harassment, spousal abuse, pornography, gynecological dysfunctions, female ordination, and the maltreatment of Anita Hill. CBS, reacting to the reaction, canceled the series in 1987 and was promptly inundated with some 50,000 letters of outraged protest. Quickly restored, the program began a very satisfying Neilsen climb to a position of durable popularity. It proved especially attractive to Southern women, to many of whom it brought a feeling of release.

Her next effort, with her husband as director and executive producer, was *Evening Shade* (title suggested by Hillary Clinton), a series fondly and rather nostalgically depicting the glacial lifestyle of a minuscule Southern town where "every day that passes is slower than molasses." Premiering in September 1990, it too began a gratifying Nielsen ascent and brought her compliments on her talent for creating a character out of an actor's personality. Its success inspired CBS into a 45-million-dollar deal with Mozark Productions for five more shows between 1991 and 1999. The first of these, the romantic Beltway sitcom *Hearts Afire*, premiered in September 1992 and was immediately criticized for Clintonesque sound bites related to the current Presidential campaign. She admitted to them but insisted that they were just as fully Bloodworth-Thomason-esque. Campaign advising was bound to involve some occupational hazards, especially for FOBs (Friends of Bill).

All this feverish creative activity proved quite lucrative, raising the monthly family income to well over a million dollars (estimated, of course, by calculating observers). Her sharing of the output of the cornucopia, especially with less fortunate women, has brought her a number of humanitarian awards, such as 1992's commendation from the Women's Legal Defense Fund. That year she also was named by *Newsweek* as one of the year's "most influential women."

It was never likely that she'd be commuting incessantly to Washington. Afraid of flying, she rides only trains and buses. Nor does she enjoy the satirical media attention characteristic of the Beltway milieu. It has indeed brought her, she has reportedly said, to a sympathetic reconsideration of FORNs (Friends of Richard Nixon).

Hillary Rodham Clinton
First Lady (1947–)

In the 1992 Presidential campaign Bill Clinton happily pointed out that he had something special to offer the voters: the high competence of his wife Hillary, who would be of incalculable help in his Presidency. We're a package, he promised: "Buy one, get one free." And that indeed is how it's turned out, whatever one may think politically of the bargain.

She was born Hillary Diane Rodham in October 1947 in Chicago, but she and her two brothers grew up in nearby Park Ridge. If spunk is one of her characteristics, she may owe it primarily to the unwelcome attention paid her by a local bully, a girl whose attacks ended after Hillary, urged by her mother, finally gave back as good as she got. Thereafter her standing among her playmates rose as high as her grades in school, which got her into the finals in the National Merit Scholarship competition as well as into the National Honor Society. She played piano, danced ballet, participated in team sports, and, during her summers, lifeguarded at a city pool—and, under Methodist Church sponsorship, set up baby-sitting arrangements for migrant workers.

For all her growing sympathy for underdogs like migrant workers, in her senior high school year she trod in her parents' solid Republican footsteps as a fervent campaigner for Barry Goldwater in 1964 and, after her graduation with honors, as leader of the Young Republicans at Wellesley College. The social turmoil of the next few years, however, affected her deeply, and in the 1968 campaign she worked for none other than the Democratic left-winger

Eugene McCarthy. At the college she spoke up for the admission of more black students and against the war in Vietnam, and she devoted her senior thesis to community development, particularly with reference to the poor. When she graduated in 1969, as president of the student government, she followed Senator Edward Brooks' speech at commencement with a speech of her own suggesting that his remarks had been largely meaningless—a speech that brought her some national publicity with a photo and a brief story in *Life* magazine. This notice, combined with some renown as a winner on the TV quiz program *College Bowl*, as well as her decision to follow law as a career, made her a likely candidate for the more prestigious law schools.

Despite a preference for Yale, she decided to check things out at Harvard. There she was told that the school already had more women in its classes than it, er, needed. In her first year at Yale, inspired by a speech by Marian Wright Edelman, Mississippi's first black woman to pass a bar exam, she became an unpaid worker in Edelman's lobbying program in Washington that would later become the Children's Defense Fund. She took her degree in 1973, a year later than scheduled, because of her work at the school's Child Study Center, her help in researching for a book by Anna Freud et al., *Beyond the Best Interests of the Child*, and her further research work, for the Carnegie Council on Children, on educational and medical entitlements for children.

Her second year at Yale was the fateful year when she noticed Bill Clinton staring at her in the library and, after some staring back, introduced herself. Although she was a year ahead of him, her year's delay (who can know about motivations?) allowed them to graduate together in the class of '73 (after spending the summer of '72, incidentally, campaigning and voter-registering for George McGovern). But after graduation they were separated, what with her lawyering for the Children's Defense Fund in Massachusetts and his teaching law in distant Arkansas.

In January 1974 she was asked to be one of the three female lawyers on the 43-lawyer staff of the House Judiciary Committee, then busily investigating the nefarious activities of the Nixon Administration with an eye to impeachment. By the time of Nixon's resignation and the end of the investigation her work had attracted enough favorable notice to inundate her with lucrative job offers. She opted, however, to join Bill at the university in Fayetteville, where he was engaged in a contest for a Congressional seat, and to work informally but energetically as his campaign manger. Although they lost, they were comforted by the unprecedented closeness of the 4 percent margin.

The campaign provided plenty of opportunities for networking, which in turn helped her to see surprising opportunities for enjoyable work in Arkansas—teaching, operating a legal clinic, engaging in community projects and political activities. Arkansas became irresistibly attractive when Bill asked her to marry him. She most readily accepted his offer, and they were married in October 1975. Her feminine instincts prompted her to keep her family name, an option that would later crop up sporadically as a ponderous political issue.

In the autumn of 1976 she and Bill, now state attorney general, moved to Little Rock. After a spell of teaching law at the University of Arkansas and managing its law clinic, she was appointed in 1977 by President Jimmy Carter, for whom she had campaigned, to the board of directors of the Legal Services Corporation. Later that year she organized and supervised the Arkansas Advocates for Children and Families to focus on problems of children, especially poor children. Her own finances were greatly improved that same year when she took a lucrative job with an eminent local law firm that paid her four times what Bill was then earning. Some celebrated market speculating helped.

She naturally worked in Bill's successful campaign for governor in 1978, and shortly thereafter he appointed her to chair the state's Rural Health Advisory Committee, created to promote good health in rural communities. Early 1980 brought two gratifying developments, a partnership in the law firm and the arrival of daughter Chelsea. But it was also the year that the Federal interning of thousands of Cuban refugees in Arkansas provoked a racist reaction that (along with that maiden-name issue) contributed to Bill's defeat. Apparently his repeated apologies for his mistakes in office and her assumption of the Clinton name (along with a weight loss, some hair styling, contact lenses, and fancier clothes) were enough to restore him, them, to the good graces of the electorate, who, with her amicable but effective prodding, elected him again in 1982, as well as in '84, '86, '88 and '90. Gratefully and confidently, he appointed her to various state administrative jobs, especially jobs dealing with child care and education. In her spare time she worked with the American Bar Association's Commission on Women in the Profession (that's *the* Profession) and served on several boards of directors for commercial firms. In 1988 and 1991 the *National Law Journal* listed her among the country's hundred most prominent lawyers.

How much this activity strained the Clintons' marriage bond is their business, but when rumors of his infidelities cropped up during the 1992 Presidential campaign, spectacularly abetted by reportedly paid testimony from a quite vocal cocktail-lounge entertainer named Gennifer Flowers, the couple met the issue directly on television, with an admission of marital strains but with her insistence on their right to privacy in the matter. In a tone of finality she declared, "We've gone further than anybody we know of, and that's all we're going to say." Later her casually adversarial remark about pursuing her profession rather than staying home and baking cookies and giving teas got her an outsized share of publicity that started talk about "Bill's Hillary Problem" but she managed to recapture some homebody support with an equally public if less widely publicized apology—and her recipe for chocolate-chip cookies.

It will be news only to a comatose Australian aborigine that as First Lady she had led the labyrinthine Task Force on National Health Care Reform with its three dozen working groups, apparently garnering more popularity than her husband not only in some polls but even in the White House, despite her ban on smoking. And (whatever the implications of the tangled Whitewater affair) her popularity remains intact on Capitol Hill as well, where her factual, reasoned, articulate defense of the Administration's health care plan (in danger from Republicans who don't want to pay for anything, with "No New Taxes" still ringing in their ears) inspired former Ways and Means Chairman Dan Rostenkowski to gush quite uncharacteristically, "In the very near future, the President will be known as your husband."

Joan Lunden
Television Morning News Anchor
(1950–)

Maybe "video mom" isn't quite fair. Too stereotyping. Although her career has been notable for its emphasis on pregnancy, motherhood, child care, and family life, it has also included a great variety of other activities unrelated to human procreation.

Joan Elise Blunden was born in September 1950 in Fair Oaks, California. (The name change, to avoid any phonetic connection with "blunder," was made at others' urgent request in 1975.) Her father, a doctor and private-flying enthusiast, flew into a storm and to his death when she was in her midteens, and thereafter she and her brother were raised by an actively devoted mother who supported them by selling real estate. Inspired by her energetic example, the daughter not only did well academically in high school but also completed some correspondence courses from the University of California before graduating. The combination kept her busy, but not too busy to keep her from less scholarly pursuits, including dance and piano lessons, strutting in parades as a drum majorette, and displaying her considerable charms in beauty contests.

After graduation at a precocious sweet sixteen, she spent the summer working in an X ray lab in the hope of becoming a surgeon like her father, but she soon discovered that dealing with others' pain was too painful to make a career out of it. Somewhat at loose ends, she enrolled in an imaginative program combining travel and education that trained her in psychology while sailing her from Spain to Japan by way of southern Africa, with plenty of fascinating stops along the way. The four-month experience opened her eyes to "contrasts of wealth and poverty, sickness and health, black and white and brown skins" and introduced what she has called her "flaky period" in Mexico City in 1968. There she studied anthropology at the Universidad de

Las Américas, did some clothes-modeling, and developed enough fluency in Spanish to act in TV commercials despite her light good looks. She also had a part in a cowboy movie that didn't require any Spanish from her (or any English for that matter).

Back in the U.S. in 1972, she settled in Sacramento, where she earned an arts degree at the local junior college and, after completing a two-month course in modeling, founded a charm school of her own This led to her being hired briefly by the local NBC-TV affiliate for hand modeling in commercials, and *that* led to her being hired in 1973 by the news director, who found her both attractive and intelligent. This led to her doing weather reports, and *that* led to reporting on consumer issues, about which she knew nothing at first but learned very quickly. Within a couple of years, after a spell of newscasting at noon, she was assigned to the News at Six as its first female anchor.

Over the next two years, despite some slings and arrows from outraged and outrageous masculinity, she attracted enough favorable attention to be offered a reporting job by New York's WABC-TV for its *Eyewitness News*. (A rival Sacramento station had been mailing out tapes of her TV appearances to cities around the country to eliminate the competition.) In the Big Apple, assigned mostly to rookie-level stories of unpalatable character, she had as well to live through a baptism of ridicule from her virile colleagues, who took to calling her a Barbie doll. To add insult, or further insult, it was under these circumstances that she was asked to change her name, although not unreasonably. She lived through the ham-handed abuse by shrugging it off, by working hard, and, in her words, by "hanging in there [until] I finally got to the point where it stopped."

In 1976 she joined the *Good Morning America* program as a kind of unconventional consumer reporter, presenting newsworthy and often bizarre products like floating transistor radios. She declined offers to play Dustin Hoffman's attorney in the movie *Kramer vs. Kramer*, to emcee a game show on TV, and to star in a sitcom, opting instead to continue working for the local station *and* the network between naps. Her importance to the network program progressed slowly, ever so slowly, until finally, in the summer of 1986, a new contract identified her formally as cohost with David Hartman.

That contract carried an unprecedented clause for child care which permitted her to have a nursery next to her office for breast-feeding her baby daughter. (She had married TV producer Michael Krauss in 1978.) Her maternal cares and consolations, before and after the birth, became popular grist for her TV mill. They did nothing, however, to contribute to her efforts to be assigned to some of the heavy stuff being handled on the bulls' side of the fence, stuff like the national debt or Congressional gridlock. This lack of "significance" in her work was frustrating but, at the urging of the more ruefully experienced Barbara Walters, she converted any resentment into energetic, capable work performance.

This tactic required a good deal of patience. She became quite celebrated for her interviews of fellow celebrities, but it wasn't until early 1987, after Hartman had left the show and she had become senior cohost, that management began grudgingly to assign her to important stories and newsmaker interviews, foreign and domestic. On the side she continued regaling the mothers in her audience with informative shows on cable and daytime network TV and even had her own syndicated talk show, *Everyday with Joan Lunden*. Despite her solicitous mother's concern over her breakneck schedule, in her spare time she has produced a couple of how-to maternity books, co-authored with her husband, as well as a related syndicated column and a 60-minute informational video cassette on baby care. Given this output it is hardly surprising that among her many awards is one from the National Mother's Day Committee in 1982 honoring her as an Outstanding Mother of the Year.

Ten years later a bitter divorce, with shared custody and much legal wrangling over money, gave that Mother's Day award a rather hollow ring and made life pretty miserable for all concerned. Heartened by much supportive reaction from her viewers, however, she has survived, becoming TV's most durable morning anchor of either, or any, gender.

Peggy Noonan
White House Speechwriter (1950–)

In the mid–1970s she was enough of a flaming liberal to join in student demonstrations against the war in Vietnam. Ten years later she was enough of a flaming reactionary to crank out cosmetic verbiage for the impoverishment of America by the Reagan-Bush regime. Her conversion to political reaction was indeed personally reactionary, arising chiefly out of her negative reaction to the excesses and superficiality of many of her fellow student demonstrators.

She was born in Brooklyn in September 1950 to very Irish, very Catholic, very working-class parents. She attributes her eloquence to her early experience competing with six siblings for her parents' attention: she would *plan* her verbal approach, and phraseology became her specialty. This technique proved much less effective in the educational environment, which she tolerated very casually. Waiting on tables on the side, she did make it through high school by 1968.

During a couple of catatonic years as an insurance adjuster, she took up English literature and journalism at Fairleigh University until, in 1970, she became a full-time student, an editor of the student paper, and a political activist. She also began reading William F. Buckley's *National Review* and became enchanted with its righteous views on God and country and the scourge of government. Turned on by its siren song (she later wrote that it "sang" to her), she was equally turned off by liberal college elitists, so much so that she turned from one form of ideological straitjacketry to another. Eventually, her heroes would be "Reagan, Thatcher, John Paul II, perhaps Gorbachev."

Her B.A. degree and a bit of luck got her a job writing news for a CBS radio station in Boston. ("I began my career writing for the ear.") Her performance there earned her a promotion to editorial director and then, in the fall of 1977, an assignment to CBS in New York as a writer-editor. Such work schooled her in rhetorical discipline the hard way, but it also allowed her to practice the art of the verbal flourish. She found the CBS ambiance invigorating despite a head-on encounter with sex discrimination when, after auditioning for a speaking role, she was told that she couldn't cut the mustard because her voice had "no balls." (A dozen years later in her autobiography she had to confess, "I still haven't come up with the right answer to that.") However, her prose had balls enough to get her assigned to writing commentary for Walter Cronkite's radio broadcasts and then for his TV successor Dan Rather, with whom she entered into a political truce for reasons of symbiosis.

Meanwhile Ronald Reagan's tentative anarchy, based solidly on fiscal nihilism, was coming into full flower, and in the mid–1980s she realized that "I wasn't a journalist, I was a partisan—a star-struck partisan." Reagan, she now surmised and later confirmed, was, like Barry Goldwater before him, a man who "knew, just knew, that he was right." She longed to be of help, to write for him. After some amateur networking she formally joined the White House speechwriters in March 1984. Again encountering sex discrimination, she wrote for Nancy—briefly, until she threw down the resignation (and intimidating PR) gauntlet. She met with it again in objections to her writing a speech commemorating the Normandy landings on D-Day because of her distressing lack of combat experience, although in the end the speech earned her a great many emotional responses and congratulations from the President— whom she also greatly pleased with her glowing depiction of the Nicaraguan contras as "the moral equal of our Founding Fathers." Yet most of the objections to, and editing of, her scripts had little or nothing to do with gender except perhaps in the sense that her macho beware-the-bear fulminations against the metamorphosing yet still godless Soviet Union often had to be softened or deleted. The meddling came largely from what she came to call the bureaucratic mice. (The term was leaked and made her the focus of some bureaucratic nibbling.)

After two years of bucking cautionary trepidation, she quit. But, unable to resist the sight of a beleaguered George Bush emerging crestfallen from the Iowa caucuses in February 1988, she began writing for him; helped him win in New Hampshire; inspired his constituency with phrases like "Read my lips—no new taxes!" and "a kinder, gentler America" and "a thousand points of light"; and eventually provided him with his unexpectedly presentable acceptance speech at the convention. Half a year later, after furnishing Reagan with a farewell and Bush with an inaugural speech, she decided to hang up her rhetorical gloves.

In her couple of dozen months as ventriloquist she had learned some things. Her bedazzlement at the Reagan Revolution dimmed: "This White House is like a beautiful clock that makes all the right sounds, but when you open it up, there is nothing inside." And despite her affection for Reagan himself politicians were a vacuous breed: "Don't fall in love with politicians, they're all a disappointment. They can't help it, they just are."

By the fall of 1990, having moved to the Upper East Side of Manhattan with her husband (now divorced) and young son, and having received an honorary doctorate in humane letters from Fairleigh Dickinson, she was busy freelancing for various newspapers and magazines, writing her entertaining political autobiography and a novel, and, she reported, enjoying a more private and less political life.

As for the political life, as she put it in an article for *Forbes*, the "voters think Washington is a whorehouse and every four years they get a chance to elect a new piano player."

Sally Ride
Astronaut (1951–)

As an undergraduate at Stanford University she loved Shakespeare. She "really had fun reading Shakespeare's plays and writing papers on them," she told an interviewer years later. "It's kind of like doing puzzles—you had to figure out what he was trying to say and find all the little clues inside the play that you were right." Eventually, however, she found that physics also had plenty of puzzles for her.

Sally Kirsten Ride was born in Encino, just north of Los Angeles, in May 1951, ten years before the United States launched its first manned (but not womaned) space capsule and 32 years before Navy Captain Robert Crippen, commander of an upcoming shuttle mission, chose her to join his crew as the first woman in space and courageously faced reporters' chauvinist questions about her adequacy. "She's flying with us, " he asserted, "because she's the very best person for the job. There's no man I'd rather have in her place."

Her father was a college professor (political science), her mother a prison counselor. Her sister Karen became a Presbyterian minister, another distaff pioneer, offering a spiritual balance to the physical. Sally the child played corner-lot football and baseball with the fellas until her mother recommended that she switch to something less potentially injurious, like tennis. She switched and soon, under the tutelage of tennis great Alice Marble, was good enough to rank 18th in the national ratings. Meanwhile, in her junior year in high school, she took a course in physiology from a gifted teacher, Dr. Elizabeth Mommaerts, and found herself hooked on science.

And so it was as a physics major that she entered Swarthmore College in 1968. Tennis, however, had lost none of its attraction, and in her sophomore year she dropped out to concentrate on it. To her surprise, she seemed to hit a ceiling, an inability to direct the ball to exactly where she felt it should go. Despite the urging of another tennis great, Billie Jean King, she deserted tennis in 1970 and enrolled at Stanford University with a double major in physics and literature, earning her a B.A. in addition to her B.S. on graduation day.

She continued thereafter at Stanford, aiming for a doctorate in astrophysics. As she approached it, while working on her dissertation, she started a job hunt for something in research physics and came across a report in the school paper that the National Aeronautics and Space Administration needed people with her kind of scientific training for space missions. She sent in an application; she had nothing to lose. She didn't know that hers was one of some 8000 applications, more than a thousand of them from women. Nor did she know that part of NASA's recruitment problem was that male scientists tended to demand more money than NASA could afford, and it was felt that women would be willing to work for less. A reasonable expectation, however unfair, leading to the abandonment of sex discrimination and the selection of six women for the 1978 class of 35 astronauts.

As one of them, she embarked on a course of training in safety procedures (parachute jumping, sea survival), jet flying, engineering, operations in weightlessness. For two of the early shuttles she was the communicator, relaying messages from the flight director to the orbiting crew. For the seventh mission, scheduled for June 1983 (in the ill-fated *Challenger*), Navy Captain Crippen appointed her flight engineer, relying on her for critical information during launch, reentry, and landing. As George Abbey, director of flight operations, had said in an interview, "She can get everything she knows together and bring it to bear where you need it."

The June 1983 liftoff was perfect, to the delight of hundreds of thousands of onlookers, many of them sporting T-shirts inscribed with "Ride, Sally Ride!" And ride she did over the next six days, busily engaged with the crew in more than thirty scientific experiments, rehabilitating faulty equipment, trying out the mechanical arm, deploying a couple of communication satellites for Canada and Indonesia, testing products and chemicals (and ants and seeds!) for their behavior in zero gravity, and, especially, using the mechanical arm to deploy and then recapture a 1½-ton West German space lab. There weren't many dull or idle moments. In a press conference after the flight she remarked that "the

thing I'll remember most about the flight is that it was fun. In fact, I'm sure
that it was the most fun that I'll ever have in my life."

Journalists besieged her for interviews, as a woman who could *do* something, but she refused unless her fellow globe-circlers were included. Assigned
by NASA to conduct liaison between the agency and various contractors wish-
ing to buy space on future shuttle flights, she flew again in October 1984, performing much the same duties as before, but this time with another woman
in the crew, Kathy Sullivan. Some fifteen months later, in January 1986, after
Challenger tragically exploded soon after takeoff, she was appointed to the
Presidential commission investigating the accident.

In 1987 she left NASA for a fellowship at Stanford and in 1989 joined
the University of California at San Diego as a professor of physics and as director of its California Space Institute. Her 1982 marriage to fellow astronaut
Steven Hawley having ended in divorce, she could devote herself to a busy life
in science. And for leisure moments there was always Shakespeare.

Jeana Yeager
Record-setting Pilot (1952–)

Her first love was horses. At the age of three or four she taught herself
to ride, bareback, at first precariously but soon with panache. Eventually, however, that first love would take second place. Although neither related to Chuck
Yeager nor particularly inspired by him, she would become fascinated with
flying.

Jeana Yeager was born in or near Fort Worth around 1952. (She's no gold
mine of personal information.) School wasn't the thrill of her young life,
although a course in drafting interested her and would prove useful later when
she got into aircraft design. After a five-year childless marriage ended in
divorce, she left Texas to join her older sister in Santa Rosa, California. There,
as a release from the static quality of a drafting job, she resorted to sky diving, but "what first attracted me to flying was a fascination with helicopters."
Here she was, at the ripe old age of 24, and she couldn't fly a helicopter! First,
she was advised, she ought to learn how to fly a conventional, fixed-wing airplane. And so she did.

Over the next ten years she flew airplanes a great deal, competitively, setting records for speed and endurance. In 1980, at an air show, she met a stunt
pilot (and former fighter pilot) named Dick Rutan, also divorced. It was a fateful meeting, evidently arranged in heaven by Daedalus and Aphrodite. At his
invitation she returned home with him to Mohave, where he worked for his
brother Burt as principal test pilot for the Rutan Aircraft Factory. Soon she

was a test pilot too, putting the factory's products through their dizzying paces, checking their performance, recommending design changes, and in the process setting more speed and endurance records.

During lunch one day in 1981 she and the Rutans got into a lively discussion of the latest in plastic fiber composites for aircraft construction, reputedly much lighter yet stronger than steel. Such materials, insisted Burt, could permit breaking the record for nonstop distance flights. The current record, set by a ponderous B-52 bomber 19 years earlier, was 12,532 miles. He was sure that a plane made of these lightweight materials could be flown as much as 26,000 miles—around the world—with the proper design, of course. And that's where he came in. He showed them—on a napkin.

It wasn't a one-person job, of course, nor an overnight one. Besides helping Burt with design and fabrication, Jeana and Dick set up Voyager Aircraft, Inc.—they had decided to name their globe-circler *Voyager*—to handle the indispensable publicity effort, peddling souvenirs and soliciting contributions from aviation buffs, corporate and individual. Burt's reputation as a designer was enough to extract a gift of the magnamite graphite fiber that would comprise nine-tenths of the plane's physical structure, as well as miscellaneous items like insulation and an engine.

The design they came up with was certainly unconventional, essentially that of a fuel tank with wings. The narrow fuselage rested near its rear on a wing spanning 111 feet, more than the wingspread of a Boeing 727 passenger jet. Its front, at the cockpit area (3 feet wide by 7½ feet long), was supported on a bar stretching to the noses of the two long fuel tanks running parallel to the fuselage. Its catamaran configuration was roughly like that of the old P-38 fighter, resembling a capital H with a bar on top. With its two engines, one at the rear of the fuselage for cruising at around 90 miles an hour and the other in front for takeoff and emergencies, when power would be needed, it weighed 1860 pounds—but it could carry 1200 gallons of high-octane fuel.

It was ready to fly in the summer of 1986, and so it was given a hundred-hour nonstop test flight by Jeana and Dick, to and fro along the coast of California, affording its pilots some experience in perpetually airborne, highly compact symbiosis, including problems of proper eating and waste disposal. The engine noise proved deafening, but that was taken care of by an audio company's gift of special earphones. After the five grueling years of preparation, topped by no less than 67 test flights interlarded with restless tinkering, the actual flight itself promised to be an anticlimax.

It wasn't. For one thing, various delays had brought the scheduled flight time to the very edge of the relatively safe "weather window," yet the pilots decided to go with it despite warnings from the designer. On Sunday, December 14, 1986, they squeezed into the cockpit at Edwards Air Force Base and started off across the Pacific. That alarming scraping sound on takeoff was from the wings, which, heavy with fuel, were irreverently abrading the tarmac, but the damage turned out to be minor. They reached Hawaii without incident but near the Philippines they found themselves confronted by 80-mph breezes from Typhoon Marge—which they put to good use as tailwinds by flying to the north of the counterclockwise-rotating storm. Other storms, however, especially those over the inconsiderately high mountains of central Africa and over the mid–Atlantic, buffeted them about so severely that Jeana especially ended the trip with a painful yet proud collection of testimonial bruises.

That end came with a nearly ideal landing a day ahead of schedule on December 23, almost exactly nine days and 25,012 miles after takeoff, with 8 1/2 gallons to spare. Both pilots lost weight, but not nearly so much as the plane, which went from 9750 pounds at takeoff to 1858 pounds those nine days later. Although shrugging off her bruises, Jeana had to admit that the trip had been more perilous than anticipated and "a lot more difficult than we ever imagined." Then, after she and the Rutans were awarded the Presidential Citizens Medal, she and Dick were launched on publicity tours which, if not their cup of tea, at least would prove financially therapeutic for the debt-burdened couple.

As for *Voyager*, it rests honorably in Washington's National Air and Space Museum.

Benazir Bhutto
Pakistani Prime Minister (1953–)

She was only thirty-five, the minimum age for American Presidents, when she became the first woman political leader of a Moslem nation in which women were only slowly emerging from their chattel classification and where proof of rape requires the testimony of four Moslem male eyewitnesses!

She was born in June 1953 in Karachi, Pakistan, to a father noted for his large landholdings and his political prominence in the Pakistani government. He was a Sunni Moslem, her mother a Shi'ite, but this distinction seemed to create none of the problems in the family that it has created elsewhere. Her attendance during childhood at Roman Catholic convent schools added further variety to the family's religious ambiance.

In 1969 she entered Harvard's Radcliffe College, where she found life much different from the solicitously served and chauffeured life she'd known at home. She adapted quickly, however, even to the loquaciously sociable Americans. With her hair long her resemblance to singer Joan Baez broke a lot of ice, yet she remained devoted to the rigors of Islamic ritual. Coed bathrooms and football games made her uncomfortable. So did participating in demonstrations against the war in Vietnam, but she did it in spite of the risk of being deported.

Meanwhile in Pakistan, ironically, the military were engaged in brutally suppressing an independence movement in the eastern, predominantly Hindu, part of the country. In December 1971 that part, with India's considerable help, became the separate nation of Bangladesh, and that month the military, disgraced by the war's million deaths and ten million refugees, was replaced by her father and his People's Party. Two years later, under a new constitution, he became prime minister.

By this time Benazir was entering on a course of study (politics, philosophy, economics) at Oxford University. After graduating with honors in 1976, she took a graduate course in foreign service, during which she was elected president of the university's celebrated debating society. She was not, as another political woman might have put it, preparing herself for a life of tea and cookies.

In the summer of 1977 she returned to Pakistan in time to witness a military coup led by General Zia, one of the several tyrants coddled by the U.S. government during the Cold War. Her father was dismissed from office and imprisoned on doubtful charges of conspiring in a political murder. In April 1979, despite her desperate efforts to obtain his release, he was executed.

She didn't witness his execution because by that time she herself was under long-term arrest to discourage her anti-military civil disobedience, which she preferred to living in safe, comfortable exile. Released in April 1980, she was rearrested the following March after her two younger brothers, in exile, forced the release of some People's Party supporters by hijacking a Pakistani Airlines plane in England. This arrest lasted nearly three years, during which she continually rejected offers of freedom contingent on her promise to abandon politics. Early in 1984, however, having developed a severe and dangerous ear infection, she was allowed to seek medical treatment in England, where she joined nearly half a million refugees from Zialand. The infection wasn't the only result of the prolonged detention and persistent harassment: she often felt confused now, even incoherent. But, with characteristic determination, she recovered and embarked on a policy of inveighing publicly against the Zia regime at every opportunity. She became quite a regular on TV interview shows in Europe and the United States.

In the summer of 1985, after one of her brothers died mysteriously in France, she returned to Pakistan to arrange for the burial and was promptly put under house arrest again but then, in November, allowed to leave the country. The next month Zia lifted martial law and gradually introduced some democratic reforms—only a few, but enough to tolerate Bhutto's return in April 1986. She received a glowing welcome by hundreds of thousands of cheering people along her motorcade route and at a political rally held in her honor.

She made an extensive tour of Pakistani cities, was elected cochair (with her mother) of the People's Party, demanded Zia's resignation and new elections, and was arrested again in August. Released only three weeks later, undaunted by rumors of conspiracies to assassinate her, she continued her public defiance in honor of her father, the martyred patriot.

Rather tall and very slender, an attractive woman, she entered an arranged marriage a la Pakistani custom in 1987. She departed from custom however, in demanding a veto power over the selection process and in refusing to let marriage, including her early pregnancy, interfere seriously with her political activity. The next year, after Zia's death in a plane crash, she had her baby, a son, and led her party to victory in the November election. Also elected, as president, was Ishaq Kahn, a Zia lieutenant. Despite his former connection, he praised her as having "the best qualities of leadership and foresight as a statesman" with "the country's love in her heart," and invited her to form a government as prime minister.

In that post she faced monumental difficulties. The country was on the verge of bankruptcy. Severe poverty among its hundred million people was chronic and widespread. The military was an intolerable drain on the nation's meager resources. During Zia's eleven-year reign the number of heroin addicts had risen from a few thousand to a million. Ethnic tensions, often erupting in violence, were aggravated by the presence of several million refugees from war-torn Afghanistan and by the hostilities of religious fundamentalism. Eighty percent of the population was illiterate. Hercules faced nothing so intimidating in the Augean stables.

And then there were some personal problems. She became pregnant again, becoming in January 1990 the first leader of a modern nation to bear a child while in office. This son wasn't her husband's only contribution to her difficulties.

President Kahn's public opinion of her changed radically, and he was to prove her nemesis. Her father has been charged with corruption, and now it was her turn, or at least her government's. Her husband faced charges of monumental corruption along with several of his political cronies. She was deposed, and the People's Party lost power in the October 1990 election to a coalition backed by the military.

She had left an impression of governmental dishevelment as well as corruption. During her twenty months in office, as *Time* reported it, she had been "guilty of colossal political blundering." She had interfered in army promotions, engaged in some bribery for political gain, broken promises, and failed to control serious unrest in a southern province. Her political coup de grace may have been at the hands of the U.S. Congress, which cut off the annual aid package of $600 million in 1990 when President Bush could no longer unabashedly certify that Pakistan didn't possess a nuclear weapon, a cutoff for which she was blamed.

And so the government settled back comfortably into its accustomed virility until her return in the fall of 1993 to a term complicated by her fourth pregnancy and by a feud with her family over their contention that her young nephew is the true (i.e., male) heir to her father's political legacy.

Anna Quindlen
New York Times Columnist (1953–)

She has been happy with the *New York Times*, and the *Times* has definitely been happy with her as its enormously popular columnist. When she quit to devote her time to her family, the editors persuaded her to contribute her essays freelance. When she received offers from other papers, the *Times* offered her a column of her own "about anything you want." When she decided again to quit, she was again offered an irresistible plum. The editors evidently knew when they had a good thing going.

Anna Quindlen was born in July 1953 in Philadelphia to an Irish Catholic father and Italian Catholic mother in a very Catholic atmosphere. She and her four younger siblings naturally attended Catholic schools, but schools where they were exposed to liberal ideas somewhat above the troglodyte level. (Her own testimony about this is rather ambiguous.) In high school she concentrated on editing the paper, cheerleading, and marriage prospects, the last being stimulated in her senior year by her meeting Gerald Krovatin, whom she married in 1978.

In 1972, during her first year at Barnard College, her mother's death left her with those four younger siblings to care for. This traumatic event profoundly rearranged her young life, but she managed somehow to meld school, homework, and *home*work into a successful combination, in addition to working part-time as a stringer for the *New York Post*. After her graduation in 1974 her family responsibilities abated somewhat as she switched to full-time reporting, which she found ever more satisfying despite a deep-seated yen to write fiction. (She'd had a story published in *Seventeen* while in college.)

In 1977 she moved to the *Times* as a city reporter assigned particularly to city hall. Her writing before long attracted such favorable editorial notice that, at 28, she was given a column of her own, becoming the youngest person in the paper's history to handle its biweekly feature entitled "About New York." Handle it she did until 1983, when she was raised to the exalted level of deputy metropolitan editor. Yet in 1985 she decided to quit. By then her two very young sons needed her at home, where there was also a typewriter eager to produce a novel. Its eagerness, however, was matched by the *Times*, which soon had her contributing freelance pieces for its weekly column, "Hers." Her misgivings about the arrangement were not long thereafter thoroughly dispelled by enthusiastic reader reactions and by several offers from admiring publishers at other papers.

Within a year, in the spring of '86, the *Times*'s executive editor, inspired by news of those offers, himself offered her a column of her own in which she could "write about anything you want." That was more than any person brimming with ideas and opinions could resist, and within another year the column, "Life in the 30s," was building a large and enchanted audience among readers not only of the *Times* but of other papers as well—sixty of them by 1988. She had a knack for making readers feel that she was writing to them as individuals, individuals with problems and ideas very like her own. Yet in December of that year, growing weary of the self-revelation involved, feeling that the column was getting stale, and hearing the call of family (a new daughter) and typewriter, she wrote a good-bye column and again handed in her notice.

Oh, *no!* the *Times* responded. Take a leave, sure, but how about coming back soon to write a column for the Op-Ed page? As to content, again you can write your own ticket. And so, before spring arrived in 1990, she was again entrancing her devoted readers, this time in a column titled "Public and Private," in which she gave her views on politics, government, war, the judiciary, the economy, women's issues like nondiscrimination, child care, abortion, whatever. (Her views on abortion are not subservient. The official Church has a right to its opinions, and she has a right to hers.)

In 1992 her work earned her the most prestigious of her several awards, a Pulitzer Prize for Commentary from Columbia University's Graduate School of Journalism. She has had her critics, of course, like any other opinionated person, but she insists that as a columnist she doesn't dictate ideas and opinions but simply presents them for readers' consideration. She hopes that a reader will at least occasionally concede that here's "an argument I haven't thought of." Her use of the word "argument" probably is significant.

Her typewriter finally produced that novel in 1991, *Object Lessons*, which was followed in 1993 by a collection of her Op-Ed columns, "Thinking Out Loud." Comfortably at home with her lawyer husband, children, and typewriter, she expects the 1990s to emphasize such problems as "child care and family planning and abortion and homelessness"—"and I certainly feel that I can go on writing about them forever."

Sharon Matola
Zoologist (1954–)

One day in 1983 in Belize City, a town of some 35,000 souls in eastern Central America, an English moviemaker completed his nature documentary and left behind, to their own devices, most of the animals used in his film. As a longtime animal lover and sometime lion tamer, his chagrined assistant took the abandoned creatures under her care. Just for a while, she assumed. But then other animals were added to her collection and, as cages began to proliferate, she found herself taking things quite seriously. Almost before she realized it, she had become the director of the Belize Zoo and Tropical Educational Center. Although armed with nothing more academically prestigious than a B.S. in biology, she soon earned an international reputation among wildlife professionals, one of whom admiringly acknowledged that her "credentials are her product."

Sharon Matola was born in June 1954 in Baltimore to businesspeople parents, between an older sister and younger brother. As a child she was attracted to baseball and to natural history, the latter interest being sustained by a collection of pets, such as butterflies for their beauty and worms for their primitive yet intriguing activity. This interest was sharpened considerably when, after her high school graduation in 1972, she enlisted in the U.S. Air Force and was sent for jungle training to Panama, where she encountered wildlife in eye-opening luxuriance.

Her thirty months of the disciplined life ("too old-boy" for her, she's said) were followed by a period of almost nomadic variety. In Iowa City in 1975 she ran a food store and took courses in Russian at the university. After three years of that she moved to Sarasota, where she enrolled in the University of South Florida's New College and on the side joined in a program familiarizing juvenile delinquents with the great outdoors. For a couple of months she understudied a lion tamer in a study of animal behavior conditioning—in Belize, where again she encountered wildlife in exhilarating luxuriance.

At the college, pursuing a degree in biology, she became so interested in fungi that, after her graduation in 1981, she continued at the university for a master's in that subject. This led, incongruously, to a job with a traveling circus in Mexico that advertised for "tall white women" as dancers. It would, she assumed, provide some wherewithal and occasional opportunities to gather Mexican mushrooms and assorted fungi to supplement her work at the university. The gypsy life worked out pretty well for a while, with her in the roles of dancer *and* performer with the big cats in the main act, working with four lions and half a dozen tigers. She was unhappy, however, with the male harassment of her and of the animals, so when the circus started playing in larger towns, sans fungi, in the summer of '82, she quit with a feeling of some relief.

Not long after, in Florida, she met the wildlife movie maker who would take her to Belize as caretaker for the animals in his documentary. There, late in 1982, when his funds ran out and he took off on another project, she was left with the peccaries, jaguars, assorted primates, reptiles, etc. Having grown fond of them during their four months in the jungle together, and knowing that they could no longer make it in the wild, she couldn't bring herself simply to release them, yet neither could she afford to keep them.

And so she arranged their cages in a primitive kind of zoo in Belize City, placing a sign at the entrance identifying this as the Belize Zoo and announcing a modest admission fee. She then visited a nearby bar to ask the bartender to send any visibly bored customers to the zoo just down the road, the first zoo ever in Belize. As the number of daily visitors (uninebriated) gradually grew, she began giving conducted tours. To attract the kiddie trade she lectured at schools, complete with entwined boa constrictor, and later persuaded the Education Ministry to approve the funding of a program of regular visits for schoolchildren, including an educational program for kids living too far away to make regular visits to the zoo.

Education was sorely needed. It soon dawned on her, to her astonishment, that only a tiny few of her visitors had ever seen fascinating wild animals like these, despite their being native to Belize. That settled it. The zoo, she decided, would have to become a permanent facility, a respected educational institution. That would take money, and so she began raising chickens and, every couple of weeks, mounting her motorcycle and distributing their meat up and down the coast. She also began inviting foreign visitors to join her, for a fee, on nature tours of the countryside. It wasn't easy, doing this and taking care herself of all the zoo details, but after several months she could, and did, hire a native as an assistant. She lucked out—he proved invaluable. With his help she developed the zoo to the point where he was eventually joined by fourteen others.

In 1984 she flew to Miami on a complimentary ticket to attend a convention of the American Association of Zoological Parks and Aquariums. Still quite penniless, she couldn't afford a room at the hotel but made do in a women's restroom with her own out-of-order sign on the door. At the convention she met a zoo architect who made up a plan for her new zoo, gratis. Contacts made there also proved a gold mine, and soon she was delightedly receiving contributions from animal conservation institutions, companies with business in Belize, and all sorts of interested people—contributions of money but also of animals. In 1991, on a thousand-acre site, the Belize Zoo and Tropical Educational Center was formally opened. There would be no more restrictive cages but spacious habitat enclosures and a complex including not only operating facilities but also a library and housing for animal research and conservation studies.

When she isn't rummaging about in the jungle, hiking about the country, climbing mountain peaks or supervising her zoo, she lives in a small cottage about a mile away—with her boa constrictor.

Susan Butcher
Dogsledder (1954–)

In first grade she wrote, "I hate the city." By fourth grade she had become more expansive and analytical: "I hate the city because society is ruining the earth for animals, and people who live in the country are happier." Eventually she would wind up driving a dogsled several times across nearly 1200 Alaskan miles from Anchorage to Nome over formidable mountains, on the ice of the northern sea and several rivers, across the charred and stump-strewn remnant of a forest, through warm air at 40 degrees above zero and cold air at 50 degrees below, through hurricane winds and blinding snowstorms, and through packs of variously menacing beasts of the Arctic wilds. She was certainly a person in the country, and definitely happier.

Susan Butcher was born in December 1954 in Cambridge, Massachusetts, to a businessman and a social worker. She and her older sister were taught independence by their mother and sailing by their father, who also gave each girl a set of tools so that they could help him with his naval carpentry projects in the garage. At sixteen she tried to enroll in a class on boat-building but was turned away, as she recalls, as gender-unsuitable. In high school, however, gender unsuitability didn't stop her from competing in a wide variety of sports while pulling down good grades in science and math. (Slight dyslexia made her less comfortable in literature classes.)

Meanwhile she had developed her lifelong affection for dogs, beginning with her first canine gift, a retriever, at age four. At fifteen it was a husky, and at sixteen (after her parents' divorce) it was another husky, which inspired her mother into a not-enough-room ultimatum. Thereupon she and the dogs moved in for a while with a less dog-tired grandmother before taking off, at seventeen, for Boulder, Colorado, where she became enthusiastically acquainted with dogsled racing and with a woman breeder and racer of sled dogs. She moved in as her assistant, accumulating considerable training in veterinary science.

Although Boulder was an improvement, it included aspects of civilization that bothered her, as when one of her dogs was stolen and another was killed in traffic, and when she had to drive miles out of town to reach hiking trailheads. So in 1975 she moved again, this time to Fairbanks, Alaska, a place chock full of readily accessible trails. She had been accepted by the University of Alaska to join in a program for the preservation of the musk oxen, an endangered species. Two years earlier she had read about dog mushing in a magazine, and about the Iditarod, that 1160-mile dogsled race from Anchorage to Nome. Her mouth watering, she began collecting likely dogs and, except during summer jobs at a salmon cannery, practicing mushing with them.

For the next couple of years she lived in a mountain cabin, enjoying a remote, primitive frontier life a la Thoreau and assiduously raising and training her dogs from birth (so that they would see her first and persistently thereafter). In 1977, when the musk oxen research program moved west to the village of Unalakeet, across the Norton Sound from Nome, she went with it, and there destiny introduced her to Joe Redington, Sr., a local notable famous as an inveterate traveler about Alaska by dogsled, as owner of a number of kennels close to Anchorage, and as an organizer of the Iditarod race. (The name comes from the trail used to deliver mail and vital supplies at the turn of the century.) With his help she got a sponsor and entered the next year's race. She won—not first place but nineteenth, just well enough to earn some of the prize money awarded to the first twenty to cross the finish line. (She was the first woman ever to win *any*thing.) In 1979 she did better, coming in ninth, and then she and Redingston took off on a 44-day trip by dogsled, history's first, to the grudgingly accessible 22,000-foot peak of Mount McKinley.

She continued training and preparatory mushing—about 2000 miles for every dog before a race—and also improving, finishing fifth in 1980 and '81. In 1982, despite some injuries, blinding snowstorms, and 30-foot-deep snowdrifts, she made the grueling trip in a little over 16 days and came in second, less than four minutes behind the winner. Although falling back to ninth place in 1983, she came in second again in 1984, despite a dunking, dog team and all, through the broken ice of Norton Sound and a subsequent run of some hours behind her sled to stave off death by freezing. Next year her luck was even worse when, soon after the start, a very hungry and uncomfortably pregnant moose assaulted her team, stamping and kicking two dogs to death and maiming thirteen others while she struggled vainly to fight it off with an ax. It took a fellow contestant, who, unlike her, carried a gun, to end the fracas. With only four sound dogs left, she opted out of the race and returned to Anchorage to nurse the hurt dogs as well as her own injuries. Meanwhile, to her chagrin, another woman, Libby Riddles, became the first woman ever to win the race.

Chagrin became determination, and in 1986, '87, and '88 she won the races in record time to become the first three-in-a-row winner of any gender. Bad luck plagued her again in 1989, in the form of a retardant known as canine diarrhea, but in 1990 she won her fourth victory. She regularly entered other races as well, setting records and collecting prize money. In 1990 the Iditarod's prize of $50,000 was augmented by another $30,000 from other races.

The accumulated proceeds have helped her and her lawyer husband David Monson, also a dogsledder, to establish and operate their Trail Breaker Kennels in the cozy wilderness to the north of Fairbanks, about a hundred inhospitable miles south of the Arctic Circle. There they affectionately raise and train dogs for sale, for prices up to $10,000. A celebrity now, with an agent, she visits the warmer forty-eight states in the summer on publicity tours. She has of course received many honors, including being named Outstanding Female Athlete of the World by the International Academy of Sports in 1989. The year before however, the United States Academy of Achievement had nominated her Athlete of the Year, without the condescending "Female."

Maria Shriver
Broadcast Journalist (1955–)

With uncles like John, Robert, and Edward Kennedy, would she ever be known as anything but the niece? Yes, because her thing was broadcast journalism. She would do her thing and become known as Maria Shriver, broadcast journalist. But it would take a while.

She was born in Chicago in November 1955, the second of five children. Her mother was Eunice Kennedy, tireless founder and promoter of the Special Olympics. Her father was Sargent Shriver, lawyer, businessman, Peace Corps director, ambassador, vice-presidential candidate. It was during his vice-presidential campaigning that she discovered "her thing." How she spent her summer vacation was traveling about with his press contingent. She enjoyed the correspondents' company and respected their fascination with the news and with reporting it. She also noticed that people generally were becoming ever more dependent on television for the news.

And so she set her sights on a career in broadcast news. After earning her B.A. in American Studies from Georgetown University, in 1977 she found work as writer and producer, as well as gofer and factotum, for the news division of a Philadelphia TV station, learning the business the hard way but also thoroughly enough to be ready for whatever opportunity might strike. In 1980 she joined Uncle Ted's futile campaign against Jimmy Carter for the Presidential nomination.

The campaign was a draining experience for the niece, but it left the woman, now in her mid-twenties, more firmly committed than ever to her chosen career. To reenter it she resorted to visiting an agent in Los Angeles, only to be told, largely as a result of the rigors of campaigning, that he couldn't take her on in her current unpresentable condition. Lose some weight, take the edge off that Kennedy-eastern accent, and learn to think fast on your feet. Two years later, after losing forty superfluous pounds, undergoing some voice training, and practicing mental agility, she went back to the same agent, who this time signed her on unhesitatingly.

She also moved to work and live on the West Coast, despite some family disparagement, in the hope of at least downplaying her role as niece. After a couple of years as a reporter for *PM Magazine*, she landed a job as West Coast reporter for CBS's morning news show. Eager to be accepted as a competent professional, she reacted ambivalently to being named by *Harper's Bazaar* in 1986 as one of the country's ten most beautiful women.

But at least that nomination came a year after CBS recognized her professional competence as well as her good looks by promoting her to the job of coanchor in New York for the morning news show, the job held earlier by Diane Sawyer. Ironically, she had just become engaged to the West Coast

Hercules Arnold Schwarzenegger and thus faced the prospect of a time-consuming, demanding job a continent away from him. He understood its importance to her and her career, however, and even urged her to resist any network tendency to give her any less on-air time than her male coanchor. She wound up with equal pay, equal billing.

The job proved demanding indeed, requiring her presence at the studio at four in the morning, three hours of preparation with newspapers and potential questions for interviewees, two hours of broadcasting plus three more hours for updated news bulletins then an afternoon of cleaning up paperwork and getting ready for the following day. If lucky, she'd get home in time for the evening news on TV, for such chores as inevitably would have been overlooked, and for horizontal collapse. Her schedule was hectic, but she preferred being "on the edge of hysteria," she said, to being bored. A calming influence was her genuine friendship with her male co-anchor, Forrest Sawyer, who has described her as "totally professional."

Her performance received generally good reviews from TV critics, with the notable exception of the *Washington Post*'s acerbic Tom Shales, but her popularity and strenuous work routine weren't enough to win out over the competition supplied by the other networks. The show's cancellation in 1986 was a hard blow. Yet she received enough offers from local TV stations to boost her morale. Rather than go local, however, she accepted an offer from NBC to cohost a news show opposite Charles Kuralt's *Sunday Morning* and to anchor a monthly evening news show called *Main Street*. In addition, she was assigned to a variety of news specials. By 1989 she was valuable enough to be signed by NBC News to a four-year contract at a salary approaching half a million a year. For this tidy sum she coanchored weekends with Garrick Utley and cohosted a prime-time weekly special, in addition to replacing anchors as needed on the regular morning and evening news shows.

In 1990 she gave up coanchoring to star in her own prime time show, *Cutting Edge with Maria Shriver*, interviewing people on the cutting edge of their professions, and then, in 1991, to host a similar show, *First Person with Maria Shriver*, which she could handle from California, eliminating the cross-country ping-pong. Her routine was much less hectic now, requiring less time away from her two very young daughters. (After nine years of intermittent courtship, she had become Mrs. Schwarzenegger in April 1986, respecting but by no means sharing his political views.) Her daughters are important to her: in early October 1992, for instance, she was granted an opportunity for a rare interview with Uncle Jack's old enemy, Fidel Castro, and summarily postponed it to take daughter Katherine to her first day in school. Held later, the interview proved downright epochal.

Family life, indeed, had become so important that she turned down a CBS offer of a prime time coanchor job in New York. Her good friend Oprah Winfrey admires her scale of values, her "sense of balance." People tell her how wonderful her life is, how "nothing's going wrong." "Yeah," she often replies, the black Irish in her recalling the mishaps and failures, "not yet anyway."

Mae Jemison
Astronaut (1956–)

As a child she dreamed of space travel, and as an adult she held on to the dream until it finally came true. Meanwhile she earned a medical degree, practiced medicine, served with the Peace Corps, studied chemical engineering, and worked actively for Afro-American causes, among other things. No devil owned *her* workshop.

Mae Carol Jemison was born in October 1956 in Decatur, Alabama, but fortunately she and her older sister and brother grew up in Chicago, where her father was a maintenance supervisor and her mother a teacher. Her school years were the years of the Apollo flights to the moon (and back), inspiring her into reading omnivorously about stars, planets, the moon, satellites—especially manned but not yet womaned satellites circling the earth. In addition, Chicago's magnificent Museum of Science and Industry was close enough to home for frequent periods of educational enchantment.

Although her interests in high school included art, dance, archeology, and anthropology, among other things, in her senior year she decided to make a career of biomedical engineering. Graduating precociously in 1973, she enrolled at Stanford University on a National Achievement Scholarship, opting for majors in chemical engineering and African/Afro-American studies; participating in sports, dance and theater activities; and being the first of her gender to be elected president of the Black Student Union. She was intent on being a well-rounded person with a well-rounded background. She was still focused on space—especially after NASA in 1977 began recruiting women and minority candidates—but she wanted to have alternatives available.

After receiving her B.S. and B.A. degrees in both majors, she began that same year (1977) working toward an M.D. at Cornell while serving in her spare time as president of the school's Medical Students' Executive Council and of its chapter of the National Student Medical Association. In her *additional* spare time, sponsored by the American Medical Student Association, she undertook further graduate study in Cuba and, under the aegis of the African Medical and Research Foundation, nursed the sick in Kenya and, a bit later, refugees from Cambodia in Thailand. All this would prove to be relevant background when, after receiving her M.D. in 1981 and interning for a year, she began practicing medicine in polyglot Los Angeles.

But not for long. From early 1983 to mid–1985 she worked in western

Africa as a medical officer in the Peace Corps learning to "assert" herself, as she put it, as a physician despite her very conspicuous female youthfulness. Back in the U.S. in 1985, working for an HMO and taking night classes in chemical engineering, she decided to assert herself into the space program and submitted her application to NASA. But that agency's shuttle program came to a virtual halt shortly thereafter as a result of the tragic *Challenger* disaster in January 1986. It wasn't until mid-1987 that she moved to Houston as the first black woman in NASA's training program for astronauts. She and her 14 fellow trainees had been selected from a total of 2000 applicants.

After a year of training and about three more years of working on various assignments, she began planning experiments, with American and Japanese fellow scientists, for her first flight, the "STS-47, Space Lab-J" mission. In September 1992 she and six others took off in the shuttle *Endeavor* for 127 encirclements of the earth over the next eight days. It was, she later conceded, an act of faith, but she had plenty of *that*. Among other things.

Besides gazing wistfully down on her old hometown, as the medic on board she was kept busy conducting an experiment with biofeedback methods, designed to determine their value as therapy for motion sickness, which can interfere with astronaut effectiveness especially during the early days of a flight. She measured the loss of bone calcium, which can limit the amount of time that humans can spend in uninterrupted flight, and studied the impact of weightlessness on the development of frog embryos and tadpoles—and was delighted to find later that they became strapping young adults.

Her achievements have brought her celebrity, which in turn has brought her many honors and awards, including the naming of a Detroit public school after her. (It specializes in science and technology.) She resigned from NASA in March 1993 to found a corporation, the Jemison Group, for research into and development of technological advances. But she'd like to return to space travel if the opportunity arises. Indeed, she has her eye on Mars.

Katie Couric
Television News Anchor (1957–)

In the mid–1980s she was a news reporter for a Miami TV station developing considerable competence in her off-camera work, but according to her producer, she was "terrible live," unable to handle the earpiece properly, awkward in speaking to the camera. Katie Couric agreed: she considered herself "the workhorse, street-reporter type" whose bosses never encouraged her to be anything else. And so in 1991, soon after she became co-anchor on NBC's morning show *Today* a network vice president, impressed by the sharp rise in the show's ratings, decided that she was "a pleasant surprise."

Katherine Anne Couric was born in January 1957 in Arlington, Virginia, thereby with her two older sisters outnumbering her lone older brother. Her father, earning a satisfying living in journalism and public relations, would prove a major influence in her choice of career. Her homemaking mother was a major influence in other ways, preparing her for doing as well as she did in school, pulling down grades good enough for the National Honor Society while doing her more energetic bit in cheerleading and in the gym and on the track, as well as contributing to her high school paper. After four years at the University of Virginia, helping to edit the college newspaper and earning honors in American studies, she graduated in 1979 and, with her father's advice, set her career sights on television news.

An entry desk job with ABC News in Washington, D.C., soon led to her being made an assignment editor for CNN's Washington bureau—unfortunately, since the job necessitated her being on the air occasionally. Her voice, it turned out, had a tin-whistle quality so grating that the president of CNN ordered the station never to let her appear before another camera. She was transferred as an associate producer to Atlanta, where, after recovering from an understandable bout of depression, she took speech lessons to learn about voice control and projection. Promoted to producer, she was assigned a daily CNN show featuring news and general information. Using the job to improve her reporting and interviewing techniques, as well as her voice quality, before long she was made a regular correspondent, assigned to cover a number of races in the 1984 election. To her dismay, however, the job proved only temporary. Indeed, her resignation was requested and accepted.

With discouragement fading in the light of determination, she found herself a reporting job with a Miami TV station. For the next couple of years she covered the standard local fare of fires, crime, etc. for a twice-daily news show, but she also wrote, produced, and presented a series of reports on child pornography that won her an award for excellence. "She was smart and knew how to put stories together," explained the producer quoted above, "but her presentation was terrible."

Nevertheless she managed to return to Washington and land a job as a reporter for a late-night news show on KRC, an NBC affiliate. Again she was assigned to cover the standard local fare, but, also again, she was responsible for an award-winning series, this one exposing the crafty shenanigans of a dating service for handicapped people. Thoroughly reliable and capable as a reporter, she was as thoroughly a flop as an anchor. She ought to find a job an anchor with a smaller station, for experience, her news director advised her in July 1989, or, better, fill a current opening at NBC as a second-level reporter at the Pentagon. She chose the better alternative.

This was fine with Tim Russert, chief of the network's Washington bureau, who had seen her on-camera reporting (though not her anchoring) and had found her invariable "competent and unflustered" in covering all kinds of stories. Soon her reports from the Pentagon during the American invasion of Panama brought her an invitation to anchor the *Nightly News* on Saturdays, and in February 1990, to fill in as substitute coanchor on the *Today* show.

A few months later, having been promoted to national correspondent, she was reporting from the Pentagon on the Great Persian Gulf War and making herself enough of a celebrity to be asked to replace the regular *Today* coanchor Deborah Norville during her maternity leave. Six weeks later, after impressive interviews with war-related figures like General Schwartzkoph and Jordan's King Hussein and after a network-titillating 13 percent rise in the program's ratings, Norville's decision not to return brought Couric her formal assignment as regular coanchor with Bryant Gumbel, confirmed after a successful year with a five-year contract at a reported million a year. The rookie with the vocal squeal had become a poised, natural (and contralto) performer on the anchor desk, quick-witted and quick to smile, as well as an adroit interviewer of myriad celebrities, including David Duke, Ross Perot and Bill Clinton, Luciano Pavarotti and Placido Domingo, Warren Beatty and Whoopi Goldberg, and George and Barbara Bush. (George had wandered into the room simply to say hello, but she started questioning him about various policies and held him there for nearly twenty minutes. As he was leaving she kiddingly suggested that she'd been able to do so "because I'm so easy." He grinned. "Easy? I don't want to get in a fight with you." The ultimate masculine accolade?)

Wife of a lawyer (and supportive husband), Jay Monahan, and mother of a young daughter, she is a bundle of sparkling energy at work and at home. The number and character of the tributes from her male colleagues are remarkable. From Bryant Gumbel have come adjectives like terrific, easygoing, curious, bright, fun to be with. According to Jeffrey Zucker, *Today's* executive producer, when NBC "found Katie" it may have almost inadvertently "defined morning television for the nineties." Perhaps "morning" is too restrictive. As of August 1993 she's been coanchoring *Now, with Tom Brokaw and Katie Couric* in *prime* time.

She couldn't be happier. She feels she's putting her skills to good use, and she can hardly remember those ugly-duckling days.

Rigoberta Menchú
Nobel Peace Prize Winner (1959–)

In 1979 her teenage brother was dragged out of his village, tortured for a couple of weeks, then flayed alive, set afire and burned to death. The following year her father died with 38 others in the Spanish embassy when the besieging Guatemalan soldiers tossed a number of hand grenades into the building. A few months later her mother was kidnapped, tortured, and raped over several weeks and then taken out to a hill and left there to die, her body prey to wild animals. Such was the treatment the daughter could expect if she continued her alleged "Communist" opposition to Guatemala's official reign of terror. Yet continue it she did.

Rigoberta Menchú was born in 1959 in Chimel, a village in northern Guatemala, where her father, a catechist, held a position of leadership and her mother served as midwife and herbalist. They and their nine children were eleven of the six to eight million Maya Indians making up most of the country's population, the tyrannized majority. Parents and children spent their summers eking out a subsistence living from their tiny bit of acreage and their winters being suffocatingly trucked south to work on the coastal cotton and coffee plantations. The hours were long, from well before sunrise till sunset. During those hours the owners at times had the fields sprayed with insecticide, asphyxiating one of her brothers, among others. (When her family asked that he be buried, they were summarily discharged without pay.)

In 1971 she spent several months in Guatemala City as a slave in an affluent household, until brutal drudgery and employer contumely forced her to return home. There she found her father in prison for leading the villagers' resistance against the attacks of soldiers hired by landowners to drive the Mayas away and take over their farms for more profitable consolidation. Released about a year later, he was shortly thereafter kidnapped, tortured, and nearly killed, yet he continued with his rebellious activity as soon as he was able, traveling about the country for support from the sympathetic influential, including some Europeans. This time he had a companion, already a fellow catechist and rebel, his teenage daughter.

In 1977 he was arrested and imprisoned for life for his "Communist" intransigence. The Mayas' reaction to this was so angry and menacing that the local authorities released him after a fortnight, threatening him with assassination, however, if he didn't just *stop*. Far from stopping, of course, he went further, joining other political perseverants in founding a Committee of Peasant Unity and persisting in his incorrigible recalcitrance, at first secretly and then, after May 1979, more openly. The next year his sons and favorite daughter, who was learning Spanish in addition to three Mayan dialects, joined the Committee and its struggle against patrician landgrabbing. In consequence, she and her family in the fall of 1979 were compelled to witness the flaying and torching of her teenage brother.

In January 1980 her father, having long ago exhausted all his legal alternatives, joined with 38 other dissidents in taking over a radio station and airing their complaints and then seeking asylum in the Spanish embassy, where they were all killed by the disciplinary grenades described above. (The building was burned to the ground.) Three months later his widow was disciplined, also as described above.

By this time her daughter was actively organizing workers, and in early

1980 about 8000 sugar and cotton fieldworkers struck against the coast plantations, supported by ten times that many of their fellow sufferers, although the strike lasted only about two weeks. (Supporters included some nuns and priests, many of them disciplined with the customary torture.) After a Labor Day demonstration in 1981 protesting the endless working hours, she became the focus of government hostility, went into hiding, and perilously made her way to Mexico, where she settled down in comparative safety, doing whatever she could to promote the cause, among other things lobbying for Indian rights at the UN and acting as prime spokesperson for the newly formed National Organization of Guatemalan Widows.

In December 1992 she was the controversial recipient of the Nobel Peace Prize for, among other things, "maintaining a disarming humanity in a brutal world," although the head of Guatemala's military complained that she "had only defamed the fatherland" before he retaliated with attacks against the Mayas in the northern portion of that fatherland. An American critic of elitist persuasion assailed her as promoting a cause not "of peace and reconciliation, but of murder and subversion." She nonetheless accepted her award of $1.2 million to set up a foundation in her father's memory in Mexico City for the extension of her efforts to protect and educate her Indian people not only in Guatemala but also throughout Central America.

When she leaves her home in a Mexico City ghetto, she's escorted by a coterie of protective friends concerned about those death threats she continually receives. Many such threats are accompanied by bouquets of baby's breath and marigolds, customarily the flowers for funerals in Latin America. So far as she knows, only four members of her family are still alive.

Susan Faludi
Author and Gadfly (1959–)

In 1991 this *Wall Street Journal* staff writer received a John Hancock Award for Excellence in Business and Financial Journalism and then a Pulitzer Prize for a front-page treatment of the leveraged buyout of Safeway Stores. This was gratifying recognition for a young woman of 32 in a milieu of gobbler pontificating. But meanwhile she had turned her penetrating gaze from business to All That Bull about women's achievement of their feminist goals having sunk them into rueful misery. This she did especially in her physically ponderous, assiduously annotated best-selling book, *Backlash: The Undeclared War Against American Women*, which turned her from business gadfly into, as she was wryly put it, "feminist du jour."

Susan Faludi was born in April 1959 in New York, daughter of a photographer and writer-editor, both talented. She and her younger brother grew up in an environment replete with provider-homemaker families, fanning her congenital spark of rebellion. When as a fifth-grader she took a poll of her fellow inmates which revealed that they were decisively anti-war, pro-choice, and pro–ERA, a local John Bircher far-righteously condemned her for promoting godless Communism. In high school, as editor of the school paper, she inveighed against born-again Christian assemblies on school property, and her valedictory speech was similarly inflammatory. In college, on scholarship, as editor of the *Harvard Crimson* she reported on sexual harassment despite strenuous opposition from on high, directed at her until her charges were confirmed.

In 1981 she graduated summa cum laude and Phi Beta Kappa, with majors in history and literature and a history award for her senior thesis. Having spent some time as a reporter trainee with a Staten Island paper and the *Boston Globe*, after graduation she took a job as news and copy clerk for the *New York Times* but also wrote for various sections of the paper, especially the business section. From 1983 through 1989 she went peripatetic, though devotedly journalistic, working for papers in Miami, Atlanta, and San Jose, gathering assorted awards and citations as she went.

In January 1990 she joined the *Wall Street Journal's* San Francisco bureau as staff writer, and the next year won the aforementioned John Hancock Award for her business reporting. Her Pulitzer was for an investigative report on the consequences of the 1986 Safeway LBO, such as layoffs, reductions in pay, and production speedups. Doubtless as gratifying as the Pulitzer was her managing editor's praise for he "brilliant reporting and penetrating analysis," seconded by an overwhelming response from readers, favorable but for Neanderthal carping. But in the meantime...

In 1986 her curiosity had been aroused by a *Newsweek* report of a Harvard-Yale joint study of college-educated single women which concluded that such women's chances of marrying dwindled precipitously with advancing age: 30 percent at 30, 5 percent at 35, 1.3 percent at 40, when a woman was more likely to encounter a terrorist than a marriage prospect. Her own closer study of the study revealed some gross statistical errors invalidating its conclusions, yet exposés, by herself and others, failed to subdue the burgeoning extrapolations by the media in the thoughtless depiction of unsubmissive women's spouseless misery in movies, books, TV, whatever. Women today, she argued in interviews, can be more relaxed about marriage. They're taking their own sweet time. And so she quit work to write a book on the subject. After two years of dogged research she joined the Institute for Research on Women and Gender at Stanford University, and two years later the book was finished.

It was painfully obvious, she insisted in *Backlash*, that women were still victims of discrimination, harassment, even violent abuse at work, in the home, on the street, in business, sports, education, the courts, government (and the Senate Judiciary Committee). Furthermore, according to consistent poll results, most women by far believe that they still have a long way to go for anything resembling equality of treatment. Any rue with which their hearts might be laden comes not from overfulfillment of goals but from accumulated frustration. "The truth is that the last decade [the 1980s] has seen a powerful counterassault on women's rights, a backlash, an attempt to retract the handful of small and hard-won victories that the feminist movement did manage to win for women."

The book, quickly selling hotcake-fashion, was received with grateful enthusiasm and critical hostility, domestic and foreign. It was a book "guaranteed to make some readers furious," wrote one reviewer, "both enraging and hopeful," wrote another. Still another attacked it for libeling homemaking women as spineless patsies. For *Commentary*, unsurprisingly, it was "a thin book" guilty of stereotyping, and in *National Review* it demonstrated that "misreporting data appears to be something of a personal hobby with her." For the *Library Journal* it was a debunker of "shoddy scholarship and half-truths" and a "most important book."

The author's evaluation would seem to be definitive. "To the extent that *Backlash* arms women with information and a good dose of cynicism," she told Carol Pogash of *Working Woman*, "I think it will have served its purpose. It's also very large, so it can be thrown at misogynists."

Maya Lin
Artist (1959–)

In high school she took advanced courses in the literature of existentialism (Sartre, Camus, et al.), a philosophy inconclusive and depressing enough to encourage in anyone a preoccupation with death, as it did in her. In college, studying architecture, she found inspiration in cemetery headstones and monuments. On a visit to Europe she made a point of stopping at graveyards. So it was only appropriate that her design was chosen for the now celebrated Vietnam Veterans Memorial.

Maya Ling Lin was born in October 1959 in Athens, Ohio. Her father, a noted ceramist, was dean of the fine arts school of Ohio State University, and her mother taught literature there; both had come to the United States about twenty years earlier. Her father's father, a distinguished lawyer and political reformer in China between the two World Wars, spent much time in London on assignment to the League of Nations, and there he and his daughter (her aunt) were readily accepted by the literary set (Wells, Forster, Hardy, Russell, Mansfield, et al.). The daughter fell in love with a poet of later renown but married, at her father's insistence, an architect, also of later renown, and eventually, after studying architecture at Yale, embarked on her own career of designing theater sets. Such was Maya Lin's genetic predisposition, and it is hardly surprising that one of her earliest preoccupations as a child was fashioning pottery.

Nor is it surprising that at Yale she would major in architecture, or that as a senior she would take a course in funerary architecture. It was in that course that the professor whimsically asked his students to submit designs, individually, in the competition for the Vietnam Veterans Memorial. To that end she visited the proposed site in Washington, D.C., on the mall between the Capital and the Lincoln Memorial. The monument, she decided, would have to be simple and inviting, "like opening up your hands" in a welcoming, protective gesture. Thus the extended arms of the famous "V," its polished black granite incised with some 58,000 names of dead and missing veterans. It also was highly reflective, implying union with earth, sky, and the visitors, many of them in tears.

Her design was one of 1420 entries in the competition, and it took the judges a week to select it as the "superbly harmonious" winner. Their decision, however, after it was formally announced in May 1981, evoked a chorus of somewhat different viewpoints. It was, some outraged professional veterans complained, an utterly inappropriate "wall of shame," a "degrading ditch," and a memorial incongruously "built by a gook." While she went on to earn her Master of Fine Arts degree from Yale that summer, H. Ross Perot—he of subsequent political celebrity who had bankrolled the memorial competition—financed heated demonstrations by overwrought veterans against her polished black granite atrocity.

The next year the fervid dissatisfaction found expression in a proposal that another, more conventional monument—which would depict three inspirational servicemen in bronze complete with American flag, and which had placed third with the judges—be added to the site in front of the "v" at the juncture of the two wings. Her reaction was that it would be a kind of statuesque graffiti in that position, and enough critics agreed for it to be sited some 120 feet away. For the dedication in November the program's front cover carried an illustration of the third-place statuary, although a panel of critics meanwhile had independently and enthusiastically endorsed the judges' selection.

And so the shy and controversial Lin continued her studies of architecture, at first at Harvard and then back at Yale, from which she received her final degree in 1986. Thereafter she worked at her profession, designing plans for public parks, business logos and computers, houses, a glass ceiling for a railroad station in New York City. Her sculptures began appearing in various galleries. Late in 1987 she was commissioned by Montgomery, Alabama, for another memorial, this one in honor of the martyrs of the battle to end racial discrimination. Again she refused to be a slave to convention. Inspired by Martin Luther King, Jr.'s phrase that blacks' demands would not be satisfied "until justice rolls down like waters and righteousness like a mighty stream," her Civil Rights Memorial features a nine-foot-high wall with those words inscribed on it behind a crystalline sheet of flowing water, and, nearby, a twelve-foot disc of black granite with water very gently spreading out of an inconspicuous hole at its center, surrounded by an engraved stone giving a history of the civil rights movement and some of the names that inspired it. This memorial, like the one in Washington, has proved to be a site where the few initial sneers have been engulfed in a flood of heartfelt and very appreciative tears. At the dedication she was "surprised and moved when people started to cry." Indeed, some of their tears "were becoming part of the memorial."

In 1892 Yale had magnanimously begun admitting women into its graduate school, and in 1992 Maya Lin was asked to design a hundredth-anniversary memorial. Her response was an oval table of green granite (again, with water flowing over it) carrying an incised history of women's participation in the school by listing, in a spiral, the number of women graduate students each year from 1701 (Yale's founding) through 1991, with the years before 1892 wryly featuring zeroes.

Lately she has taken to designing houses and, especially, the interior for the new location of New York's Museum of African Art. However its interior decor might turn out, one can be sure that it won't be stuffy.

General References

Bird, Caroline. *Enterprising Women*. New York: W.W. Norton, 1976.

Bohigian, Valerie. *Ladybucks*. New York: Dodd, Mead, 1987.

Clark, Electa. *Leading Ladies*. New York: Stein & Day, 1976.

Fraser, Antonia. *The Warrior Queens*. New York: Knopf, 1989.

Gilbert, Lynn, and Gaylen Moore. *Particular Passions*. New York: Clarkson N. Potter, 1981.

Harrison, Patricia (ed.). *America's New Women Entrepreneurs*. Washington, DC: Acropolis Books 1986.

Jackson, Guida M. *Women Who Ruled*. Santa Barbara, CA: ABC-CLIO, 1990.

Jensen, Marlene. *Women Who Want to Be Boss*. Garden City, NY: Doubleday, 1987.

Konolige, Kit. *The Richest Women in the World*. New York: Macmillan, 1985.

Kufrin, Joan, and George Kufrin. *Uncommon Women*. Piscataway, NJ: New Century, 1981.

Lamson, Peggy. *In the Vanguard*. Boston: Houghton Mifflin, 1979.

Longstreet, Stephen. *The Queen Bees*. New York: Bobbs-Merrill, 1979.

O'Neill, Lois Decker (ed.). *The Women's Book of World's Records and Achievements*. Garden City, NY: Doubleday, 1979.

Rennert, Richard (ed.). *Female Leaders*. New York: Chelsea House, 1994.

Telgen, Diane, and Jim Kamp (eds.). *Notable Hispanic American Women*. Detroit: Gale Research, 1993.

Uglow, Jennifer S. *The International Dictionary of Women's Biography*. New York: Continuum, 1982.

Index

Abbey, George 206
Abernathy, Ralph 69
"About New York" 212
Abrams, Robert 130
Adams, Brook 107
Addams, Jane 21
Advisory Committee on Women 119
The African Elephant 156
African Medical and Research Foundation 220
African Wildlife Foundation 157
Agnew, Spiro 71
Alice Eastwood Hall of Botany 12
All Screwed Up 96
All the President's Men 71
Amboseli National Park 156, 157
Amelia Earhart Research Foundation 34
American Academy of Arts and Sciences 50
American Association of Anthropologists 37
American Association of Zoological Parks and Aquariums 215
American Athletic Union 63
American Bar Association 182, 200
American Civil Liberties Union 111–12, 143
American Enterprise Institute 93
American Medical Association 117
American Museum of Natural History 38
American National Opera Company 99
American Nuclear Guinea Pigs 143
American Red Cross 140
American Tennis Association 97

Andropov, Andrei 80
Apollo program 220
The Archeology of Beekeeping 67
Argonne National Laboratory 48
Arias Sanchez, Pedro 101
Arizona Bar Association 105
Arizona Women Lawyers Association 105
Arkansas Advocates for Children and Families 200
Around the World in Eighty Days 14
Aspin, Lee 159
Associated Press 73, 78, 98

Babbitt, Bruce 105
Bacardi Breezer 174
Backlash: The Undeclared War Against American Women 225, 226–27
The Baltimore Sun 49
Bard, Joseph 31
Barry, Marion 83, 180, 181
Bateson, Gregory 39
Beatty, Warren 110
Bee Research Association 66
Bee World 66
"Behind Asylum Bars" 14
Belize Zoo and Tropical Education Center 214–15
Bellevue Hospital 14
Bendix Transcontinental Air Race 56
Benedict, Ruth 38
Bentsen, Lloyd 134
Berkshire Music Center (Tanglewood) 98
Berson, Solomon 76–77
Bethune, Albertus 17

Bethune, Mary McLeod 17–18
Beyond the Best Interests of the Child 199
Bhutto, Benazir 209–11
Bhutto, Zulfikar Ali 209–11
Black Panthers 103
Black Student Union 228
Blackwell's Island 14
Bloodworth, C. T. 196
Bloodworth-Thomason 196–98
Blum, Richard 114
Bly, Nellie 12–14
Boadicea 1–3, 91
Boaz, Frank 38
Body and Soul 169
Body Shops 168, 169
Boggs, Hale 177
Boggs, Lindy 177
Boleyn, Anne 5
Bonner, Elena 79–81
Book of Etiquette 58
A Book of Honey 67
Bork, Robert 111, 112, 122, 182
Born, Max 47
The Boston Globe 140, 165, 226
Boston University's Opera Workshop 99
Bourke-White, Margaret 44–46
Bradlee, Ben 71
Brady, James 195
BrainReserve 173–74
Branch Davidians 149
Brandeis, Louis D. 21
Breaking with Tradition 88
Brinkley, David 178
British Beekeepers' Association 66
Brookings Institution 106, 107
Brooklyn Museum 46
Brooks, Edward 199
Broun, Heyward 30
Brown, John 9
Brown vs. Board of Education 68, 69
Bryceson, Derek 127
Buchenwald 43, 46, 74
Buckley, William F. 203
Bueno, Maria 176
Bureau of Fisheries 49, 50
Bureau of Indian Affairs 187, 188
Bush, George 120, 122, 123, 132, 139–40, 151, 167, 185, 104–5, 211, 223
Butcher, Susan 215–17
Butterfly Cooing Like a Dove 52

Caldwell, Erskine 45
Caldwell, Sarah 98–99
California Academy of Science 11, 12
Carlton Club 90
Carnegie Council for Children 199
Carpenter, "Liz" 71
Carson, Rachel 48–50
Carswell, G. Harrold 182
Carter, Jimmy 85, 110, 134, 136, 139, 141, 194, 195, 200, 218
Carter, Rosalyn 110
Castro, Fidel 101, 219
Catalyst 86–88
Catherine of Aragon 5
Catt, Carrie Chapmen 26
Cecil, William 6
Celler, William 163
Challenger 206, 207, 221
Chamberlain, Neville 27
Chamorro, Cardenal Pedro 100
Chamorro, Violeta 100–2
Charles VII 3–4
Chavez, Linda 136–37
Cherokee Nation 187–88
Children's Defense Fund 153, 199
Chimps 122
Chisholm, Conrad 85
Chisholm, Shirley 83–86
Chopin, Frederic 8
Chung, Connie 191–93
Church of the Advocate 103
Churchill, Winston 2, 19, 32
Civil Rights Memorial 229
Clinton, Bill 72, 101, 108, 112, 116, 117, 141, 142, 148, 149, 162, 196, 199–201
Coalition for a Democratic Majority 93
Coalition of Concerned Citizens for a Better D.C. 180
Cochran, Jacqueline 55–57
Cochrane, Elizabeth 13–14
Cohen, Stanley 54
Cold Springs Harbor Laboratory 41
College Bowl 199
Coming of Age in Samoa 38
Commentary 92, 93, 227
Commission on Judicial Conduct (New York) 164
Committee on Consumer Interests 138
Committee on Peasant Unity 224
Common Cause 107

Congregation of the Missionaries of
Charity 61
Congressional Budget and Impound-
ment Act 107
Congressional Women's Caucus 136
Convention on International Trade in
Endangered Species 157
Conyers, John, Jr. 69
Coolidge, Calvin 34, 93
Cornell, Douglas B. 73
Cosmopolitan 31, 34
Coughlin, Charles 31, 32
Council of Economic Advisers 167
Couric, Katie 221–23
Cousins, Norman 58
Cox, Archibald 122
Crane, Eva 65–67
Crane, James Alfred 66
Cressman, Luther 37, 38, 39
Cresson, Edith 123–25
Crippen, Robert 205, 206
Cronkite, Walter 204
Croze, Harvey 156, 157
Cutting Edge with Maria Shriver 219

Dachau 74
Dade County 147, 148
The Dallas Times-Herald 107
D'Amato, Alphonse 104, 130
Davis, Nelson 10
Daytona Normal and Industrial Insti-
tute 17
DeGaulle, Charles 123
Delco, Wilhelmina 119
Delta Sigma Theta 82
Democratic Party Committee 120
Department of Energy 141–43
Department of Health, Education and
Welfare 107, 108, 138, 160, 162
Department of Housing and Urban
Development 160, 161
Department of Justice 149
Department of Labor 140
Department of Transportation 139
Designing Women 196, 197
The Dial 7
"Dictatorship and Double Standards"
92, 93
Didrikson, Babe 61–63
Dirksen, Everett 36

Diversity of Life 146
Dixon, Arrington L. 179
Dole, Elizabeth 137–41
Dole, Robert 138–39
Donaldson, Sam 178, 191
Douglas, William O. 189
Douglas-Hamilton, Ian 156
Downs, Hugh 108–10
Drake, Francis 6
Dudley, Robert 6

Earhart, Amelia 32–35
Earle, Sylvia 130–32
Eastwood, Alice 10–12
Edelman, Marian Wright 151–53, 199
Edelman, Peter 153
The Edge of the Sea 50
8½ 95
Eisenhower, Dwight D. 28, 43, 65
Elders, Jocelyn 116–18
Elders, Oliver 110
Elephant Memories 157
Elizabeth I 5–6
The End of the World... 94
Endeavor 221
Enigma Project 51
Entertainment Tonight 179
Equal Employment Opportunity Com-
mission 144
Equal Franchise Society 21
Equal Rights Amendment 16, 113, 119,
129, 136, 163
Equal Suffrage Association 21
Europe: A Tapestry of Nations 79
Europe in the Spring 42
Evening Shade 196, 197
Everyday with Joan Lunden 203
Exploring the Deep Frontier 131
Eyes on Russia 45

Face the Nation 160
Falkland Islands invasion 91
Faludi, Susan 225–27
Families in Peril 153
Farmer, James 86
Federal Communications Commission
165, 192
Federal Trade Commission 138
Feinstein, Bertram 113, 114

Feinstein, Dianne 112–16
Fellini, Federico 95
Fenwick, Hugh 58
Fenwick, Millicent 57–59
Fermi, Enrico 46, 48
Ferraro, Geraldine 127–30
Ferraro, Nicholas 128
Filthy Rich 197
First Person with Maria Shriver 219
Fleas, Flukes and Cuckoos 52
Flowers, Gennifer 200
Foch, Ferdinand 19
Forbes 205
Ford, Gerald 122, 139, 146
Forest Hills 97, 176
Fortune 44, 45, 171
Fortune, Reo 38, 39
Frankfurter, Felix 111
Freud, Anna 199
Fugitive Slave Act 9
Fuller, Margaret 9

Gandhi, Mahatma 46
Gardner, John 107
Gault, Ronald 171
Gelbert, Larry 196–97
Genetics Society of America 41
Gentle Giants of the Pacific 131
Gere, Richard 110
Gerson, Allen 93
Giannini, Giancarlo 93
Gibson, Althea 96–98
Giddings, Al 131
Ginsberg, Douglas 182
Ginsberg, Martin 111
Ginsberg, Ruth Bader 111–12
Glenn, John 134
Goeppert-Mayer, Maria 46–48
Golden Gate Park 12
Goldovsky, Boris 98
Goldwater, Barry 37, 43, 106, 198, 204
Gombe National Park 126–27
Good Morning America 202
Goodall, Jane 125–27
Gorbachev, Mikhail 81, 91
Graham, Katherine 70–71
Graham, Philip 70
Greeley, Horace 7
Green Belt Movement 154–55
Gridiron Club 26, 73

Growing Up in New Guinea 39
Gruson, Sydney 78
Gumbel, Bryant 223

Hall, William 75
Hamburger, Victor 54
Hamilton, Alice 15–16
Harper's Bazaar 58
Harris, Barbara 102–4
Harris, Marcelite Jordan 171–73
Harris, Maurice Anthony 173
Harris, Patricia Roberts 82–83, 180
Harris, William Beasely 82
Hartman, David 202, 203
The Harvard Business Review 88
Harvard Club 16
The Harvard Crimson 226
The Harvard Law Review 116
Harvard University 7
Haskell, Floyd 183
Hatch, Orin 186
Hawkes, Graham 131
Hawkins, Augustus 151
Hawley, Steven 207
Head Start 150, 152, 153
Hearst, William Randolph 93
Hearts Afire 196, 197
Heath, Edward 90
Helms, Jesse 112
Henry V 3
Henry VIII 5
Hepburn, Katharine 65
"Hers" 212
Hewitt, Don 160
Higgins, Marguerite 73–75
Hill, Anita 115, 182, 197
Hills, Carla 120–23
Hills, Roderick 121–23
Hitler, Adolf 27, 30, 45, 53
Hodgkin, Dorothy Crowfoot 59–60
Hodgkin, Thomas 60
Holmes, Hamilton 170
Holt, Edward 38
Holt, Ruth 38
Holtzman, Elizabeth 130, 162–64
Home for Dying Destitutes 61
Honey: A Comprehensive Survey 67
Hoover, Herbert 23
Hoover, J. Edgar 181

The Horse Soldiers 98
House Armed Services Committee
  158, 159
House Budget Committee 107
House Judiciary Committee 199
*How to Go to Work When Your Husband
  Is Against It...* 88
How to Talk with Practically Anybody...
  109
Howe, Louis 29
Hull House 15–16, 21, 24
Human Rights Commission (New
  York) 144
Humphrey, Hubert 93
Hunt, Al 195
Hunter College 161, 162
Hunter-Gault, Charlayne 169–71

I Always Wanted to Be Somebody 98
I Saw Hitler 31
Iditarod 216, 217
Industrial Poisons in the United States 16
Institute for Research on Women and
  Gender 226
International Academy of Sports 217
International Botanical Congress 12
International Flying Organization 57
"Iron Lady" 90
Ivins, Molly 166–68

Jackson, Jesse 144
James I 6
Jemison, Mae 220–21
Jemison Group 221
Jensen, Hans 48
Joan of Arc 3–5
Job, Enrico 95
Johnson, Don 110
Johnson, Lady Bird 71
Johnson, Lyndon 72, 82, 133, 150, 178
Jordan, Barbara 120, 132–35
The Journal of Theoretical Biology 140

Kahn, Ishaq 211
Kelly, Sharon Pratt 179–81
Kennedy, Edward F. 106, 151, 218
Kennedy, Eunice 268
Kennedy, Jacqueline 72, 109

Kennedy, John F. 23, 28, 30, 36, 71, 72,
  133, 218
Kennedy, Robert 152–53, 218
Kertes, Stan 64
King, Billie Jean 175–77, 206
King, Coretta Scott 23
King, Larry 175–76
King, Martin Luther, Jr. 69, 228
King, Rodney 151
Kirkpatrick, Evron M. 92
Kirkpatrick, Jeane 92–94
Koop, C. Everett 186
Kopp, Maxim 32
Koppel, Ted 179
Koussevitsky, Serge 99
Krauss, Michael 202, 203
Krovatin, Gerald 212
Kuralt, Charles 189, 190, 219

Ladies Professional Golf Association
  65
Lake Manyara National Park 156
Lane, George 52
Latham, Aaron 165, 166
The Lawmakers 178
League of Women Voters 29, 159
Leakey, Louis S. B. 126
Leakey, Mary 126
Legal Services Corporation 200
Lend-Lease 21, 36
Lenihan, Brian 184
Let's Talk About Men 95
Letterman, David 179
Levi-Montalcini, Rita 53–54
Lewis, Flora 77–79
Lewis, Sinclair 24, 29–30
Library of Congress 46
Life 42, 45, 199
"Life in the 30s" 213
Lime Street 197
Lin, Maya 227–29
Lindberg, Charles 33, 34
Lindsay, John 163, 165
Lippmann, Walter 32
The Lizards 95
Llewellyn, Sidney 98
Locarno Film Festival 95
The Los Angeles Times 78
Louis Philippe 8
Love and Anarchy 95

Lovelock, James 146
Luce, Clare Booth 42–44
Luce, Henry R. 44
Lulu 99
Lunden, Joan 201–3

Maathai, Wangari 154–55
MacArthur, Douglas 74
McCarthy, Eugene 199
McCarthy, Joseph 16, 30, 32, 35–36
McClintock, Barbara 40–41
McCormack, John 86
McCormick, Anna O'Hare 26–28
McCormick, Francis J. 26
McGovern, George 93, 162, 190, 192, 193
Macmillan, Harold 89
MacNeil, Robert 171
The MacNeil/Lehrer News Hour 167, 171, 178, 196
Main Street 219
The Man from Hope 196
Manhattan Project 47, 48
Mankiller, Wilma 187–89
Marble, Alice 97, 206
Margaret Chase Smith Library 37
Margulis, Lynn 145–47
Maricopa County Supreme Court 105
Marshall, Thurgood 112, 163
Mary, Queen of England 19
The Mary Tyler Moore Show 197
*M*A*S*H* 196, 197
Mastroianni, Marcello 95
Mathias, Charles 136
Matola, Sharon 213–15
Mayer, Joseph 47
Mead, Margaret 37–39
The Measure of Our Success 153
Menchú, Rigoberta 223–25
Mercer, Lucy 29
Metropolitan Club 138
Metropolitan Opera 98, 99
Mikulski, Barbara 134–37
Milk, Harvey 113, 114
Mimi the Metalworker, His Honor Betrayed 85
Missing 79
Mitchell, Martha 71
Mitterrand, François 81, 123–25
Moi, Daniel Arap 155

Molly Ivins Can't Say That, Can She? 166
Mommaertz, Elizabeth 206
Monahan, Jay 223
Mondale, Walter 120, 129–30, 196
Monson, David 217
Moody Bible Institute 17
Morning Edition 178
Morning with Charles Kuralt and Diane Sawyer 190
Morse, Wayne 43
Morton, Bruce 134
Moscone, George 112–13
Moses and Aron 99
Moss, Cynthia 155–58
Mozark Productions 197
Municipal Assistance Corporation 161
Museum of African Art 229
Museum of Modern Art 46
Museum of Science and Industry 220
Muskie, Edmund 107
Mussolini, Benito 27, 32, 53

The Nation 31
National Academy of Sciences 41
National Aeronautics and Space Administration 206–7
National Air and Space Museum 209
National American Women Suffrage Association 22
National Association for the Advancement of Colored People 18, 68, 69, 87, 101, 119, 149, 152
National Association of Colored Women 18
National Association of Women Judges 105
National Black Feminist Organization 144
National Council of Negro Women 18
National Council of Women of Kenya 154
The National Geographic 125, 127
National Herbarium 12
National Honor Society 122, 198
National Labor Relations Act 25
National Labor Relations Board 158–59
The National Law Journal 200
National Merit Scholarship 198

The National Observer 181
National Oceanic and Atmospheric Administration 132
National Organization of Guatemalan Widows 225
National Press Club 73
National Public Radio 178
National Research Council 40, 41
The National Review 203, 227
National Scholarship and Fund for Negro Students 87
National Science Foundation 146
National Security Council 92
National States Rights Party 144
National Student Medical Association 220
National Task Force on Equal Rights for Women 159
National Taxpayers Union 140
National Urban League 18
National Youth Administration 17–18
Naval Affairs Committee 35
Nellie Bly's Book 14
Nero 1
New England Conservatory of Music 98
New England Opera Theater 98
The New Russia 31
New Times 181–82
New York City Division of Day Care 85
New York Cosmopolitan Club 97
The New York Evening Journal 14
The New York Herald-Tribune 32, 73–75
The New York Post 31, 72, 78
New York School of Philanthropy 21
New York School of Social Work 96
The New York Times 27, 28, 39, 58, 71, 78, 88, 93, 136, 161, 167, 178, 212–13, 226
The New York Tribune 7
New York Welfare Department 96
The New York World 13–14
The New Yorker 171
Newsbreak 190
Newsday 75, 78
Newsweek 70, 71, 220
Nichols, Mike 191
Nightline 178, 183
Nightly News 223

Nixon, Richard 71, 72, 110, 122, 134, 138, 162, 165, 190, 192, 199
Noonan, Peggy 203–5
North, Oliver 182
North American Free Trade Agreement 122
North of the Danube 45
Norton, Edward 143
Norton, Eleanor Holmes 143–45
Norville, Deborah 223
Not for Women Only 109
Nothin' but Good Times Ahead 168
Novello, Antonia 185–87
Novello, Joseph 186
Now, with Tom Brokaw and Katie Couric 223
Nuremberg trials 28

Object Lessons 213
Occupational Safety and Health Administration 142
O'Connor, John Jay 104–5
O'Connor, Sandra Day 122
Odlum, Flord 56
Office of Management and Budget 107, 108
O'Leary, Hazel 141–43
O'Leary, John F. 142
Olivier, Laurence 110
O'Neill, Thomas P. 129
Opera Company of Boston 99
Origin of Eukaryotic Cells 146
Ortega Saavedra, Daniel 101–2
Ossoli, Marchese 8
O'Sullivan, Maureen 109

Paisley, Ian 184
Panetta, Leon 108
Parker, Dorothy 42, 43
Parks, Raymond 68
Parks, Rosa 67–70
Pat and Mike 65
Patton, George 27
Paul VI, Pope 62
Peace Corps 160, 218, 221
Peace March (1968) 23
Pearl Harbor 21, 45, 56
Pegler, Westbrook 30
Perkins, Frances 23–26

Perot, H. Ross 228
Pershing, John J. 19, 20
The Philadelphia Public Ledger 31
Philip II 6
Pierpoint, Robert 190
Planned Parenthood Federation of America 158
PM Magazine 218
Pogash, Carol 227
Police Athletic League 96
Political Woman 92
Poole, Joyce 157
Poor People's Campaign 153, 171
Popcorn, Faith 173–74
The Popcorn Report... 174
A Popular Flora of Denver 12
Portraits in the Wild 156
Potter, Lewis 182
Povich, Maury 192, 193
Pratt Institute 144
La Prensa 100–1
Presidential Commission on Housing 122
Prime-Time Live 191
Profiles in Courage 23
Proposition 13 (California) 114
Pryor, Richard 110
"Public and Private" 213
Public Broadcasting System 181, 182
Pulitzer, Joseph 13–14
Putnam, George 33

Quakers 9
Quayle, Dan 140
Quindlen, Anna 212–13

The Rake's Progress 99
Raleigh, Walter 6
Rankin, Jeannette 20–23
Rather, Dan 101, 190, 192, 193, 204
Reagan, Ronald 43, 79, 91, 92, 93, 104, 105–6, 122, 130, 136, 139, 142, 191, 195, 204, 205
Reasoner, Harry 10
Red Cross 19, 29, 33
Redingston, Joseph 216–17
Rehnquist, William H. 104, 106, 182
Reno, Janet 147–49
Reviving the American Dream 108

Rice, Grantland 62, 63
Richards, Ann 118–20, 134, 167
Richards, David 118–19
Richardson, Elliot 122
Riddles, Libby 217
Ride, Sally 205–7
Riders to the Sea 99
Riggs, Bobby 176–77
Rinehart, Mary Roberts 18–20
Rinehart, Stanley 19
Rivlin, Alice 106–8
Rivlin, Lewis A. 106
Roberts, Cokie 177–79
Roberts, Steven 178–79
Robinson, Jo Ann 69
Robinson, Mary 183–85
Robinson, Sugar Ray 96
Robinson, Edna 96
Rockefeller, Nelson 192
Roddick, Anita 168–69
Roddick, Gordon 168–69
Rodham, Hillary 198–201
Rodham, Hugh 149
Roe vs. Wade 112, 113
Roosevelt, Eleanor 18, 26, 28–30, 43
Roosevelt, Franklin 17, 18, 23, 24, 25, 26, 27, 28–30, 32, 42, 43
Roosevelt, Sara 29
Roosevelt, Theodore 28, 29
Roosevelt Medal of Honor 28
Roper, Daniel 24
Ross, Harriet 9
Rostenkowski, Dan 149, 201
Rothschild, Miriam 51–52
Royal Society 51
Russell, Bertrand 57
Russert, Tim 222
Rutan, Burt 207–9
Rutan, Dick 207–9

Sagan, Carl 145
Sagan, Dorian 146
Sakharov, Andrei 80–81
The San Francisco Chronicle 113–14
Sandinistas 100–2
Sarazen, Gene 64
Sarbanes, Paul 134
The Saturday Evening Post 18, 19
Saturday Night with Connie Chung 193
Sawyer, Diane 189–91, 218

Sawyer, Forrest 219
Scalia, Antonin 112
Schroeder, James White 158–59
Schroeder, Pat 147, 158–60
Schultz, George 166
Schwartz, Felice 86–87
Schwartz, Irving 87
Schwarzenegger, Arnold 219
The Sea Around Us 50
Seaman, Robert 14
Selective Training and Service Act 35
Senate Judiciary Committee 226
Seven Beauties 96
Seventeen 212
Shalala, Donna 160–62
Sheles, Tom 219
Shaw, Bernard 5
Shriver, Maria 218–20
Shriver, Sargent 218
Sierra Club 156
Silent Spring 50
Simpson, Alan 182
Sing Sing 7
60 Minutes 14, 164, 166, 191
Smith, Alfred E. 25
Smith, Clyde 35
Smith, Margaret 176
Smith, Margaret Chase 35–37
Smith, Samantha 197
Social Security Act 25
Somozas 150
Spanish Armada 6
Special Olympics 218
Special Victim Bureau (New York) 128
Spellman, Francis J. 29
Stahl, Leslie 164–66, 195
Stalin, Josef 27, 30
The Stanford Law Review 104
Stars and Stripes 74
Statistical Mechanics 47
Steinbrenner, George 160
Stevenson, Adlai 30
Stewart, Potter 106, 182
Stuffed Shirts 42
Suetonius Paulinus 1, 2
Sullivan, Kathy 207
Summer on the Lakes 7
Sunday Morning 219
Sununu, John 135
Sutherland, Joan 98

Swedish Royal Academy of Sciences 59
Swept Away by an Unusual Destiny… 94, 96
Symbiosis in Cell Evolution 145
Systematic Thinking for Social Action 107

Task Force on National Health Care Reform 201
Telegraph Hill 21
Teller, Edward 47, 48
Teresa, Mother 61–62
Test Ban Treaty (1963) 36
The Texas Observer 166
Thatcher, Denis 89
Thatcher, Margaret 81, 89–91, 125
"Thinking Out Loud" 213
This Week 110, 178
Thomas, Clarence 115, 182
Thomas, Helen 71–73
Thomason, Harry 197–98
Thompson, Dorothy 30–32
Three Mile Island 142, 190
"Three Women of Courage" 21
Time 42, 129
Today 108, 109, 221, 223
Totenberg, Nina 181–83
Trail Breakers Kennels 217
Trance and Dance in Bali 39
Trans-Action 171
Transcendentalism 7
Triangle Shirtwaist Company 24, 25
Tring Park 51
The Trojans 99
Truman, Harry 28, 30, 35, 137
Tsavo National Park 156
Tubman, Harriet 9–10
Tubman, John 9
Twentieth Amendment 23
20/20 108, 110
Two and Two Are No Longer Four 95

Under the Sea Wind 50
Underground Railroad 9–10
Union of National Opposition 101
United Nations 28, 92, 93, 225
United Nations Food and Agriculture Organization 58
United Press 72

Urey, Harold 48
U.S. Academy of Achievement 217
U.S. Court of Appeals (D.C.) 111, 112
U.S. Golf Association 64
U.S. House of Representatives *see*
  House of Representatives
U.S. Information Agency 160
U.S. Lawn Tennis Association 64, 97
U.S. News and World Report 108, 178
U.S. Public Health Service 106
U.S. Supreme Court 105–6, 112, 133
U.S. Trade Representative 122
Unity Democratic Club 85
University of Wisconsin 161–62
Urban Institute 122

Van Lawick, Hugo 127
The Vatican Journal 28
Verne, Jules 14
Vietnam Veterans Memorial 227, 228
Vogue 58
Voyage to the Moon 99
Voyager 208–9

Wages and Hours Act 25
Wagner, Robert 197
The Wall Street Journal 225, 226
Wallace, Alfred Russell 11
Wallace, George 143
Walters, Barbara 108–11, 202
War on Poverty 150
War Powers Bill 163
Washington, Booker T. 21
The Washington Post 70–71, 78, 115, 219
Washington Research Project 152
The Washington Star 93
The Washington Times-Herald 70
Washington Week in Review 171
Watergate 71, 132, 133, 164, 165, 182,
  190, 192, 199
Waters, Edward 149
Waters, Maxine 149–51
Weddington, Sarah 119
Wertmuller, Lina 94–6
White, Byron 112

White, Wallace 35
White House Office of Consumer
  Affairs 138
Whitewater 201
Will, George 129, 178
Williams, Sydney 151
Willis, Cecil 118
Willkie, Wendell 32, 40
Wilson, Paul 25
Wilson, Woodrow 22
Wilson Sporting Goods Company 64
Wimbledon 97, 175–77
Winfrey, Oprah 219
Witness 103
Woman in the Nineteenth Century 7
The Women 42
Women in Communications 196
Women's Air Force Service Pilots 56
Women's Armed Services Committee 35
Women's Legal Defense Fund 198
Women's Political Caucus 119
Women's Tennis Association 177
Woodruff, Judy 193–96
Woods Hole Biblical Laboratory 49
Woodward, Bob 165
Working Women 227
The World at Home 28
Wright, James 136

Yalow, Aaron 76
Yalow, Rosalyn 75–77
Yeager, Chuck 207
Yeager, Jenna 207–9
You Have Seen Their Eyes 45
Young, Andrew 133
Young Women's Christian Association
  82

Zaccaro, John 128, 129
Zaharias, Babe Didrikson 62–65
Zaharias, George 64
Zeffirelli, Franco 95
Zia ul-Haq, Mohammad 210–11
Ziegler, Ron 190
Zucker, Jeffrey 223